A Special Issue of
Aphasiology

Aphasia therapy workshop Current approaches to aphasia therapy: Principles and applications

Edited by

Jacqueline Stark
Austrian Academy of Sciences, Austria

Nadine Martin
Temple University, USA

Ruth B. Fink
Moss Rehabilitation Research Institute, USA

Psychology Press
Taylor & Francis Group

HOVE AND NEW YORK

Published in 2005 by Psychology Press Ltd
27 Church Road, Hove, East Sussex BN3 2FA
www.psypress.co.uk

Simultaneously published in the USA and Canada
by Taylor and Francis Inc.
270 Madison Avenue, New York NY 10016
Psychology Press is part of Informa plc
© 2005 by Psychology Press Ltd

British Library Cataloguing in Publication Data
A catalogue record for this book is available from the British Library

ISBN 1-84169-800-8 (hbk)
ISSN 0268 7038

Cover design by Jim Wilkie
Typeset in the UK by DP Photosetting, Aylesbury, UK
Printed in the UK by Hobbs the Printers, Totton, Southampton, UK
Bound in the UK by TJ International, Padstow, Cornwall, UK

CONTENTS

* This book is also a special issue of the journal Aphasiology, and forms issues 10 &11 of Volume 19 (2005). The page numbers are taken from the journal and so begin on p. 903.

APHASIOLOGY, 2005, 19 (10/11), 903–905

Editorial

Current approaches to aphasia therapy: Principles and applications

Jacqueline Stark

Austrian Academy of Sciences, Vienna, Austria

Nadine Martin

Temple University, Philadelphia, PA, USA

Ruth B. Fink

Moss Rehabilitation Research Institute, Philadelphia, PA, USA

When the decision was made to hold the 41st Academy of Aphasia meeting in Vienna, Austria, in 2003, Jacqueline Stark proposed holding a concurrent aphasia therapy workshop, because so many prominent clinical researchers would be in attendance and it would be an ideal forum to discuss current perspectives on aphasia rehabilitation.

The workshop was held on 22nd and 23rd October 2003 at the Austrian Academy of Sciences following the annual meeting of the Academy of Aphasia. The general consensus was that the meeting was very productive. We were very pleased that colleagues from neighbouring new European countries—Czech Republic, Slovakia, Hungary, Slovenia, Croatia, and others—were able to attend the workshop. Student and other submissions were welcomed in the form of poster presentations. In addition to the platform sessions, two poster sessions were organised.

Six main topics were selected to be discussed in sessions organised by experts in each area. These included:

1. Functional communication: Psychosocial aspects. Organiser: Linda Worrall
2. Technological advances in language rehabilitation. Organisers: Ruth Fink and Myrna Schwartz
3. Aphasia therapy: Best when intensive and prolonged? Organiser: David Howard
4. Cognitive neuropsychological approaches. Organiser: Argye Hillis

---

Address correspondence to: Jacqueline Ann Stark, Department of Linguistics and Communication Research, Austrian Academy of Sciences, Kegelgasse 27/1, 1030 Vienna, Austria.
Email: Jacqueline-ann.stark@univie.ac.at

The contributions of Nadine Martin and Ruth Fink to this project were supported by grants from the National Institutes of Health (NIDCD), DC 01924-11 (PI: N. Martin) to Temple University and DC 00191-21 (PI: M. Schwartz) to Moss Rehabilitation Research Institute.

          DOI:10.1080/02687030544000119

5. (Psycho-) Linguistic approaches. Organisers: Cynthia Thompson and Na'ama Friedmann
6. Beyond language: Cognitive aspects of language therapy. Organisers: Gail Ramsberger and Jacqueline Stark.

The papers in this special issue of *Aphasiology* are based on the peer-refereed papers from the workshop.

The first set of papers addresses the current emphasis on functional communication and psychosocial aspects of aphasia rehabilitation. Byng and Duchan's paper discusses aphasia rehabilitation within a framework of a social model of disability. This model is illustrated with examples from the team at the Connect Disability Network in the UK. Worrall, Rose, Howe, Brennan, Egan, Oxenham, and McKenna report three studies investigating the use of aphasia-friendly written material to break down the informational barriers (''the digital divide'') experienced by people with aphasia.

The second set of papers explores the role of computer technology in studying, treating, and compensating for language disorders. The Linebarger and Schwartz paper discusses the use of a computer program designed to facilitate aphasic sentence production by compensating for processing limitations such as impaired retention of linguistic material. The authors discuss the design and deployment of this ''processing prosthesis'' and its implications for research and treatment. The Fink, Brecher, Sobel, and Schwartz paper discusses computer-based treatment protocols for impaired naming and the kinds of evidence that they may provide about treating lexical retrieval in aphasia. The Stefanatos, Gershkoff, and Madigan paper describes how computer-based analysis and manipulation of speech waveforms may facilitate research (by allowing controlled studies of the impact on language perception of different acoustic/phonetic elements), treatment (by allowing for ''supported'' speech perception), and potentially even assistive communication (via computer-based manipulation of waveforms to make spoken input more comprehensible).

The third set of papers addresses the question of whether there is a better outcome with more intensive therapy. Hinckley and Carr compare the outcomes of intensive and non-intensive context-based aphasia treatment to achieve improvement in a catalogue-ordering task. The implications of their findings are discussed in terms of the principles of whole-task training. Basso considers the importance of intensity and duration of aphasia therapy, and using a meta-analysis she provides evidence in support of intensive, prolonged therapy. In light of these findings Basso maintains that the role of the speech and language therapist as the sole person providing the necessary intensive and prolonged therapy must be reconsidered.

The fourth set of papers highlights the contributions and limitations of treatment approaches based on cognitive neuropsychological models. Hillis and Heidler provide a useful state-of-the-art assessment of efforts to use such models to guide and inform therapy approaches. Additionally, they discuss the potential usefulness of neuropharmaceutical adjuncts to treatment, an exciting new area of aphasia rehabilitation research. Rapp examines the relationship between deficit type and responsiveness to treatment by applying a single remediation protocol on deficits affecting different components of the spelling process. Marshall and Cairns discuss evidence for pre-verbal conceptual processes that support language production and the need to consider these processes in treatment. Results from two studies are discussed in support of their hypothesis.

The fifth set of papers discusses linguistic approaches to treatment of agrammatic aphasia. These approaches exploit what is known about normal and disordered sentence processing and production as well as syntactic theory. The underlying theory as well as data supporting these approaches are presented. Thompson and Shapiro provide a summary of their studies that apply linguistic theory to the treatment of agrammatic aphasia, and discuss their complexity account of treatment efficacy (CATE). Using a single case study, Friedmann demonstrates how the syntactic tree can be used to characterise the severity of impairment in agrammatic aphasia as well as the recovery process. She accounts for degrees of severity and the process of recovery in agrammatic aphasia in terms of three levels on the syntactic tree.

The final set of papers addresses the influence that non-linguistic cognitive skills such as attention, memory, executive functions, and visuospatial skills may have on language recovery. Nicholas, Sinotte, and Helm-Estabrooks examine the effect of executive functions on treatment of patients with severe non-fluent aphasia learning to use an alternative communication programme (C-speak Aphasia). Ramsberger investigates the importance of focusing on non-linguistic cognitive skills to improve conversational competence. Stark introduces a therapy programme aimed at improving oral sentence production—the ELA-syntax programme—and considers the role of learning and memory in the language therapy process.

We would like to thank the organisers for their assistance in getting an exciting final programme together for the meeting, and all the authors for presenting papers on their ongoing clinical research, for writing their papers for this special issue, and for helping with the refereeing process.

APHASIOLOGY, 2005, 19 (10/11), 906–922

Social model philosophies and principles: Their applications to therapies for aphasia

Sally Byng

Connect – The Communication Disability Network, London, UK

Judith Felson Duchan

Buffalo, New York, USA

Background: The social model of disability has, on occasion, created confusion and contention among those working in the field of aphasia. Some have treated it as an alternative or substitute for traditional therapies.

Aims: This paper makes an effort to clarify the issues surrounding discussions of the social model, and attempts to reduce some of the disagreement associated with its use. It is argued that the social model can provide principles for practice that can be used as a guide for any types of therapies.

Methods & Procedures: The study examines the literature on the social model. A distinction is drawn between social model philosophies and social model principles. Once the distinction is made, a set of principles is presented as a guide for planning and evaluating support services for people with aphasia.

Outcomes & Results: The particular principles drawn from the social model philosophy are: equalising social relations, creating authentic involvement, creating engaging experiences, establishing user control, and becoming accountable to users. Illustrations are given of how each of these social model principles was used by staff and people with aphasia to guide different support services offered by a UK charity called Connect – The Communication Disability Network. The principles were also found useful in evaluating social model activities.

Conclusions: A case is made that the social model principles can provide speech therapists with a guide for conducting their therapies, whatever form those practices take.

The social model of disability has been attracting some attention in aphasiology in recent years. From the tenor of discussions that we have been involved in, it appears that this model has begun to be seen as an alternative type of therapy. However, we see the model as one that can interact with current therapies. Having worked within this frame of reference for several years now, we want to clarify some of the social model philosophies underpinning therapy and describe how we have incorporated the social model into our practices. We will conclude the paper by discussing how social model philosophy can be applied to any type of therapy for aphasia, including therapies that focus on impairment.

Address correspondence to: Sally Byng, Connect – The Communication Disability Network, 16–18 Marshalsea Road, Southwark, London SE1 1HL, UK. Email: sallybyng@ukconnect.org

Thanks are due to Maxine Bevin, Katerina Hilari, Alan Hewitt, Sally McVicker, Susie Parr, Tom Penman, Carole Pound, Kate Swinburn, and Linda Worrall, who have all contributed to the development of the ideas and work described in this paper.

http://www.tandf.co.uk/journals/pp/02687038.html   DOI:10.1080/02687030544000128

WHAT IS THE "SOCIAL MODEL" ANYWAY?

We see the social model as a philosophical framework for provision of therapy, *not* an "approach" to therapy in itself. It is the conceptual frame that has emerged powerfully from the disability movement (e.g., Oliver, 1996, 2004; UPIAS, 1976), and the one that has influenced the new model from the World Health Organisation (2001). Much has been written about it, but it is rarely defined. It seems to be assumed that there is a shared understanding of what the model entails, but our sense is that there are many different definitions or interpretations of the model. We once heard social model practices described negatively and narrowly as "being nice to someone, having a cup of tea and saying that it is all the fault of the rest of the world"!

Our understanding of the social model might best be cast in terms of its ramifications for practice. We see the most important ramifications of the social model as the following points.

Confronting disabling societies

There are significant disabling impacts of an impairment that are caused by the attitudes, and practices of other people and by the environment, rather than by the impairment itself. That is, if other people behaved differently and if environments were changed, then many of the challenges associated with an impairment would be considerably reduced.

This perception of disability as being caused by sources other than impairment has underpinned much of the recent move towards anti-discrimination legislation, such as the Disability Discrimination Act in the UK (1995), the Americans with Disabilities Act in the US (1990), the Disability Discrimination Act in Australia (1992), the New Zealand Disability Strategy (2001). This kind of legislation also reflects the increasing move in many societies towards respecting and valuing difference. The legislation acts to reduce discrimination related to ethnicity and race, gender, sexual orientation, as well as disability.

Challenging the relationships between service users and service providers

Within the social model, people with disabilities are seen as experts in their own conditions. They are not patients but people. The usual power relationships between service providers and people with disabilities, in which service providers generally hold more power, should be challenged. This would ensure that service providers (professional and non-professional) deliver what people with disabilities need and want, rather than what providers think they need (Davis, 2004; Morris, 1993).

This aspect of the social model has probably been one of its more contentious features. In the more politicised parts of the disability movement, people with disabilities have described their relationship with service providers as being oppressive—having to take what is on offer rather than being in the position of choosing from a range of options.[1]

---

[1] Note that there may also be cultural differences at work here too. For example, the British response to "experts" may be different from that of other cultures. The UK disability movement sometimes expresses a considerable degree of scepticism about what "experts" can offer, while in other cultures people may be more inclined to seek the opinion of, and be guided by, an expert.

Addressing social exclusion and isolation

The social model also emphasises how people with disabilities often become socially isolated and are excluded from participating in many aspects of life. Much disability-related legislation is intended to reduce social exclusion and the isolation that can follow from it.

In practice, many of the processes through which people with disabilities are excluded are quite subtle and difficult to address through legislation. They are perhaps more related to a lack of awareness and recognition, and to habitual ways of doing things. They are therefore more intractable and complex to address directly (see Parr, 2004, for an analysis of the subtle processes of social exclusion that affect the experience of people with aphasia).

Valuing the lived experience and expertise of people who live with a disabling condition

Much of the impetus for the social model of disability has come from a recognition that there is often a marked difference between ''insider'' and ''outsider'' perspectives on disability (Boazman, 2003; Gillman, Swain, & Heyman, 1997; Pound, 2004); that is, between the experience of people who live with a disability, and those who do not. Service provision that fails to address the issues and priorities of people with disabilities does so because it tends to be shaped by professionals who are outsiders (Beresford, 2004; Gillman, 2004; Phillips, 1992).

The social model, like the medical model, is an underlying frame of reference and set of attitudes towards impairment and disability (Duchan, 2004). One can use it to design principles of practice and to design and evaluate therapies. This means that any kind of therapy can be delivered within a social model frame of reference.

SOCIAL PRACTICE PRINCIPLES ARISING FROM THE SOCIAL MODEL

We have translated the social model philosophy into five principles, as follows.

1. Equalising the social relations of service delivery

As outlined above, the social model directly challenges the relationship between service provider and service user (Abberley, 2004; Goble, 2004). The focus of therapies based on the social model is to support people to have more control over their own healthcare services. This shift in control changes the relationship between the service user and the service provider from one of dependency of the user on the provider to one of colla-boration between the two parties, where both parties bring expertise, knowledge, and experience to the collaboration.

2. Creating authentic involvement

It is also fundamental to proponents of the social model that service users should be involved in the process of decision making about services to be offered, not only at the personal level about their own care, but care in general. This involvement needs to be authentic, not tokenistic (Beresford, 2003). For example, tokenistic involvement would be where users of a service are consulted about a proposed service development or set of options about treatment choices, but given either inaccessible information or too little information for them to be able to give an informed view. Authentic involvement would mean that service users are given all the information they need to be able to contribute a considered view about what services would best address their need, and in a form which ensures that they can understand it adequately. But note that this should not detract from the expertise and experience that professionals can contribute to the planning and decision-making process. Expertise is needed to reach a negotiated and shared decision about the choices and direction for treatment. This is particularly challenging when the service users have communication problems.

3. Creating engaging experiences

Therapies should include experiences where service users take part in "work" that they find engaging. Associated with the idea of "work" is that their contribution is worthwhile, fulfilling a purpose that is not only valued by them, but also by others. Also tied to the idea of work is that the experiences relate to the day-to-day reality of living with disability, and are oriented to personal meanings about what makes life worth living.

Engaging experiences may be had during real-life activities as well as activities created for a therapeutic purpose. For example, service users can make contributions to provider organisations, such as staff recruitment or acting in an advisory capacity. For some people, this kind of engaging activity can be as therapeutic as, for example, learning non-verbal communication skills in a one-to-one or group environment. (For more on the difference between passive participation and active engagement, see Hewitt & Byng, 2003.)

4. Establishing user control

User control is a fundamental part of the disability movement (Barnes, Mercer, & Morgan, 2000). Authentic control by users of organisations that deliver services to them requires that people with disabilities be involved in organisational decision making at all levels of the organisation's structure, and that their viewpoints become incorporated in the philosophy and activities of the whole organisation. This control needs to be exercised in an environment of authentic involvement. Some proponents of the social model of disability would argue that organisations working for people with disabilities should be controlled entirely by those people. Other proponents would argue for shared control, with the key issue being that organisations should be properly accountable to the people whom the organisation is seeking to serve (see the next point).

5. Becoming accountable to users

Here we are referring to the responsibility taken by the people working in organisations to the key interested parties or "stakeholders" of that organisation. Accountability is a concept that was created in management contexts, rather than the disability movement. However, we feel it can serve as a powerful way to evaluate whether service users are involved meaningfully in organisational decision making (see Mercer, 2004, for an example). There are various stakeholders in organisations, each requiring different sorts of accountability. This accountability might relate to good use of financial resources, relevance of services provided to the users of the service, efficiency and effectiveness of services, or the ethos of the organisation. Accountability requires not only the provision of high-quality direct services but also that organisations involve, listen to, and inform users in understandable ways about various facets of the organisation.

It is one thing to write about the social model—it is another to try to work in ways that are consistent with its principles. In the next section of this paper we describe how social model principles have influenced practice at Connect, an organisation set up in the UK to promote services to people living with aphasia.[2]

We will take each of the principles outlined above and illustrate what they look like in practice within different aspects of the organisation of services: developing a new service, service users as advisers, and co-delivery of services by service users. We acknowledge that many organisations are developing innovative practice around working collabora- tively with service users (e.g., Kagan & Duchan, 2004), however the purpose of this paper is not to review practice in this arena but rather to analyse our own practices to illustrate the implementation of the principles of social model practice we have outlined.

APPLYING PRINCIPLES OF SOCIAL MODEL PRACTICE: SOME EXAMPLES

To illustrate what our social model principles look like in practice at Connect, we will identify the facilitators and barriers we have met at Connect. We acknowledge throughout the challenges and difficulties of actually living up to the ideals set forth in the principles.

Developing a new service for people living with aphasia

In 2002 we began to consult people living with aphasia about the development of a second centre for Connect's operations in the south-west of England. As a result of this consultation, we piloted the delivery of one-off workshops for people living long-term with aphasia, taking these workshops out ''on the road'' across the south-west. This area is largely rural, making regular attendance for therapy at a fixed centre too difficult for most people with aphasia.

Each of these workshops focuses on a specific topic. There is no assumption that people will attend more than one workshop, so each event has to be complete in itself. As individual topics are addressed (such as having better conversations, access to the creative arts, trying out computers) participants get information and advice from people with and without aphasia. They have a chance to feel competent and be listened to, to meet and network with other people coping with the same issues, and a chance to have a good time.

Each of the principles of social model practice can be applied to this service initiative. The principles can thereby serve as a type of test for the initiatives, to see if they are accomplishing our various aims derived from the social model.

   1. *Equalising the social relations of service delivery.* Within each of the workshop events, we usually have a session called ''Ask the expert''. In this session, two or three people with aphasia are the experts, receiving questions from the floor about their experience in relation to the topic under discussion. For example, in the

---

[2] Connect is a charity promoting innovative therapy and support services for people living with aphasia to meet their long-term needs. As part of this work we deliver therapy and support services ourselves, free of charge (all funding for the services provided is achieved through grants and donations). In addition, we provide courses to other service providers about our service and therapy innovations and our research findings, through which we aim to support people in reflecting upon and changing their own services. Our current activities can be found at: www.ukconnect.org.

workshop on "Having better conversations", questions might be asked such as "I always ask my wife to repeat words she can't say – does that help conversation?" The experts with aphasia will then give their experience of whether repetition helps or not, and ask for other experts in the audience to offer their experience. In this way, people with aphasia are seen as authorities on their own condition and thereby qualified to offer advice that may be helpful for other people. Speech and language therapists also give their perspective from their experience and knowledge from their expertise. This sharing and pooling of expert knowledge and experience provides a rich source of information for people with aphasia, and their relatives and friends. These events also allow people with aphasia to experience, display, and share their expertise. They convey to other people with aphasia that they can view aphasia as a phenomenon about which they have unique knowledge rather than something wrong that must be put right. This sharing of expertise is seen as entirely commonplace within other disability groups (UK Department of Health Expert Patient Programme, 2004). However people with aphasia too often find themselves marginalised and not treated as people who "know best" about their condition, partly because they cannot communicate about it, and partly because they are not given sufficient time to communicate about it.

2. *Creating authentic involvement.* People with aphasia have been authentically involved in the development of these workshop events in a genuine way that makes a qualitative difference. The idea for these events came from a consultation exercise that we ran when we listened to what over 200 people with aphasia wanted from long-term services. This involved listening, questioning, probing, querying, and interpreting what people with aphasia and family members were saying. This consultation revealed to us that the experience that people wanted did not have to be delivered from a "bricks and mortar centre". Rather it could be delivered from a "virtual" centre—that is, it could be delivered on the move and was more dependent on the resources, dynamics, and opportunities provided within the event than on a specific place. The concept for these days was discussed with a group of people with aphasia, who advised on the content and format for the events. They then also began to collaborate in the development of materials and content, and to participate in presentations at workshops.

3. *Creating engaging experiences.* The opportunities for people with aphasia to share the running of these events has meant that they have been involved with purpose. This has included working as "welcomers" to the events, and as facilitators of small groups in the introduction sessions, contributing their own experiences to illuminate specific issues or as experts in the "ask the expert sessions" described above. These roles are all required to make the events work well. Under these circumstances, people with aphasia have reported their feelings of strong engagement.

4. *Establishing user control.* People with aphasia have become increasingly involved in development of the overall content in the programme of events and in making decisions about the specific topic to be covered within each day. These events are not actually controlled by people with aphasia; they involve a collaboration between people with and without aphasia. No structure has yet been created which enables these events to be solely user controlled.

5. *Becoming accountable to users.* The progress of these events—where they are being run, the topics covered, the number attending, and the feedback received—is all reported back to a planning group of people with aphasia. These events are also

reported to Connect's Governing Board, of which one third of members are people with aphasia, trained and supported to contribute. In this sense, everything that Connect does in these events is referred back to people with aphasia at various levels of responsibility, meeting our organisation's strong commitment to accountability to our service users.

Creating an advisory panel of service users

Connect is experimenting with a forum of people with aphasia called *Live-Wire*, whose purpose is to monitor how Connect is involving people with aphasia in all aspects of what it does, such as the development and delivery of therapy and support services, training, staff recruitment, governance, etc. The *Live-Wire* forum meets every 2–3 months and hears a presentation from staff members about a specific area of activity. The presentation details how people with aphasia are involved in that activity. *Live-Wire* members are then asked to address some specific questions about how people with aphasia could be involved either differently or more extensively.

How do we invoke the five principles of social model practice within the *Live-Wire* forum?

1. *Equalising the social relations of service delivery.* The very nature of the *Live-Wire* forum means that people without aphasia have to report to people with aphasia. We are asking for advice, explaining what we do and why in relation to involvement, taking knotty issues that we cannot solve alone and asking for advice about how to do better. This immediately changes the dynamics and the power relations between service user and provider, since people with aphasia in this context are the experts or points of reference.

2. *Creating authentic involvement.* In order to ensure that *Live-Wire* forum members can participate, we have to make all the information that we have given them communicatively accessible (see Pound & Hewitt, 2004). Without this, *Live-Wire* forum members would not be able understand or contribute to the issues that we are discussing and asking for advice about. In addition, we devised a comprehensive training programme for *Live-Wire* members, to ensure that they were able to participate. And we provide communication supporters to make sure that people with no verbal communication are able to contribute.

3. *Creating engaging experiences.* The issues that we take to the *Live-Wire* forum are real issues that Connect needs to address, such as how do we manage the problem of the number of people with aphasia waiting to access Connect's services? Discussing this with the *Live-Wire* forum has involved setting out how the current entry arrangements work. It has also involved talking about why arrangements have been set up the way they have. The result is that forum members have become better informed about Connect's rationales and constraints, so they can offer relevant suggestions for alternative options to a waiting list. People with aphasia regard the time that they put in to *Live-Wire* forum as valued work—doing something purposeful and necessary.

4. *Establishing user control.* The *Live-Wire* forum itself is chaired by a person with aphasia, who is an employee of Connect and who sets the agenda, in discussion with Connect staff members without aphasia. The topics that *Live-Wire* forum discusses are progressively enabling people with aphasia to have greater say over what happens at Connect and why it should happen.

5. *Becoming accountable to users*. The very nature of *Live-Wire* forum is about being directly accountable to people with aphasia. The notes from the *Live-Wire* forum go to the Senior Management Team, and the *Live-Wire* forum is given a report back from the Senior Management Team describing what action has been taken in relation to the recommendations or comments that were made. This allows the forum members to keep track of Connect's responsiveness to the issues they raise.

Co-delivery of services with people with aphasia

Connect involves people with aphasia as co-deliverers of therapy and support services. In so doing, we offer our users another arena for assessing how we are doing in light of our five social model principles.

1. *Equalising the social relations of service delivery*. People with aphasia sometimes facilitate groups on their own. They plan and direct the groups from week to week, with access to regular supervision from trained staff without aphasia. They may well have volunteers without aphasia in their group acting as communication supporters to group members who have more difficulty getting messages in or out.
2. *Creating authentic involvement*. Group facilitators with aphasia are trained and supported in their roles. Very often they begin their role in a small working party collaboratively with trained non-aphasic staff, in which the purpose of the group is formulated and the means of carrying out the work is discussed. An example would be an art group at Connect, which was co-facilitated by a therapist, a volunteer artist, and two women with aphasia, neither of whom had access to any spoken or written language. Together they planned the aims and objectives, and a programme of activities to deliver those objectives. People with aphasia were then supervised and supported in running the group, and were recognised as leaders by members of the art group. The facilitators would meet prior to each session and plan the direction and focus of each session together. They would also discuss ways of facilitating particular individuals to engage with the exploration of their aphasia through art. In each session each of the facilitators would have responsibility for watching out for when people needed drawing out, supporting, and extending, and they would intervene appropriately, including the facilitators with aphasia.
3. *Creating engaging experiences*. The kind of experiences involved in the art group, described above, represented real-life ''work'', where the contribution of the two group facilitators with aphasia was integral to the development of the group. It was also stimulating, positive, and enhancing for the women concerned, and because of this, it provided them with a therapeutic experience, although therapy was not the focus.
4. *Establishing user control*. Connect is still at a stage where the content of the therapy programme is determined by non-aphasic staff, on the basis of a considerable amount of careful listening to service users' needs. However, as a result of suggestions from the *Live-Wire* forum, another advisory group of people with aphasia will be working with the therapy and support delivery team to devise the menu of therapy and support services to be offered. This should result in a more equitable contribution to the formation of the menu on offer.
5. *Becoming accountable to users*. Currently Connect's therapy services are reported to and monitored by Connect's Board. We hope in the future to establish

intermediary accountability for service user involvement in Connect's offerings through such mechanisms as the *Live-Wire* forum.

Learning from experience

We have found our efforts to create practices grounded in the social model complex but convincing. We commissioned a study to evaluate the impact of our therapy and support services, delivered within the context of the social model philosophy. The outcomes of this quantitative and qualitative study suggested that both the communication skills and the quality of life of people with aphasia attending Connect improved significantly (see van der Gaag, Smith, Mowles, Davis, Moss, & Laing, 2005, for more detail).

These three experiences, developing a new service, creating an advisory panel of service users, and working with people with aphasia to deliver services, offer examples of how we have gone about trying to apply social model principles. The activities associated with the experiences are not traditionally thought of as therapy, although all involved have seen that they have had a therapeutic impact.

APPLYING SOCIAL MODEL PRINCIPLES TO DIFFERENT TYPES OF THERAPIES

Much of the literature on the social model has portrayed it as a different type of therapy, contrasting it with "impairment-focused" therapies (Byng, 2001; Duchan, 2001a, 2001b; McNeill, 2001). These therapies have often been contrasted as follows: impairment-focused therapy aims to fix the problem in the person, socially focused therapy aims to remove the barriers to successful communication, social engagement, and inclusion. This distinction often seems to presume that one must choose between them. People also seem to assume that the social model "belongs" to the socially focused therapies, not the impairment-focused therapies. We see this as a false contrast and false assumption.

It is probably true that some therapies (and methods of assessment) lend themselves more naturally to being implemented within a social model philosophy, as we have described it above—for example, therapies and assessments that address social or physical barriers experienced by people with aphasia and therapies that promote social participation (e.g., Beukelman & Mirenda, 1998; Kagan, 1998; Simmons-Mackie, 2000, 2001; Threats & Worrall, 2004). And certainly, therapies that focus on the social ramifications of a disability are consistent with the central tenets of the social model and in keeping with its principles.

However, we believe that this dichotomy is to miss the point of what the social model means. The social model is a philosophy and a way of working, not a form of or approach to therapy in itself. Thus it is perfectly possible to carry out impairment-focused therapies in a social model way of working (e.g., Cairns, in press; Elman & Bernstein Ellis, 1999). Conversely, socially focused therapies could also be delivered in a way that does not conform to social model principles for practice and reinforces individual/medical model ways of working. The form that therapy takes is determined as much by the way that therapists think and act, their values and beliefs (about disability, power, and difference), as by what the "tasks" or "events" of therapy consist of. These values and beliefs are rarely made explicit.

We will illustrate what we mean by suggesting what the principles of social model practice might look like when applied to any "impairment-focused" or "socially focused" therapies[3] as well as to other types of activities.

1. Equalising the social relations of service delivery

People with aphasia have the inside knowledge of what that impairment feels like, their own understanding of what that impairment means, and their own priorities for which impacts of the impairment need to be addressed (for examples, see Black & Ireland, 2003; Boazman, 2003; Hewitt & Byng, 2003; Khosa, 2003). Therapists know about the form of the impairment and its impact. This knowledge is an insufficient basis for therapy without being combined with the understanding and priorities of the person with aphasia.

Therapies that conform to the equalising principle would be ones focused on a shared meaning of the impairment that includes: (i) the perception of the person with aphasia, (ii) a shared perception of the priority issues to address, and (iii) a shared understanding of how therapy is trying to relate to that meaning and address the priorities. For example, therapists can design language tasks that will enable those with aphasia to understand the form of their impairment. This understanding can serve as one means of gaining control over that impairment. However, language tasks can be delivered in such a way that they do not convey understanding about the language impairment. Therapists' expertise in this kind of therapy does not have to be used in a dominant way—with skilled interaction it can be supportive and educative.

Therapists may assume that they are already doing this kind of negotiation. However, we find that many people with aphasia do not understand what therapy they have received, nor how it is meant to make a difference to their life. This suggests that accessible, meaningful negotiation between therapist and client is not always taking place, and that therapies are not always based on the priorities of people with aphasia.

In a therapist–client relationship there is always potential for an imbalance of power, with the power being weighted in most cases away from the person with aphasia. Socially focused therapies are just as likely to be vulnerable to power imbalances as impairment-focused therapies. It is possible, for example, for an autocratic clinician to control group therapy that aims to develop social support among people with aphasia. Examples of this kind of power imbalance as well as that addressing impairment have been documented in the literature (Simmons-Mackie & Damico, 1999; Parr, 2004).

Fundamental to equalising the social relations of service delivery are the following:

- Recognising and explicitly acknowledging the competence and contribution of the person with aphasia at all times, whatever the setting, context, or activity. For example, clinicians can acknowledge the competence of someone with aphasia when interacting with them, or when talking about or writing about them. Acknowledging competence can serve as a model for others such as family members, friends, and those working with the individual. It can be more difficult to reinforce competence in the context of therapies that focus on impairment, since focusing on the impairment often involves

---

[3] We note, however, that the term "impairment-focused therapies" has probably become as misused as the term "social model", with again many differing operational definitions being employed. For the purposes of this paper we are defining as "impairment-focused" therapies those therapies that aim to change impaired language and communication systems through activities that focus directly on those systems. These therapies represent, of course, the vast majority of therapies for aphasia described in the literature.

concentrating on what someone cannot do. Repeated emphasis on aspects of language that are difficult may make it hard to retain a sense of oneself as a competent person (although, of course, this is not necessarily true for everyone). In the context of impairment-focused therapies, tasks that use errorless learning (e.g., Montagu & Marshall, in press) may be more effective in sustaining a sense of competence and make people less vulnerable to a negative view of themselves as communicators.

- Working constructively with one's knowledge and position to allow for an egalitarian, negotiated interaction. There is a difference between being knowledgeable and authoritative and being authoritarian and controlling (cf. Simmons-Mackie & Damico, 1999)
- Developing listening, interpreting, and interactional skills that are needed to discover the meaning and experience of impairment and disability felt by the person with aphasia

2. Creating authentic involvement

One way for people with aphasia to become authentically involved in therapy that focuses on impairment is for clinicians to provide clear choices about what to work on and how to carry out the work. The service provider should not make an assumption about what kind of therapy will be best for a person, but rather should discuss options and dilemmas, and negotiate what therapy experiences would most benefit the person with aphasia. For therapists to do this effectively requires them to suspend their own agendas, be honest about what they can offer, and be knowledgeably self-aware of their own biases and skills. People living with aphasia (those who have it and those who live with them) need to be able to select, with the therapist, from among a variety of services that address the impact of the aphasia. Different people living with aphasia need different therapy services at different times.

This may sound familiar—it is probably stated in every undergraduate speech and language pathology/therapy textbook. Yet, in practice, how many therapists actually offer a range of different therapy approaches? Do we not tend to offer what we feel most comfortable delivering? This may be a sensible strategy to ensure that people get well prepared and delivered therapy. However, do we also acknowledge what we are *not* offering, because it either lies outside our expertise, or is beyond the resources we have available?

For example, at Connect we have opted to offer a service to as many people with aphasia as possible, because we are aware of the huge need that exists for services that enable people to get on with their lives. This immediately precludes us from offering some kinds of therapy that require intensive one-to-one resources. We are explicit with people who come to the centre that this is the case, so that they know what they can expect from us and what they cannot. We have discussed this issue with our advisers with aphasia. Their view has been that we should seek to serve as many people as possible, and if that means not providing intensive one-to-one therapy then so be it, provided that our services still result in gains to communication and quality of life, which our evidence-base suggests that they do.

The choice agenda has more impact than may appear at first sight. Giving people real choice means a number of things:

- Service providers need to set out the available choices. *This may include clarifying what services are not being offered as well as those that are.* This means that service providers have to be able to account for why they are not offering a particular type of therapy opportunity, when there may be reason to believe that it could be effective. Services not offering opportunities to focus on language change need to make clear why that therapy is not available, and services that do not offer therapy opportunities to work on confidence, self-esteem, and lifestyle change also need to explain this option and why it is not available.

- The process of making clear what your service offers and what it does not offer requires time and negotiation to make it explicit and accessible.
- People with aphasia may choose not to take up what is on offer, when they clearly understand the choices available. This is entirely reasonable of course, but can be challenging for service providers, whose preferred options have been "rejected".

3. Creating engaging experiences

Therapies need to relate to the life of the person with aphasia. This has been well understood by therapists for many years, as can be seen in the way they choose their materials and activities to fit the life circumstances and interests of particular service users. However, engaging people involves more than relating tasks to life. Engagement involves enabling people to feel more connected to the business of real life. Therapies that focus on the impairment are sometimes so removed from real life that it becomes unclear how they are intended to make a difference to the business of day-to-day communicating, and they fail to carry over to contexts other than those used in therapy.

The end product of therapy for most people needs to be that they feel more equipped to exchange opinions, provide comments, negotiate, express affection, express needs, and so on—the real-life purposes to which most of us put our communication. Therapies need to facilitate people to achieve these communications, and they need to achieve these gains in the most economical way possible.

This real-life criterion can be a challenge for therapies that focus on specific aspects of the language impairment. However there are more examples in the literature where the link between language gains in therapy and the real application of those gains in day-to-day life is made explicit and built in to the therapy (e.g., Montagu & Marshall, in press).

Our experience has shown us that many of our attempts to increase user participation and control have provided ideal contexts for engagement. Therapists offering any kind of therapy service in any kind of context are in a position to develop engaging experiences for people with aphasia. We have found a fruitful source of engagement in those activities that involve people in shaping and influencing the services.

4. Establishing user control

For users to have some control over the therapy services being offered, they should have an opportunity to contribute to decisions about what is available, choosing from a wide range of services available elsewhere. Further, as part of the information for making an informed choice, users need to know the effectiveness of different options.

It is only recently that professionals have begun to provide service users with outcome information about different therapies. Indeed, information may be impossible to come by, since we do not yet have an evidence base for many of our services. In the case where there is little information about outcomes, people with aphasia must evaluate their options by relying on the opinions and experience of professionals.

An informed choice, then, rests on the provider's ability to give a fair and balanced picture of a full range of therapies. Service providers offering primarily therapy for the language impairment need to inform service users about the other possibilities for therapy that exist, and vice versa—in both cases recognising and explicitly acknowledging the benefits and limitations of the forms of therapy being offered

The need to provide outcome information to service users also has implications for how the research community chooses what to study. Outcome-based research, done in accord with social model principles, should provide the research base for the therapies that are required and valued by people with aphasia. The long-term implication for this is that the research agenda underpinning aphasia therapies will become more wide ranging and extensive than is currently the case (Byng, Parr, & Cairns, 2003; Sarno, 2004).

5. Becoming accountable to service users

Developing user accountability is a major implication of a social model. Service providers and researchers of all types of therapy should explain to service users and their families and friends about why the services are provided in the way that they are. For example, in keeping with this tenet, service providers favouring individually based therapies, as well as those favouring group therapies, would need to explain to service users why that is the therapy on offer. This is not to say that service providers would need to provide all possible services (there may be legitimate reasons why a particular range of services is provided), but rather, if they are being accountable, they need to explain their choices of offerings. In this way, service providers as well as service users can be more explicit about the decisions that go into service planning and design.

Researchers and therapists following this accountability principle would also find themselves needing to ascertain whether therapy provided in one way is the most efficient way of achieving a particular outcome. There may be different ways of achieving the same outcome from therapy, which have different implications for delivery. For example, one-to-one therapy addressing the impairment might be an effective way of gaining control over, and insight into, one's own language. Being in a group with other people with aphasia talking about what aphasia means to them can be another powerful way of understanding one's impairment.

Different people may prefer different ways of gaining insight and control over their language and communication impairment, and the two methods might work at different speeds and require different resources. It may be that both methods would achieve the same outcomes but might work at different rates, with consequent cost implications.

At the moment, data demonstrating comparative cost effectiveness barely exist. Yet if we are to be more accountable to people who use our services, it follows that we should provide them with this kind of information. For a long time, the aphasiology community has protested about the lack of resources going into aphasia therapy. Yet we have done little to provide data on how much it costs to achieve particular outcomes. Without this kind of evidence the credibility of arguments about the need for more resources is hard to sustain. This sets an agenda for the research community in aphasia therapy.

CONCLUSION AND SUMMARY

The social model has the potential to be misinterpreted when applied to aphasia therapy. In particular, it is sometimes mistakenly seen as a therapy approach that is an alternative to impairment-focused therapies.

We view the social model as a philosophy rather than as a therapy approach, and have tried to outline its key philosophical components. We have also derived a set of principles growing out of the philosophy—principles that we feel can be well used when developing and evaluating therapies for people with aphasia.

In order to show how the principles work, we described three projects that we have been engaged in at Connect. Table 1 outlines how the principles have helped us structure and evaluate our projects.

We have tried to show in this paper that the social model philosophy can apply to various kinds of therapies, regardless of their theoretical standpoints, goals, or purposes. This application is feasible because the social model relates to the underpinning beliefs, attitudes, and behaviours of the service provider, which in turn affect their relationship with the service user. Therapies should be evaluated by determining the most effective and efficient means of achieving what people with aphasia want to achieve. One therapy does not fit all, and we should be tailoring what we do to who people are and where they are in their personal process of learning to live with aphasia.

Some people will want to make most sense of their aphasia and to gain quality of life by focusing directly on improving or compensating for their impaired language and communication. Others will want to focus more broadly. They may want to learn to communicate differently, to create their new identity, or to find other ways to enhance their quality of life. Therapies for these different goals could include practising communication skills, having conversations, accessing the creative arts, exploring the potential of technology, changing environments for communication. We feel that many options should be made available and that people should also regularly be given chances to revise their choices.

The social model principles outlined in this paper provide a way of designing and evaluating different sorts of therapies, whether impairment focused or socially focused. The principles can be converted into the following guiding questions:

- Do I treat service users as knowledgeable (e.g., discuss their concerns, solicit ideas and opinions about therapies, create discussions between experienced service users and newer ones)?
- Have I involved service users in decisions about their course of therapy and how it is conducted (e.g., offering choices from what is offered and explicitly discussed what is not being offered)?
- Are the therapies my service offers engaging (e.g., are they seen as worthwhile and connected to the business of life)?
- Do the service users in my organisation have control over various aspects of therapy (e.g., the range of therapies on offer, selection, execution, evaluation)?
- Is my organisation accountable to its users (e.g., are users represented on executive and non-executive boards, advisory committees, panel presentations)?

We are aware that there is sometimes debate about whether the wide range of therapies that we are describing here should all be offered and engaged in by speech and language therapists. There is a view that speech and language therapists should only carry out therapies that directly target the language impairment. The social model philosophy makes clear that speech therapists are there to provide the service and resources needed by people learning to live with aphasia, by offering a variety of ways to address the impairment, and identity and lifestyle changes experienced by people with aphasia.

We believe that the principles of the social model come into play, whatever the therapy, because the model is fundamentally about the relationship between healthcare provider and healthcare user. Indeed, speech-language therapists and researchers are now

TABLE 1
Social model principles, some practice manifestations, and examples of applications to different projects or therapies

		Connect's projects		
Social model principles	Manifestations of principles	Project 1 Starting a new Connect service	Project 2 Live-Wire advisory panel	Project 3 Co-delivery of services
Equalising social relations	Service user brings own expertise to the project or therapy	Created an expert panel of people with aphasia for workshop presentations	Created an advisory panel of people with aphasia to report to senior management	Involved people with aphasia in Connect's service delivery programmes
Creating authentic involvement	Service user is involved in decision making in relation to the project or to the therapy. Support and training are provided to ensure that participation is not tokenistic. Input of service user is solicited and valued	People with aphasia are supported as they develop workshop ideas and participate in presentations	Provision of communication access support during meetings. Developed accessible minutes and presentations	Training and support provided to people with aphasia so they could facilitate groups
Creating engaging experiences	Participation seen as fulfilling a worthwhile purpose by service user, professionals and other participants and considered indispensable by all. Participation connected with the business of real life	The participation of people with aphasia has a well-defined purpose that was seen as relevant and important	Presented real issues to advisory panel, solicited their input, and acted on their recommendations	Leadership of people with aphasia in individual groups is indispensable to the group
Establishing user control	People's viewpoints and suggestions are responded to and acted on	Events are not yet controlled by people with aphasia, but they have considerable influence as co-planners and participants	The chair of the panel is a person with aphasia, as are all of its participants	Beginning to work with people with aphasia to enable them to influence the "menu" of services available at Connect
Becoming accountable to users	All members of organisation are responsible to service users. Decisions about issues that affect service users are made with the involvement of service users All in the organisation listen to and inform users in understandable ways about specific facets of the organisation	Reports of the events given to planning group and input solicited. Reports also made to Connect's governing board	The purpose of this group is primarily one of accountability. The organisation is accountable to members of the group	This still needs work. The service users/facilitators are supervised, but not yet accountable to anyone except to their immediate supervisor

living in a cultural and healthcare context where the social model principles are being legislated and discussed (although the full implications are not always fully understood). We fear that unless our clinical and research communities respond to these changes we will find ourselves left out of the healthcare delivery agenda.

REFERENCES

Abberley, P. (2004). A critique of professional support and intervention. In J. Swain, S. French, C. Barnes, & C. Thomas (Eds.), *Disabling barriers – enabling environments* (pp. 239–250) London: Sage Publications.

Americans with Disabilities Act (1990). http://www.usdoj.gov/crt/ada/adahom1.htm

Barnes, C., Mercer, G., & Morgan, H. (2000). *Creating independent futures: An evaluation of services led by disabled people.* Leeds, UK: The Disability Press.

Beresford, P. (2003). User involvement in research: Connecting lives, experience and theory. In J. Swain, S. French, C. Barnes, & C. Thomas (Eds.), *Disabling barriers – enabling environments* (pp. 246–250). London: Sage Publications.

Beukelman, D., & Mirenda, P. (1998). *Augmentative and alternative communication: Management of severe communication disorders in children and adults* (2nd ed.). Baltimore: Paul H. Brookes.

Black, M., & Ireland, C. (2003). Talking to ourselves: Dialogues in and out of language. In S. Parr, J. Duchan, & C. Pound (Eds.), *Aphasia inside out: Reflections on communication disability* (pp. 21–31). Berkshire, UK: Open University Press.

Boazman, S. (2003). A time of transition: A matter of confidence and control. In S. Parr, J. Duchan, & C. Pound (Eds.), *Aphasia inside out: Reflections on communication disability* (pp. 32–40). Berkshire, UK: Open University Press.

Byng, S. (2001). Integrating therapies. *Advances in Speech-Language Pathology, 3,* 67–71.

Byng S., Parr, S., & Cairns, D. (2003). The science or sciences of aphasia? In R. De Bleser & I. Papathanasiou (Eds.), *The science of aphasia.* (pp. 201–226). Elsevier.

Cairns, D. (in press). Controlling language and life: Therapy for communication and identity in a bilingual speaker. In S. Byng & J. Duchan (Eds.), *Aphasia therapy files* (Vol. 2). Hove, UK: Psychology Press.

Connect – The Communication Disability Network. www.ukconnect.org

Davis, K. (2004). The crafting of good clients. In J. Swain, S. French, C. Barnes, & C. Thomas (Eds.), *Disabling barriers – enabling environments* (pp. 203–205). London: Sage Publications.

Department of Health. (2004). *The expert patient: A new approach to chronic disease management in the 21st century (2001).* London: Department of Health. Retrieved from http://www.dh.gov.uk

Disability Discrimination Act, Australia (1992). http://unpan1.un.org/intradoc/groups/public/documents/apcity/unpan004021.pdf

Disability Discrimination Act, UK (1995). http://www.hmso.gov.uk/acts/acts1995/1995050.htm

Duchan, J. (2001a). Impairment and social views of speech-language pathology: Clinical practices re-examined. *Advances in Speech-Language Pathology, 3,* 37–45.

Duchan, J. (2001b). Social and impairment approaches viewed in a forest and in the shadows of a city street. *Advances in Speech-Language Pathology, 3,* 73–76.

Duchan, J. (2004). *Frame work in language and literacy: How theory informs practice.* New York: Guilford Press.

Elman, R. J., & Bernstein-Ellis, E. (1999). The efficacy of group treatment in adults with chronic aphasia. *Journal of Speech, Language, and Hearing Research, 42,* 411–419.

Gillman, M. (2004). Diagnosis and assessment in the lives of disabled people: Creating potentials/limiting possibilities? In J. Swain, S. French, C. Barnes, & C. Thomas (Eds.), *Disabling barriers – enabling environments* (2nd ed., pp. 251–257). London: Sage Publications.

Gillman, M., Swain, J., & Heyman, B. (1997). Life history or "case" history: The objectivication of people with learning difficulties through the tyranny of professional discourses. *Disability and Society, 12,* 675–694.

Goble, C. (2004). Dependence, independence and normality. In J. Swain, S. French, C. Barnes, & C. Thomas (Eds.), *Disabling barriers – enabling environments* (pp. 41–46). London: Sage Publications.

Hewitt, A., & Byng, S. (2003). From doing to being: From participation to engagement. In S. Parr, J. Duchan, & C. Pound (Eds.), *Aphasia inside out: Reflections on communication disability* (pp. 51–64). Berkshire, UK: Open University Press.

Kagan, A. (1998). Supported conversation for adults with aphasia: Methods and resources for training conversation partners. *Aphasiology, 12,* 816–830.

Kagan, A., & Duchan, J. (2004). Consumers' views of what makes therapy worthwhile. In S. Byng & J. Duchan (Eds.), *Challenging aphasia therapies* (pp. 158–172). Hove, UK: Psychology Press.

Khosa, J. (2003). Still life of a chameleon: Aphasia and its impact on identity. In S. Parr, J. Duchan, & C. Pound (Eds.), *Aphasia inside out: Reflections on communication disability* (pp. 10–20). Berkshire, UK: Open University Press.

LPAA Project Group. (2000). Life participation approach to aphasia: A statement of values for the future. *ASHA Leader, 5*(3), 4–6.

McNeill, M. (2001). Promoting paradigm change: The importance of evidence. *American Journal of Speech-Language Pathology, 3*, 55–58.

Mercer, G. (2004). User-led organisations: Facilitating independent living. In J. Swain, S. French, C. Barnes, & C. Thomas (Eds.), *Disabling barriers – enabling environments* (pp. 176–182) London: Sage Publications.

Montagu, A. & Marshall, J. (in press). ''What's in a name? A therapy study with proper names using an errorless approach to treatment. In S. Byng & J. Duchan (Eds.), *Aphasia therapy files, Volume 2.* Hove, UK: Psychology Press.

Morris, J. (1993). *The shape of things to come? User led services.* London: National Institute for Social Work.

The New Zealand Disability Strategy (2001). http://www.odi.govt.nz

Oliver, M. (1996). *Understanding disability: From theory to practice.* Basingstoke, UK: Macmillan.

Oliver, M. (2004). If I had a hammer: The social model in action. In J. Swain, S. French, C. Barnes, & C. Thomas (Eds.), *Disabling barriers – enabling environments* (2nd ed., pp. 7–12). London: Sage Publications.

Parr, S. (2004). *Living with severe aphasia: The experience of communication impairment after stroke.* Brighton, UK: Pavilion Publishing.

Phillips, M. (1992). ''Try harder'': The experience of disability and the dilemma of normalization. In P. Ferguson, D. Ferguson, & S. Taylor (Eds.), *Interpreting disability: A qualitative reader.* (pp. 213–227). New York: Teachers College Press.

Pound, C. (2004). Dare to be different: The person and the practice. In J. Duchan & S. Byng (Eds.), *Challenging aphasia therapies: Broadening the discourse and extending the boundaries* (pp. 32–53). Hove, UK: Psychology Press.

Pound, C., & Hewitt, A. (2004). Communication barriers: Building access and identity. In J. Swain, S. French, C. Barnes, & C. Thomas (Eds.), *Disabling barriers – enabling environments* (2nd ed., pp. 161–168). London: Sage Publications.

Sarno, M. T. (2004). Aphasia therapies: Historical perspectives and moral imperatives. In J. Duchan & S. Byng (Eds.), *Challenging aphasia therapies: Broadening the discourse and extending the boundaries.* Hove, UK: Psychology Press.

Simmons-Mackie, N., (2000). Social approaches to the management of aphasia. In L. Worrall & C. Frattali (Eds.), *Neurogenic communication disorders: A functional approach.* New York: Thieme.

Simmons-Mackie, N. (2001). Social approaches to aphasia intervention. In R. Chapey (Ed.), *Language intervention strategies in aphasia and related neurogenic communication disorders* (4th ed., pp. 246–268). Philadelphia: Lippincott, Williams & Wilkins.

Simmons-Mackie, N., & Damico, J. (1999). Social role negotiation in aphasia therapy: Competence, incompetence and conflict. In D. Kovarsky, J. Duchan, & M. Maxwell (Eds.), *Constructing (in)competence: Disabling evaluations in clinical and social interactions* (pp. 313–342). Mahwah, NJ: Lawrence Erlbaum Associates, Inc.

Threats, T., & Worrall, L. (2004). The ICF is all about the person, and more: A response to Duchan, Simmons-Mackie, Boles, and McLeod. *Advances in Speech-Language Pathology, 6*, 83–87.

UPIAS. (1976). *Fundamental principles of disability.* London: Union of Physically Impaired Against Segregation.

van der Gaag, A., Smith, L., Mowles, C., Davis, S., Moss, B., & Laing, S. (2005). Therapy and support services for people with stroke and aphasia and their relatives: A six month follow up study. *Clinical Rehabilitation, 19*, 372–380.

World Health Organisation. (2001). *International Classification of Functioning, Disability and Health.* www.who.int/classification/icf.

APHASIOLOGY, 2005, 19 (10/11), 923–929

Access to written information for people with aphasia

Linda Worrall, Tanya Rose, Tami Howe, Alison Brennan, Jennifer Egan, Dorothea Oxenham, and Kryss McKenna

The University of Queensland, Australia

Background: Accessibility is often constructed in terms of physical accessibility. There has been little research into how the environment can accommodate the communicative limitations of people with aphasia. Communication accessibility for people with aphasia is conceptualised in this paper within the World Health Organisation's *International Classification of Functioning, Disability and Health* (ICF). The focus of accessibility is considered in terms of the relationship between the environment and the person with the disability.
Aims: This paper synthesises the results of three studies that examine the effectiveness of aphasia-friendly written material.
Main Contribution: The first study (Rose, Worrall, & McKenna, 2003) found that aphasia-friendly formatting of written health information improves comprehension by people with aphasia, but not everyone prefers aphasia-friendly formatting. Brennan, Worrall, and McKenna (in press) found that the aphasia-friendly strategy of augmenting text with pictures, particularly ClipArt and Internet images, may be distracting rather than helpful. Finally, Egan, Worrall, and Oxenham (2004) found that the use of an aphasia-friendly written training manual was instrumental in assisting people with aphasia to learn the Internet.
Conclusion: Aphasia-friendly formatting appears to improve the accessibility of written material for people with aphasia. Caution is needed when considering the use of illustrations, particularly ClipArt and Internet images, when creating aphasia-friendly materials. A research, practice, and policy agenda for introducing aphasia-friendly formatting is proposed.

Most people are familiar with the concept of accessibility as they go about their daily lives. Buildings have ramps, pedestrian crossings have both auditory and visual signals, lifts use Braille numbers, kerbs have cut-outs, and there are many other less visible ways in which society accommodates people of different abilities. As a parallel concept to wheelchair ramps, Kagan and Gailey (1983) challenged aphasiologists to consider ''communication ramps'' for people with aphasia. What is the equivalent to wheelchair ramps for people with aphasia? That is, how can society accommodate people with aphasia to enable improved communication access?

The conceptual framework of the World Health Organisation's *International Classification of Functioning, Disability and Health* (ICF: WHO, 2001) provides a common understanding of accessibility. Figure 1 shows the interrelationship between a person's health condition and its effects on his or her body structures and functions, everyday activities, and participation in life roles. It also shows that environmental and personal factors mediate the effects of a health condition on functioning. Accessibility focuses on

---

Address correspondence to: Associate Professor Linda Worrall, Communication Disability in Ageing Research Centre, School of Health and Rehabilitation Sciences, The University of Queensland, QLD 4072, Australia. Email: l.worrall@uq.edu.au

DOI:10.1080/02687030544000137

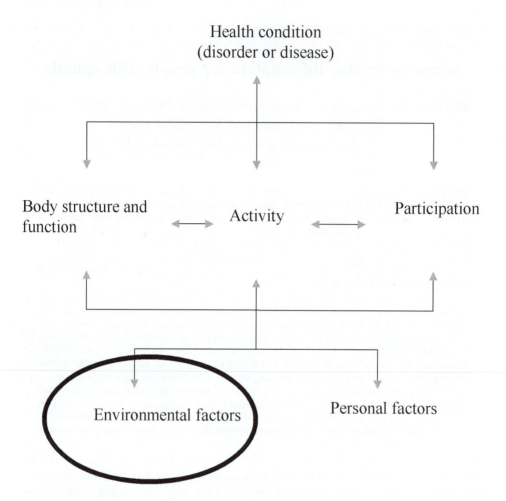

Figure 1.   Accessibility within the ICF.

the relationship between environment and the person. In the ICF framework, this means that accessibility focuses on the specific relationship between environmental factors and all other constructs in the framework. While most aphasiologists are familiar with characterising the functioning of a person with aphasia, environmental factors that impact on communicative functioning are not so well known.

Environmental factors within the ICF refer to physical, social, and attitudinal factors and can act as either barriers or facilitators to the functioning of a person with aphasia. The three levels of environmental factors are immediate personal environment (e.g., family, work), services (e.g., rehabilitation services, government agencies), and cultural/ legal systems (e.g., cultural beliefs, laws). The classification categories are Products and technology; Natural environment and human-made changes to environment; Support and relationships; Attitudes; and Services, systems, and policies.

Howe, Worrall, and Hickson (2004) have reviewed the environmental factors in these ICF categories that have been found to act as either a barrier or facilitator to communicative functioning in aphasia. While Howe et al. conclude that no study has systematically investigated accessibility issues for people with aphasia using a recognised framework such as the ICF, a study by Parr, Byng, and Gilpin, with Ireland (1997) that conducted in-depth interviews with 50 people with aphasia was the first to shed light on the possible barriers that people with aphasia experience in their everyday lives.

Parr et al. (1997) reported that the primary barriers were informational, structural, attitudinal, and environmental. Informational barriers were defined as a lack of information that is relevant, timely, and accessible. Lack of support, resources, services, and opportunities were described as structural barriers. Attitudinal barriers were primarily negative reactions of other people, while environmental barriers were described as background noise, and people speaking too fast, simultaneously, or using complex language.

The focus of this paper is informational barriers. People with aphasia have different information needs at various stages post-onset of aphasia. While the verbal medium is often used to transmit information, written media, in particular patient education materials (PEMs) such as brochures, fact sheets, or booklets about stroke or blood pressure, have many benefits. According to Bernier (1993), PEMs are beneficial because they supplement and reinforce verbal information; they are cost effective; they allow people to learn at their own pace; they offer message consistency; they can be referred to when and as often as desired, in the location preferred by the client; and they are an effective method for enhancing information recall. Hoffmann, McKenna, Worrall, and Read (2004) found that 12–22% of clients with stroke reported receiving written information about stroke before leaving hospital. The mean reading grade level of this information was Grade 11 as assessed by the SMOG (McLaughin, 1969), a level too high for the general public, let alone people after stroke who were found to read at a mean of Grade 7–8. Hence many people with stroke are not receiving PEMs, and when they are provided, they may be too complex for their reading ability.

If people with strokes do not receive adequate written health information, then it is likely that people with aphasia are being further marginalised. In addition, it is known that a reading impairment is a common symptom of aphasia, yet it is not known whether information is being modified to increase the likelihood of a person with aphasia understanding PEMs.

In recent years, some aphasia service providers around the world have embraced a functional or social approach to aphasia services and have sought to overcome informational barriers by providing aphasia-friendly websites or written material relevant to people with aphasia. Aphasia-friendly websites include:

- Talkback Association for Aphasia in Adelaide, Australia:
  http://aphasia.asn.au/aphasiafriendly/index.htm
- Connect Communication Disability Network in London, United Kingdom:
  www.ukconnect.org
- Aphasia Help website: www.aphasiahelp.org
- Communication Disability in Ageing Research Centre in Brisbane, Australia:
  www.shrs.uq.edu.au/cdaru/aphasiagroups

An example of an aphasia-friendly booklet about aphasia is *What is Aphasia?* from the Aphasia Institute in Canada (http://www.aphasia.ca). At the Communication Disability in Ageing Research Centre, the four main principles used in aphasia-friendly formatting are to: simplify the text (vocabulary and syntax), use large font, format using plenty of white space, and use relevant illustrations (www.shrs.uq.edu.au/cdaru/aphasiagroups).

The aim of this paper is to synthesise the results of three studies that have empirically examined some issues surrounding aphasia-friendly formatting. The first study (Rose, Worrall, & McKenna, 2003) examined whether aphasia-friendly formatting improved the comprehension of written health information for people with aphasia. The second study (Brennan, Worrall, & McKenna, in press) sought to determine which of the formatting principles made a difference in comprehension. The formatting principles of simplifying text, using large font, using pictures, and incorporating large amounts of white space were tested in this experiment. Finally, aphasia-friendly formatting principles were used to design a printed manual that taught people with aphasia how to use the Internet (Egan, Worrall, & Oxenham, 2004). The effectiveness of this aphasia-friendly training was evaluated.

DO APHASIA-FRIENDLY WRITTEN MATERIALS WORK?

While many speech pathologists are developing aphasia-friendly materials, there has been no study that has examined whether these modifications increase the comprehension of the material by people with aphasia. Rose et al. (2003) asked 12 people with aphasia to read and answer questions about four brochures on different health topics (stroke, motor neurone disease, arthritis, and osteoporosis). Brochures were selected from hospital waiting rooms. Two versions of each brochure were presented (i.e., an aphasia-friendly version and the original version). Knowledge scores significantly increased after reading any brochure, but there was a significantly greater increase in knowledge after reading the aphasia-friendly versions. Knowledge increased by 29.6% for the aphasia-friendly versions compared to an 18.4% increase for the original versions—hence 11.2% more information was comprehended when the aphasia-friendly versions were read.

While there was no significant correlation between aphasia severity and the benefit that the aphasia-friendly versions provided, there was a trend showing that people with moderate-mild aphasia benefited most. It was suggested that people with mild aphasia have adequate reading skills to gather sufficient knowledge from the original brochures and possibly do not need the aphasia-friendly formatting. On the other hand, people with a severe aphasia had such a reading disability that they were not greatly assisted by the aphasia-friendly formatting. In addition, they may have had difficulty processing the knowledge questions that assessed their comprehension of the brochure.

Interestingly, only half of the people with aphasia preferred the aphasia-friendly version. Those who did not prefer the aphasia-friendly versions complained about the increased length of the aphasia-friendly brochures. Others thought that the use of pictures (Microsoft ClipArt and black and white line drawings) indicated a lack of respect for people with aphasia. Also of interest was that 40.6% of participants preferred versions that did not improve their comprehension. Again, this may be a reaction to the perceived stigmatising nature of aphasia-friendly brochures.

In summary, the aphasia-friendly formatting increased comprehension by approximately 11%. People with mild-moderate aphasia appeared to benefit most from the modified formatting. However, while the aphasia-friendly brochures may have increased comprehension, people with aphasia may not prefer them. Some complained that they were too long and that the pictures, in particular, were stigmatising.

This study indicated that further research into the effectiveness of each of the four aphasia-friendly formatting principles is required. In particular, the helpfulness of the pictures was questioned.

WHAT APHASIA-FRIENDLY MODIFICATIONS MAKE THE DIFFERENCE?

Brennan et al. (in press) further investigated the effectiveness of each of the four aphasia-friendly formatting principles in increasing comprehension of written paragraphs. This study investigated whether each single aspect of aphasia-friendly formatting (i.e., simplified vocabulary and syntax, large print, increased white space, and pictures), used in isolation, would result in increased comprehension compared to control paragraphs. Nine people with mild to moderately severe aphasia read a battery of 90 paragraphs and selected the best word or phrase from a choice of four to complete each paragraph. The paragraphs were formatted using single aspects of aphasia-friendly formatting and the results compared to the combined aphasia-friendly formatting (i.e., all four principles) and the original format. The results supported the Rose et al. (2003) study which showed that people with aphasia comprehended more information if it was in aphasia-friendly format. They also comprehended significantly more paragraphs that had simplified vocabulary and syntax, large print, or increased white space. Although people with aphasia tended to comprehend more paragraphs with pictures added than control paragraphs, this difference was not significant. A likely explanation for the lack of significant improvement when pictures augmented the text in this study was that the pictures may have been distracting. In this study, pictures were obtained from Microsoft ClipArt and Internet searches using Google Image Search. This method is believed to reflect the sources likely to be used by clinicians when creating therapy materials. However, it is acknowledged that purpose-drawn illustrations and photographs may have provided a more appropriate illustration to the text. The pictures used were not always as appropriate to the text as purpose-drawn illustrations or photographs might have been, although whether different pictures would work better is still an empirical question.

USING APHASIA-FRIENDLY WRITTEN MATERIAL TO TRAIN PEOPLE WITH APHASIA TO USE THE INTERNET

In an initiative to overcome the digital divide, Egan et al. (2004) sought to examine whether people with aphasia could learn to use the Internet with specialised training materials. Since the Internet is a major source of information, communication, and leisure opportunities, it is important that all people from society can access its benefits. People with aphasia are not only disadvantaged by inaccessible websites, they are also marginalised when they attempt to access training.

Training in groups does not allow the person with aphasia to receive the individual assistance they need. Published textbooks that aim to simplify the process of using the Internet are not sufficiently modified for people with aphasia. On-line or computerised tutorial programmes require computer skills to access the training, while tutoring in the home can be expensive and the tutor may not understand the limitations that aphasia places on an individual.

Hence, this study developed a training programme that included an aphasia-friendly training manual (free download available at: www.shrs.uq.edu.au/cdaru/aphasiagroups), a trained and supervised volunteer tutor, and an accessible public Internet-linked computer. Twenty people with aphasia participated in the programme. Their skills in using the Internet were assessed before and after the training programme. The program consisted of $1\frac{1}{2}$ hours training each per week for a period of 6 weeks.

There was a significant increase in the independence of people with aphasia in the skills required to use the Internet. The skills that remained most difficult were saving favourite sites (Microsoft Internet Explorer) or bookmarking them (Netscape), and sending and receiving email. Participants were asked if they were able to use the student-training manual without assistance. Of the 20 participants, 12 said they could use the Internet manual independently, 2 said they ''sometimes needed help'', 3 said they ''often needed help'', and 3 said they ''always needed help''. One participant, an 89-year-old lady with severe aphasia, remained fully dependent after the training, but frequently used the Internet as a shared activity with her granddaughter.

While the individualised tutoring of the volunteer was instrumental in the success of this programme, participants viewed the aphasia-friendly training manual as an essential component of the training. They noted that they could refer to it at any time, they could understand the manual, and they could practise at home using the manual.

In summary, this study showed that providing aphasia-friendly written material to support individual training by volunteers can enable people with aphasia to access the Internet. This is just one way in which the concept of aphasia-friendly formatting can be used to improve accessibility of information for people with aphasia.

FUTURE RESEARCH, PRACTICE, AND POLICY ISSUES

Some of the remaining questions about aphasia-friendly formatting that are being investigated by our research team include: Do people with aphasia receive less information than non-aphasic stroke patients while they are in hospital? Do their information needs change? Is aphasia-friendly text formatting different from best practice guidelines for general readability? How do people with aphasia respond/react to aphasia-friendly written materials? Are websites for people with aphasia aphasia-friendly?

In practice, the limited evidence to date suggests that aphasia-friendly formatting improves comprehension of written health information for people with aphasia. While more research is necessary, accessible versions of written material should be an available option for people with aphasia. For example, information provided by speech-language pathologists (e.g., directions to clinics, minutes of meetings, brochures about aphasia) can be modified to be aphasia-friendly. Written information in hospitals and rehabilitation facilities (e.g., stroke booklets, menu cards, phone instructions, consent forms for medical procedures) can be formatted according to these principles. Written information at home (e.g., personal phone books, calendars) can also be made aphasia-friendly.

There is also much to be done at a policy level so that ''communication ramps'' become as accepted as ''wheelchair ramps''. Aphasiologists need to ensure that policy makers understand that ''accessibility'' does not just mean physical accessibility (e.g., wheelchair ramps or cut-outs in kerbs). In addition, frequent monitoring of communicatively inaccessible services by consumers is needed so that service providers are reminded of their accessibility obligations. The website ''Ouch'' (http://www.bbc.co.uk/ouch) is an example of how people with disabilities are publicising accessibility issues.

The focus of the studies summarised here has been the effectiveness of aphasia-friendly formatting for written material. These studies have shown that there can be benefits to providing aphasia-friendly brochures, booklets, and manuals, but not all people with aphasia benefit from or prefer these modified formats. Caution is required when considering how aphasia-friendly formatting is used, particularly the use of illustrations. Further investigation into the type of illustrations (e.g., photos, ClipArt, hand-drawn illustrations) and method of selecting illustrations (keyword, verb only, concrete words only, low-frequency words, etc) is warranted.

In conclusion, while most aphasia rehabilitation to date has been directed at the person with aphasia, this paper has suggested there can be considerable gains made by making the environment more accessible. One key way to do this is to provide people with aphasia with aphasia-friendly written materials.

REFERENCES

Bernier, M. J. (1993). Developing and evaluating printed education materials: A prescriptive model for quality. *Orthopedic Nursing, 12*, 39–46.

Brennan, A., Worrall, L., & McKenna, K. (in press). The relationship between specific features of aphasia-friendly written material and comprehension of written material for people with aphasia. *Aphasiology.*

Egan, J., Worrall, L., & Oxenham, D. (2004). Accessible Internet training package helps people with aphasia cross the digital divide. *Aphasiology, 8*(3), 265–280.

Hoffmann, T., McKenna, K., Worrall, L., & Read, S. (2004). Evaluating current practice in the provision of written information to stroke patients and their carers. *International Journal of Therapy and Rehabilitation, 11*, 303–309.

Howe, T., Worrall, L., & Hickson, L. (2004). What is an aphasia-friendly environment? A review. *Aphasiology, 18*(11), 1015–1037.

Kagan, A., & Gailey, G. P. (1993) Functional is not enough: Training conversation partners for aphasic adults. In A. L. Holland & M. M. Forbes (Eds.), *Aphasia treatment: World perspectives* (pp. 199–225). San Diego, CA: Singular Publishing Group.

McLaughlin, H. (1969). SMOG grading: A new readability formula. *Journal of Reading, 12*, 639–646.

Parr, S., Byng, S., & Gilpin, S., with Ireland, C. (1997). *Talking about aphasia: Living with loss of language after stroke*. Buckingham, UK: Open University Press.

Rose, T., Worrall, L., & McKenna, K. (2003). The effectiveness of aphasia-friendly principles for printed health education materials for people with aphasia following stroke. *Aphasiology, 17*(10), 947–963.

World Health Organisation (WHO). (2001). *International Classification of Functioning, Disability and Health.* [http://www3.who.int/icf].

APHASIOLOGY, 2005, 19 (10/11), 930–942

AAC for hypothesis testing and treatment of aphasic language production: Lessons from a "processing prosthesis"

Marcia C. Linebarger

Psycholinguistic Technologies, Inc., and Moss Rehabilitation Research Institute, Philadelphia, PA, USA

Myrna F. Schwartz

Moss Rehabilitation Research Institute, Philadelphia, PA, USA

Background: The design of augmentative and alternative communication (AAC) technology for aphasic individuals must be informed by a theory of the underlying disorder in order to determine what kind of assistance will be most effective. AAC devices may therefore serve to test competing theories, each predicting the efficacy of a different kind of support for language production. They may also serve as heuristic tools, affording the opportunity to observe language production under radically altered conditions. A communication system that we have termed a "processing prosthesis" was directly inspired by the performance hypothesis, the view that processing factors rather than loss of linguistic knowledge underlie aphasic language production disorders. Unlike AAC technology, which focuses on the provision of *direct* linguistic support in the form of vocabulary items and pre-stored utterances, this system (referred to here and in previous literature as the "CS") emphasises *indirect* support to allow the user to more fully exploit his or her retained language production capabilities. If the CS is effective in facilitating aphasic sentence construction, this may be taken as evidence in support of the performance hypothesis embodied in its design. *Aims*: We illustrate the interplay between AAC technology and psycholinguistic theory by reviewing studies of the CS, and describe some approaches to language remediation that have emerged from this work. *Contributions*: We review three published studies and preliminary data from a fourth. These studies demonstrate the efficacy of the CS through "aided" effects (i.e., the extent to which utterances produced on the system are more structured and/or informative than those produced without the system) and treatment effects (i.e., the impact of a period of CS use on the aphasic individual's spontaneous, unaided speech). *Conclusions*: The CS data suggest that "indirect" support may play an important role in facilitating and treating aphasic sentence production; and, more generally, they demonstrate the bidirectional flow of insight between assistive technology and the psycholinguistic analysis of aphasic disorders.

Address correspondence to: Dr Marcia Linebarger, Psycholinguistic Technologies, Inc., 93 Old York Road, Suite 1#447, Jenkintown, PA 19046, USA. Email: Linebarger@psycholinguistic-technologies.com

Preparation of this manuscript was supported by NIH/NICHHD R01HD043991 to M. Schwartz. The work reviewed in this paper benefited from the collaboration and assistance of many individuals, including Rita Berndt, Megan Bartlett, Roberta Brooks, Monica Chun, Ted Kantner, Susan Kohn, Denise McCall, John Romania, Paula Sobel, Diane Stephens, and Telana Virata.

http://www.tandf.co.uk/journals/pp/02687038.html

DOI:10.1080/02687030544000146

Augmentative and alternative communication (AAC) technology designed for individuals with aphasia—in contrast to people with severe motor disabilities but unimpaired sentence formulation—must provide assistance with the process of sentence construction itself. Therefore, the design of an AAC device must draw on a theory of the underlying language deficit; and, importantly, the efficacy of this device may provide a test of this theory. That is, if a theory posits that the absence of X underlies an aphasic language disorder, and if a device is created to provide X, then the efficacy of this device can be used to test the claim about the role of X in the disorder. (Positive evidence is more definitive than negative evidence in this regard, since the latter may result from the failure to provide X in an appropriate form or quantity.) By "efficacy" we refer here to two related measures.[1] First, what we will term the *aided effect* is the extent to which productions created with the help of the device are superior—structurally, lexically, or otherwise—to the user's spontaneous speech. A second measure of the efficacy of an AAC device is its *treatment effect*, the impact of language practice with the device on the user's unaided, spontaneous speech. If an AAC device does show an aided effect—if it facilitates the creation of more structured or informative utterances—then the expectation arises that this practice may carry over into unaided speech. Such a carryover would add additional support to the theory embodied in the AAC device. Note that we restrict our attention here to the impact of the device on structural and informational properties of language produced under laboratory conditions. The important question of whether and how the device enhances functional communication outside the laboratory is beyond the scope of this paper.

We will follow common practice in distinguishing two broad families of theories about aphasia: *competence* versus *performance* accounts. Competence-based accounts invoke a loss of linguistic knowledge or ability. The essential claim is that language breaks down along linguistic lines, that aphasic disorders are most plausibly defined in terms of some specific kind of linguistic information that is not processed correctly (e.g., wh-gaps or the mapping between syntactic structure and thematic roles). In contrast, performance-based accounts are rooted in the belief that linguistic knowledge is largely preserved in aphasia but cannot be used effectively in real time due to performance factors: difficulties in accessing, retaining, or selecting linguistic information under the temporal constraints that normally obtain in spoken language production. For example, Kolk and colleagues have argued for a slowing down of the syntactic component, and concomitant reduction of the temporal window for syntactic computation (Kolk, 1995). Reduction in the span of lexical-semantic STM has been shown to compromise phrase and sentence production by reducing the syntactic workspace (Martin, Katz, & Freedman, 1998). And word-finding problems, which may contribute to syntactic fragmentation, have been linked to performance-based factors such as interference among co-activated elements, so that words that can be produced in isolation may fail to be retrieved in connected speech (Schwartz & Hodgson, 2002; Williams & Canter, 1982).

Competence and performance accounts suggest different approaches to assistive technology. The competence account would seem to be most consistent with what we will term *direct support*: the provision of linguistic information—words, phrases, sentences, or structural templates—which the user is anticipated to require. Most AAC devices currently used by aphasic individuals provide such direct support (although we do not suggest that their design was in fact motivated by the competence account). For

---

[1] Neither of these senses corresponds to the use of this term in the clinical trials literature.

example, C-VIC (Weinrich, McCall, Shoosmith, Thomas, Katzenberger, & Weber, 1993) and its descendants allow the user to select among pictographic icons and/or printed text, using dynamic displays whose size and complexity can be customised to the user's cognitive/linguistic skills. For more recent exemplars of the C-VIC paradigm, spoken output is provided: touching or clicking icons triggers the output, via synthesised speech or another individuals' recorded speech, of utterances pre-programmed by the clinician or family member.

In contrast, the performance account suggests a different approach, one that we will term *indirect support*. On this account, the goal of an AAC device is help the user to exploit her or his preserved language-production abilities rather than attempting to compensate for linguistic lacunae. Let us consider what kind of support this might entail. A common theme in all the performance-based accounts is *time*: the aphasic speaker needs some way to "stop the clock", to retain sentence elements already produced while laboriously accessing additional material. It was observed in the C-VIC literature that iconic AAC devices can perform this function in a limited way: the icons selected by the user remain visible while the sentence is completed, thereby providing a record of the partially completed structure. The superior performance of people with severe aphasia on C-VIC as contrasted with their spoken output was attributed in part to this memory support, as well as to the fact that the system bypasses the user's verbal expression altogether; lexical retrieval reduces to icon selection.

However, it is this last feature, the bypassing of spontaneous speech, that limits the effectiveness of such systems for many aphasic users. For severely aphasic individuals with little or no verbal output, selecting from a pre-stored set of elements may be required in order to communicate at all. But many individuals with aphasia, even those with fragmentary and ungrammatical speech, are nevertheless able to produce some appropriate material, in most contexts; and they may strongly prefer to rely on their spontaneous speech rather than on the output of a mechanical device. The goal of the indirect support approach to AAC is to allow the user to build on this retained ability.

The CS[2] (Linebarger, Schwartz, Romania, Kohn, & Stephens, 2000), a communication system that we have characterised as a "processing prosthesis", is designed to provide processing support in order to build on whatever spoken language the user is able to produce. The system links spoken words or phrases recorded by the user with visual icons which can be moved around on the screen, replayed, and built up into sentences and narratives. The memory support provided by the system essentially "turns off the clock", allowing the user unlimited time to compose sentences and narratives. In this paper, we will review data from recent studies of the CS in order to characterise more fully the indirect support approach to AAC technology, and its implications for remediation and for the analysis of aphasic disorders. Although we will focus on research incorporating this processing prosthesis, the lessons we have learned may also be applicable to other AAC technologies and to non-computerised language therapy.

---

[2] We use the term "CS" to refer to the original research prototype employed in the studies reviewed here. A commercial version of the system is soon to be distributed by Psycholinguistic Technologies, Inc. (www.SentenceShaper.com) under the name "SentenceShaper". Therefore a potential conflicting interest should be noted, as ML owns shares in Psycholinguistic Technologies. In order to avoid conflict of interest, ML has not participated in testing or in scoring of raw data in any of the studies reviewed here.

OVERVIEW OF THE CS

The system can be operated with either a touch screen or a mouse. To record an utterance of any length, the user speaks into a microphone, touching buttons at the bottom of the screen to register the beginning and end of the utterance. A coloured shape then appears; touching this shape causes the recorded material (referred to below as a ''chunk'') to be played back. The user can build these individual chunks into sentences by dragging them to a *Sentence Assembly Area* at the top of the screen. The chunks lined up in the sentence assembly area can be played back in sequence, so that the user can monitor his or her productions. If dissatisfied, the user can re-order the chunks, delete a chunk that sounds wrong, or move one or more chunks back into the work area. When the user is satisfied with the contents of the sentence assembly area, he or she can click a button to have the contents combined into a single, larger unit and represented as a single icon in a second staging area, the *Narrative Assembly Area* at the side of the screen. The entire sequence in the narrative area can be replayed by touching another button. This whole process is repeated until an entire narrative is composed. The functionality described above represents purely indirect support: no linguistic information is provided. By allowing the user to replay material already recorded, and to replay and correct different orderings of sentence elements, the CS functions as a kind of externalised working memory.

Although its primary function is to serve as a processing prosthesis, the CS can be configured to provide two forms of lexical support. The *WordFinder*, a hierarchical list of printed words and phrases, is accessed from a button on the screen. The *Side Buttons* surrounding the main work area of the CS display (unless customised by the clinician) 10 prepositions and 10 high-frequency, predominantly ''light'' verbs (e.g., ''make'', ''have'', ''go''). In both these tools, touching a printed word causes the system to play its pronunciation; the user must then record the word him/herself to incorporate it into a production.

Is the CS an effective communication system? Below we review several recent studies assessing the two sorts of efficacy discussed above: aided effects and treatment effects.

"AIDED" EFFECTS FROM PURE PROCESSING SUPPORT

Does the CS allow users to create richer or more structured utterances than they could create without the system? The clearest evidence on this point comes from a study (Linebarger et al., 2000) in which six agrammatic aphasic subjects were trained to use the CS, and were then provided with computers in their homes in order to use the system independently, constructing narratives on topics of personal interest. Because our intention was to assess the impact of indirect support alone, the lexical tools (Side Buttons, WordFinder) were not available during testing. After approximately 15 hours of system use, subjects were asked to create narratives on the CS to describe two silent videos, which had not been viewed during training. Using an ABBA design (A = unaided; B = aided), the narratives were elicited over four sessions. For data analysis, we collapsed data across the two videos per condition. Performance was analysed using the Quantitative Production Analysis (QPA) methodology (Saffran, Berndt, & Schwartz, 1989) which indexes both structural and morphological properties of narrative production. Structural QPA measures include, e.g., Proportion of Words in Sentences, Mean Sentence Length, and Median Length of Utterance (the measures that we will track in the discussion below); morphological/closed-class measures index the presence of determiners, verb inflections, auxiliaries, and the closed-class vocabulary taken as a whole.

In the QPA analysis of these video narratives (Tables 1 & 2 in Linebarger et al., 2000,), the aided narratives contained longer and more sentential utterances than the unaided versions, as evidenced by increases in a variety of QPA structural measures. These effects were significant for the group, in the right direction in five of the six subjects, and quite marked for two subjects. These two subjects' aided transcripts differed from their aided transcripts in the three structural measures noted above: Proportion of Words in Sentences (.11 in DD's unaided narratives, .86 in the aided counterparts; .34 in DB's unaided transcripts and .82 in the aided counterparts); Mean Sentence Length (3.4 unaided and 6.5 aided for DD, 3.9 unaided and 5.3 aided for DB); and Median Length of Utterance (2 in DD's unaided narratives, 4 in the aided counterparts; 2 in DB's unaided transcripts and 5 in the aided counterparts). Examples of these two subjects' unaided and aided descriptions of the same video events are provided below.

Subject DB:
(*Unaided*) The, the maid, the maid, the maid, uh, uh, upstair and she, uh, the maid upstairs and "scuse me" and um … *go* around but now uh the …. The policeman, she she?, no, the man, two men, and the uh, oh, she, uh, her, she … *knock* them out, knock them out, um hum, knock them out, two men.
(*Aided*) The man goes around them. She did not do it. The nurse goes around the baby carriage. The policeman, she fights the, the two men.

Subject DD:
(*Unaided*) "Ooh! A fish! Ah, water" and …. uh mmm and attendant, "here," and bumped his head. "Oh boy, oh my hand, my hand, my hand."
(*Aided*) The boy and the fishmonger is taking the fish. The boy hit his hand.

It should be stressed that these two subjects showed the strongest aided effects, and one of the six subjects showed no significant aided effects at all. Interestingly, the reliable aided effects were all observed in structural QPA measures, in contrast to morphological/closed-class measures, which were largely unaffected although the auxiliary and inflection measures showed a trend in the predicted direction. The distinction between structural and morphological aided effects may be seen as providing support for those who posit distinct agrammatic deficits, one a "constructional" agrammatism marked by impoverished structure and the other a "morphological" agrammatism characterised by the omission and mis-selection of closed-class elements (e.g., Saffran, Schwartz, & Marin, 1980). On this account, the CS results could be taken to indicate that constructional agrammatism—in contrast to morphological agrammatism—derives from processing limitations, and is therefore ameliorated with processing support such as the CS provides.

The aided effects observed in this study illustrate how AAC technology may emerge from a theory of the underlying deficit, and may in turn be used to assess the validity of this theory. The CS was directly inspired by the performance hypothesis and, in turn, provides quite strong support for it, because the structural enhancement of sentences produced on the CS in this study derived entirely from the processing support that the system provided.

TREATMENT EFFECTS FROM CS USE

We would argue that narrative production, as contrasted with more constrained language tasks such as single picture description, should be used to assess the efficacy of virtually any treatment protocol targeting aphasic sentence production. One reason is that gains in narrative production may correspond more directly to changes in functional communication. Several studies (Doyle, Tsironas, Goda, & Kalinyak, 1996; Jacobs, 2001; Ross & Wertz, 1999) have linked measures of connected speech with naïve listeners' perceptions of communicative competence, while other studies (Doyle, Goda, & Spencer, 1995; Thompson, Shapiro, Tait, Jacobs, Schneider, & Ballard, 1995) have reported strong similarities between the narrative and conversational speech of individuals with aphasia. The prominent role of storytelling in much of human conversation certainly engenders the expectation that gains in measures of connected speech would be reflected in subjects' functional communication. Unfortunately, treatment gains have rarely generalised from more constrained laboratory tasks to the production of connected speech (see, e.g., Berndt & Mitchum, 1995, for a review). In recent years, however, several approaches to the treatment of aphasic language production have reported gains in connected speech, although the changes observed have been variable across subjects and across discourse measures: Mapping Therapy (reviewed in Marshall, 1995), the "Linguistic Specific Treatment" of Thompson and colleagues (e.g., Thompson, Shapiro, Kiran, & Sobecks, 2003), and treatment studies incorporating the CS. The latter are reviewed below.

CS in conjunction with other software

Two subjects participated in an extended treatment programme (Linebarger, Schwartz, & Kohn, 2001) in which the CS was used alternately (but not concurrently) with another language therapy programme. As indicated in Linebarger et al. (2001, Tables 7 & 9), the first 15 hours of home CS use (in addition to several hours of CS training) impacted various discourse measures of both subjects' *unaided* retellings of silent videos viewed before and after (but not during) training. For example, both subjects showed changes in Median Length of Utterance (JT: 2 pre, 4 post; JW: 3 pre, 5 post) and Mean Sentence Length (JT: 3.7 pre, 5.1 post; JW: 6.4 pre, 7.7 post). These gains are particularly encouraging because they were achieved through largely independent home use of the CS. Although subjects came to the lab weekly to be observed using the CS, there was very little instruction from the experimenters. Advice was limited to reminders to replay and monitor material already produced, and to try to create full sentences. Neither subject received any assistance from family members or friends in their home use of the system.

CS with lexical support

A second study (Linebarger, McCall, & Berndt, 2004a) used the CS with both lexical tools described above: the Side Buttons and the WordFinder. Two nonfluent aphasic subjects were trained to use the CS, and then engaged in 11 weeks of independent home practice (approx. 5 hours/week), with weekly visits to the lab (where they were given minimal instruction in system use). They were provided with videotaped, edited episodes of a television show to describe during home practice. The WordFinder vocabulary was customised to include words used by unimpaired control subjects describing the videotaped episodes. Pre and post training, subjects described an unpractised silent video in the unaided mode. Both subjects used the CS effectively, but only one subject made significant gains in unaided language. As indicated in Linebarger et al. (2004a, Table 2), the latter subject (S2) showed gains in most structural QPA measures (Median Length of Utterance: 4 pre, 6 post; Mean Sentence Length: 4.78 pre, 6.35 post; % Words in Sentences: .73 pre, .81 post) and increases in informativeness under the Nicholas and Brookshire (1993) Correct Information Unit (CIU) analysis (%CIUs: .46 pre, .71 post;

CIUs/min: 41 pre, 51 post). Neither subject made significant improvement in morphological measures.

Three additional aphasic subjects participated in a subsequent study (Linebarger, McCall, Virata, & Berndt, 2004b) in which the WordFinder was disabled and CS lexical support was limited to the Side Buttons. After CS training, subjects used the CS at home for 10–28 weeks, with weekly visits to the lab. Unaided retellings of the same short silent videos were elicited weekly for 8 weeks prior to the introduction of the CS and every 3–5 weeks following the start of CS home use, in order to assess the impact of extended CS use on structural (QPA) and informational (CIU) properties of unaided speech. The test videos themselves were never practised on the CS. Repeated elicitation of the same video narratives over the eight baseline sessions did not result in upward trends in structural measures for any of the three aphasic subjects in this study, and only one of the three subjects showed a positive trend at baseline on any of the measures studied. Treatment effects from CS use were assessed by comparing the mean scores for all baselines with the mean scores for all narratives produced post-onset of CS home use. All three subjects made significant gains on a variety of QPA and CIU measures following the start of CS use, suggesting that the support provided by the CS played a critical role in the observed treatment gains.

CS combined with supported conversation groups: The "CS + Groups" study

Further data regarding the impact of CS use on unaided spoken language production are emerging from a recently concluded study employing the CS in the context of aphasia groups (Schwartz, Linebarger, Brooks, & Bartlett, 2005). In this project, subjects met weekly in 90-minute, supported conversation groups led by a speech language pathologist and research assistant. For 1–2 hours each week, group participants also underwent training on the CS. After achieving mastery of CS mechanics, each subject was provided with a computer, for independent practice at home; the CS was augmented to automatically transfer homework productions onto a zip disk for transport between home and lab. Weekly 1-hour training sessions in the lab continued after that, with emphasis on replaying and revising homework productions.

During this study, we explored several new uses of the CS, which aimed at deepening social contacts among group members. As an AAC device, the CS is most appropriate for communicative situations that allow unlimited time for message creation. And so, for example, aphasic individuals have occasionally used the CS to create and deliver speeches or other public presentations (two of which are reported in Fried, 2002, pp. 150, 262).In the CS + Groups Study, we piloted two other CS applications which allow the user unlimited time to compose: *CS-based email*, a version of the CS with a simple interface allowing aphasic individuals to send their CS narratives as compressed sound file attachments to emails (Linebarger, Schwartz, Kantner, & McCall, 2002), and a *group website* (run locally on subjects' home computers, for reasons of privacy and expense). The latter played CS productions in conjunction with photographs provided by the subjects, and functioned as a "virtual scrapbook" to describe their families, interests, and opinions. Subjects were encouraged to send each other emails, and to view fellow members' web pages in order to identify areas of common interest that could be discussed in emails.

We will focus here on the final two of the four groups, during which—more than in earlier groups—we emphasised home use of the CS and encouraged sub-

TABLE 1
QPA Scores

Subj	WAB Sub type	WAB AQ (Pre)	Test	Cinderella				Silent video				Wordless story book			
				Mn. S	WIS	MLU	VPU	Mn. S	WIS	MLU	VPU	Mn. S	WIS	MLU	VPU
S9	A	66.8	Pre	3.92	.31	2	0.32	3.50	.24	2	.33	5.30	.34	3	.47
			Post	**5.00**	.38	**3**	**0.55**	**4.54**	**.38**	**4**	**.48**	5.07	**.51**	**5**	**.63**
S8	BA	63.2	Pre	3.63	.19	1	0.18	2.60	.15	1	.33	2.63	.29	2	.30
			Post	**4.50**	**.52**	**3**	**0.52**	**4.33**	**.35**	**2**	**.51**	**6.69**	**.82**	**6**	**1.17**
S11	BA	74.6	Pre	4.50	.37	2	0.30	4.50	.31	2.5	.60	5.25	.34	2.5	.24
			Post	**5.80**	.38	**3**	0.43	**5.00**	**.66**	2	**.70**	**6.26**	**.76**	**5**	**.83**
S16	BA	68.8	Pre	4.37	.53	3	0.63	4.57	.39	3	.67	6.43	.30	3	.60
			Post	**5.47**	**.68**	3	**0.92**	**5.50**	.51	2	.62	6.06	**.71**	**4**	.58
S14	BA	67.4	Pre	3.43	.15	2	0.43	5.00	.06	1	.48	2.93	.37	2	.44
			Post	**4.21**	**.37**	2	0.47	3.00	.08	**2**	.47	**4.13**	.42	**3**	.54
S12	BA	67.2	Pre	4.27	.48	2	0.44	3.83	. 53	3	.43	3.95	.62	3	.48
			Post	3.88	.44	2	0.46	**4.85**	. **83**	3	**.82**	**5.22**	**.90**	**4**	**.78**
S15	BA	48.6	Pre	–	–	–	–	0	0	1	.20	4.00	.11	1	.37
			Post	–	–	–	–	**2.33**	.09	**2**	.27	3.33	.21	**2**	.21
S7	BA	53.1	Pre	–	–	–	–	3.00	.08	1	.38	2.60	.21	1	.46
			Post	–	–	–	–	2.33	**.23**	1	**.54**	2.33	.26	1	.45
S10	CA	57.5	Pre	4.10	.77	4	0.86	3.85	.78	4	.93	4.78	.84	4	.80
			Post	**4.59**	.80	3	0.79	3.93	.75	3	.71	4.68	.68	4	.65
S13	BA	61.2	Pre	5.59	.82	5	0.90	5.14	.67	3	.47	4.56	.58	3	.78
			Post	4.88	.79	3	0.89	4.44	**.82**	3	**.71**	4.63	**.71**	3.5	.74

For the participants in Groups 3 and 4, Quantitative Production Analysis scores on three production tasks, pre and post study.

Mn. S = Mean number of words in sentences; WIS = proportion of words in sentences; MLU = median utterance length (sentences and non-sentences); VPU = Verbs per utterance (sentences and non-sentences); A = anomia; BA = Broca's aphasia; CA = conduction aphasia.

Post scores set in bold typeface are those that exceed pre scores by at least half the pooled standard deviation for that measure.

jects to create complex narratives (e.g., retellings of television programmes and the like) rather than the simpler and more formulaic email messages typically created in earlier groups. All subjects were chronic (15 to 72 months post-onset) and moderately impaired (as indicated in Table 1, WAB severity levels ranged from 48.6 to 74.6 prior to treatment). Pre/post changes in narrative language performance were measured with three unpractised probes administered across different days: a wordless story book, a wordless video, and fairy tale narration. Table 1 summarises the performance of these 10 subjects, reporting Verbs Per Utterance in addition to the three QPA measures that we have emphasised above (MLU, Mean Sentence Length, % Words in Sentences).

As indicated in Table 1, the subjects in this study fell into two groups in terms of their response to treatment. The six "good responders" (those in the upper grouping of Table 1) made impressive gains in a variety of measures across all three narrative tasks, in contrast to the four "poor responders" whose performance was unchanged or even declined following treatment.

DISCUSSION

Below we summarise three major lessons that we have learned from the CS studies.

Lesson 1: Efficacy of indirect support

Why does the processing support provided by the CS allow aphasic users to create more structured utterances on the system than they are capable of in their unaided speech? One reason is that it effectively *enlarges the planning window*, allowing the user to assemble and integrate into a sentence more material than would be possible under normal conditions. A second, related reason is that it *allows the user to more fully exploit lexical associations*. The inability of aphasic users—under normal, unaided conditions—to maintain in memory the material they have already produced, may deprive them of the kinds of lexical associations that normally play an important role in language production, and may force them to rely too heavily on purely "top-down" concept-driven activation of words and structures. The CS, in contrast, allows users to replay segments they have recorded (in a deliberate effort to elicit a completion) and in this way they are able to take advantage of inter-lexical associations and the cloze effect. Replay of these fragments provides a semantic, syntactic, and even prosodic context, which may help in overcoming word retrieval blocks as we know from the clinical and research literature on sentence-completion cueing. More generally, there is considerable evidence for better word retrieval in connected speech than in isolated naming e.g., (Berndt, Haendiges, Mitchum, & Sandson, 1997; Kohn & Cragnolino, 1998; Marshall, Pring, & Chiat, 1998; Williams & Canter, 1982; Zingeser & Berndt, 1990), and the various factors thought to be responsible for this effect are potentially operative in the CS environment as well.

While our CS training procedures have always emphasised the replaying of previously recorded material in order to activate an appropriate completion, another strategy for exploiting lexical associations emerged from the CS + Groups Study: the use of prepositions and light verbs to "bootstrap" lexical retrieval, as illustrated in the following example.

Nonfluent aphasic subject S11 (see Table 1) exhibited marked "content paucity" in generating narratives, producing a word or phrase and then insisting that she couldn't think of anything else to say. In response to this, we developed a strategy of insisting that she begin each production by selecting and incorporating a preposition or light verb from the CS Side Buttons into each production. Despite her protestations that none of these words were relevant to the topic at hand, the item that she selected would quite often trigger the production of highly relevant material. For example, having produced a painfully sparse narrative about her family's observance of Christmas (limited to the single word "tree"*),* she was instructed to select and incorporate into each sentence a preposition from the Side Buttons. The resulting narrative was far richer: "*Underneath* the tree is a manger. *Above* the manger is a star. *In front of* the manger Mary and Joseph were kneeling. *Behind* the tree is a plug. *From* the light *to* the plug lights are sparkling." Only the Side Button prepositions (in italics) were provided by the CS; the other material was produced spontaneously by S11 within structures initiated by these prepositions.

Similar effects have been observed in conjunction with exercises focused on the Side Button verbs. In general, it is impressive that these light verbs and prepositions—which one would assume are poor triggers for lexical associates, given their stripped-down semantics—nevertheless have a surprising ability to pull ideas and words with them. Although words such as "under" or "have" do not have strong lexical associations in isolation, they do appear to trigger associations *within more explicit contexts*, as illustrated in the example above. Our aphasic subjects have generally found this boot-strapping tactic highly counterintuitive, since in effect we are instructing them to address word-finding problems by starting with an "irrelevant" lexical item—a word such as "under" which is not itself activated in any top-down fashion by the conceptual context (Christmas, in the above example)—and to use the lexical associations of this "irrele-vant" word (in the context of Christmas, "under" immediately evoked "tree") to drive the content of their message. However, despite the perceived artificiality of this strategy, it is very effective for some aphasic subjects. For such individuals, it is possible that intensively training these words would increase their availability during unaided speech, and that this heightened activation would in itself facilitate lexical retrieval as observed above, without any conscious use of the bootstrapping techniques employed on the CS. With their more severe patients, clinicians often adopt the strategy of training a small core vocabulary. Typically, this vocabulary comprises nouns that refer to everyday objects, along with some action verbs. Our experience with the CS, however, suggests that (for some aphasic individuals) training a core vocabulary of prepositions and mul-tipurpose light verbs might ultimately impact the retrieval of a wide variety of words and structures.

Lesson 2: Prerequisites for successful CS use

We have tentatively identified two abilities that appear to be linked to successful CS use: *monitoring/metalinguistic skills* and *left-to-right fluency*. It is our hypothesis that either one of these capabilities may suffice to allow effective use of the system, and that "poor responders" to CS training evince neither. These abilities may well be linked to aphasia severity: as indicated in Table 1, the four subjects who did not show consistent treatment effects from CS use all had WAB AQs outside the range for the good responders.[3] Two quite distinct styles of effective CS use are profiled below.

The first capability (monitoring/metalinguistic skills) may be observed in what we will term the "anagram" style user who may have a limited production workspace (as evi-denced by an inability to produce more than a word or two at a time) but has good monitoring and correcting skills, which allow him/her to concatenate small chunks into larger structures. An "anagram" user attempting to describe a picture of a dog eating a bone under a table might proceed as follows:

1. Select "under" from the Side Buttons, record it, and replay it in the Work Area.
2. Subsequently record its object "table".
3. Move "under" and "table" up to the Sentence Assembly Area, yielding the sequence "*under | table*".
4. Record "the bone", replay this phrase, and then record "eat", all in the Work Area.
5. Drag both new chunks to the sentence area to form the sequence "*eat | the bone | under | table*".

---

[3] In referring to "effective" use of the CS here, we are not distinguishing between aided and treatment effects. The relationship between these two kinds of effects remains to be fully explored. While subjects who do not show aided effects rarely make treatment gains, the inverse is not true; for example, subject S1 in Linebarger et al. (2004a) showed impressive aided effects but made only very limited treatment gains.

6. Replay this sequence and add a subject noun "dog", yielding "*dog* | eat | the bone | under | table".

7. Notice the missing determiners and verb morphology, and modify the sequence—through re-recording and/or insertion of new recordings—to yield "*the dog* | *eats* | the bone | under | *the table*".

It is of considerable interest that some subjects who cannot produce more than a word or two at a time are nonetheless able to monitor and correct or expand these longer sequences, suggesting that the workspace capacity for sentence production is different from the workspace capacity drawn upon for receptive sentence monitoring. It has been our experience during the aphasia group study that subjects with a restricted production workspace appear to benefit from the task of re-recording a series of small chunks into larger phrasal chunks. In our hypothetical example, the user might re-record the five chunks above into two: "the dog eats the bone | under the table". We hypothesise that CS use, and possibly this particular exercise, may actually bring about an expansion in the user's language-production workspace.

The second capability (left-to-right fluency) may be observed in the user who has better sentence construction skills and can generate limited sentences left to right. These subjects replay their CS productions in order to trigger new material, and we hypothesise that they benefit from CS use primarily through training in exploitation of the cloze effect and other context-facilitation effects (discussed above). Such a user might record "the dog eats a" and then replay this chunk to trigger a direct object "bone"; replaying the sequence "the dog eats a | bone" in the sentence assembly area might then trigger an additional phrase "under the table". If such a user produced "bone" or "table" initially, however, he or she might be unable to proceed by going back and producing a subject and main verb, despite greater fluency in left to right generation. The inability of some "left-to-right" users to employ the anagram strategy described above further supports the distinctiveness of the production and monitoring workspaces. In fact, these two types of users—"anagram" users who cannot produce more than a word or two at a time, but are able to use their monitoring skills to build these fragments into larger structures; and "left-to-right" users who can produce longer utterances but are unable to correct or revise them effectively—provide a double dissociation in this regard.

Although we have focused here on the processing support provided by the CS, there are other ways to provide certain aspects of this support. As noted above, iconic AAC devices such as C-VIC provide a record of sentence elements previously selected. For individuals with preserved reading skills, the use of written text (possibly created through use of a speech recogniser and maintained if necessary through text to speech playback) may provide some of the functionality of the CS. For example, a recent study (Peach & Wong, 2004) reports treatment gains from a narrative-based protocol in which a human clinician transcribed each of the patient's utterances, read it aloud, and then instructed the patient to monitor it closely and edit the transcription (followed by explicit feedback).

Lesson 3: Intensive and narrative-based practice may be required for treatment gains

Our treatment studies with the CS add to the weight of evidence that chronic aphasic individuals may continue to make language gains, but that regular and fairly intensive practice may be required. In addition, we have found that narrative production exercises (e.g., retelling television shows) appear to be more effective than simpler tasks (e.g., describing single-event pictures), an argument also advanced by Peach and Wong (2004). The impact of continued practice is illustrated by subjects S8 and S11 in the CS + Groups study. Having made strong gains during the study (see Table 1), these subjects requested to participate in a second group. Both subjects' narrative measures showed further gains following this second group. For example, all three QPA measures rose for the Cinderella narrative: Median Length of Utterance (subject S8: 3 to 3.5; subject S11: 3 to 5); Mean Sentence Length (subject S8: 4.5 to 5.42; subject S11: 5.8 to 6.11), and Proportion of Words in Sentences (subject S8: .52 to .67; subject S11: .38 to .76).This suggests that the impact of CS use may not plateau early on; and since the CS can be used independently, extended CS treatment is potentially feasible. A questionnaire administered to all subjects in the CS + Groups study indicated the willingness of many participants to use the CS for the long term and with some degree of independence: 82% expressed "a lot" of interest in continuing to use the CS following completion of the study, and 63% expressed the desire to work on the CS with little or no assistance. However, the most compelling motivation for aphasic individuals to continue using the CS (or any AAC device) will come from its integration into functional contexts. The Internet-based applications piloted in the CS + Groups Study are promising in this regard, and we are currently investigating the integration of the CS with a handheld device which would extend its deployment to "real world" communicative situations.

CONCLUSIONS

The performance hypothesis has major implications for assistive technology. The "indirect support" approach that it motivates may be summarised as follows: help the user to access his or her preserved knowledge, rather than attempting to anticipate and provide specific words or utterances. The CS essentially provides an artificially enlarged language-production workspace, and in this supportive environment, many aphasic individuals are able to assemble much more elaborated structures than they can produce without processing support. Furthermore, there is increasing evidence that this greater elaboration carries over to unaided, spontaneous speech in some (but not all) aphasic individuals who engage in extended but largely independent language practice in the supportive environment of the CS. The heuristic potential of AAC technology is illustrated, albeit more anecdotally, in the work reviewed here. The strategic use of prepositions and light verbs to trigger appropriate content words, for example, is more easily induced in the artificial environment of the CS because words can be maintained long enough to evoke appropriate associations. The studies reviewed here add to the increasing evidence that assistive technology may guide both the analysis and the remediation of aphasic language disorders.

REFERENCES

Berndt, R. S., Haendiges, A. N., Mitchum, C. C., & Sandson, J. (1997). Verb retrieval in aphasia: 2. Relationship to sentence processing. *Brain and Language, 56,* 107–137.

Berndt, R. S., & Mitchum, C. C. (1995). Cognitive neuropsychological approaches to the treatment of language disorders. *Neuropsychological Rehabilitation, 5,* 1–6.

Doyle, P. J., Goda, A. H., & Spencer, K. A. (1995). The communicative informativeness and efficiency of connected discourse in adults with aphasia under structured and conversational sampling conditions. *American Journal of Speech-Language Pathology, 4,* 130–134.

Doyle, P. J., Tsironas, D., Goda, A. H., & Kalinyak, M. (1996). The relationship between objective measures and listeners' judgments of the communicative informativeness of the connected discourse of adults with aphasia. *American Journal of Speech-Language Pathology, 5,* 53–60.

Fried, S. (2002). *The new rabbi*. New York: Bantam Books.

Jacobs, B. J. (2001). Social validity of changes in informativeness and efficiency of aphasic discourse following linguistic specific treatment. *Brain and Language, 78*, 115–127.

Kohn, S. E., & Cragnolino, A. (1998). The role of lexical co-occurrence in aphasic sentence production. *Applied Psycholinguistics, 19*, 631–646.

Kolk, H. H. J. (1995). A time-based approach to agrammatic production. *Brain and Language, 50*, 282–303.

Linebarger, M. C., McCall, D., & Berndt, R. S. (2004a). The role of processing support in the remediation of aphasic language production disorders. *Cognitive Neuropsychology, 21*, 267–282.

Linebarger, M., McCall, D., Virata, T., & Berndt, R. S. (2004b). *Supported versus unsupported narrative elicitation: Impact on language production in aphasia*. Poster presented at the annual meeting of the Academy of Aphasia, Chicago, IL.

Linebarger, M. C., Schwartz, M., Kantner, T. R., & McCall, D. (2002). Promoting access to the Internet in aphasia [abstract]. *Brain and Language, 83*, 169–172.

Linebarger, M. C., Schwartz, M. F., & Kohn, S. E. (2001). Computer-based training of language production: An exploratory study. *Neuropsychological Rehabilitation, 11*(1), 57–96.

Linebarger, M. C., Schwartz, M. F., Romania, J. F., Kohn, S. E., & Stephens, D. L. (2000). Grammatical encoding in aphasia: Evidence from a ''processing prosthesis''. *Brain and Language, 75*, 416–427.

Marshall, J. (1995). The mapping hypothesis and aphasia therapy. *Aphasiology, 9*(6), 517–539.

Marshall, J., Pring, T., & Chiat, S. (1998). Verb retrieval and sentence production in aphasia. *Brain and Language, 63*, 159–183.

Martin, R. C., Katz, M., & Freedman, M. (1998). Lexical-semantic retention and language production. *Brain and Language, 65*, 99–101.

Nicholas, L. E., & Brookshire, R. H. (1993). A system for scoring main concepts in the discourse of non-brain damaged and aphasic speakers. *Clinical Aphasiology, 21*, 87–99.

Peach, R. K., & Wong, P. C. M. (2004). Integrating the message level into treatment for agrammatism using story retelling. *Aphasiology, 18*, 429–441.

Ross, K. B., & Wertz, R. T. R. (1999). Comparison of impairment and disability measures for assessing severity of, and improvement in, aphasia. *Aphasiology, 13*, 113–124.

Saffran, E. M., Berndt, R. S., & Schwartz, M. F. (1989). The quantitative analysis of agrammatic production: Procedure and data. *Brain and Language, 37*, 440–479.

Saffran, E. M., Schwartz, M., & Marin, O. S. M. (1980). Isolating the components of a production model. In B. Butterworth (Ed.), *Language production* (pp. 221–241). London: Academic Press.

Schwartz, M., & Hodgson, C. (2002). A new multiword naming deficit: Evidence and interpretation. *Cognitive Neuropsychology, 19*, 263–287.

Schwartz, M., Linebarger, M., Brooks, R., & Bartlett, M. (2005). *Combining assistive technology with conversation groups in long-term rehabilitation for aphasia*. Manuscript in preparation.

Thompson, C. K., Shapiro, L. P., Kiran, S., & Sobecks, J. (2003). The role of syntactic complexity in treatment of sentence deficits in agrammatic aphasia: The complexity account of treatment efficacy (CATE). *Journal of Speech, Language, and Hearing Research, 46*, 591–607.

Thompson, C. K., Shapiro, L. P., Tait, M. E., Jacobs, B. J., Schneider, S., & Ballard, K. J. (1995). A system for systematic analysis of agrammatic language production. *Brain and Language, 51*, 124–129.

Weinrich, M., McCall, D., Shoosmith, L., Thomas, K., Katzenberger, K., & Weber, C. (1993). Locative prepositional phrases in severe aphasia. *Brain and Language, 45*, 21–45.

Williams, S. E., & Canter, G. J. (1982). The influence of situational context on naming performance in aphasic syndromes. *Brain and Language, 17*, 92–106.

Zingeser, L., & Berndt, R. S. (1990). Retrieval of nouns and verbs in agrammatism. *Brain and Language, 39*, 13–32.

APHASIOLOGY, 2005, 19 (10/11), 943–954

Computer-assisted treatment of word retrieval deficits in aphasia

Ruth B. Fink, Adelyn Brecher, and Paula Sobel

Moss Rehabilitation Research Institute, PA, USA

Myrna F. Schwartz

Moss Rehabilitation Research Institute, and Thomas Jefferson University, PA, USA

Background: There are now numerous experimental studies demonstrating successful treatment of word retrieval deficits in aphasia. Technological advances allow us to implement many of these approaches on the computer and target the underlying impairment (e.g., in phonologically vs semantically based retrieval deficits). These computer-assisted treatments have the potential to facilitate the work of clinicians and, if geared towards independent or volunteer-assisted usage, extend the rehabilitation process beyond the period of formal therapy.

Aims: Our aim is to review the benefits and limitations of computer-assisted treatment for word retrieval deficits, focusing on the lessons we have learned from a computerised therapy system, developed in our laboratory, which was designed to be used in the clinical setting, as well as by patients working independently.

Contributions: We review relevant single and multiple case studies that use computer-assisted treatment programmes in various clinical and home settings. We then describe an outcome study that used the therapy system developed in our laboratory to deliver a hierarchical, multi-modality cueing protocol under clinician-guided and self-guided instruction. Through the use of mini case studies, we exemplify the system's application in the clinical setting and in home usage. Additionally we present use and satisfaction data which impact on clinical and home use.

Conclusions: Theoretically motivated, computer-assisted treatments for naming impairments can be beneficial as an adjunct to one-on-one speech/language therapy, and are an effective way to intensify and continue the rehabilitation process. While many of our patients are capable of working independently or with minimal assistance to achieve their goals, computers still represent an unfamiliar and intimidating technology for the majority of our patients and families; and access in the home remains limited. One way to provide needed support is through a computer lab, staffed by trained volunteers working under the supervision of a speech-language pathologist. Additional research is needed to replicate these findings with a larger and more diverse group of individuals with aphasia and to evaluate the effectiveness of the Multi-modality Matching Module of MossTalk Words® software in the treatment of semantically based anomia. This could potentially provide pilot data for a large-scale clinical trial.

Address correspondence to: Ruth B. Fink, MA CCC-SLP, Moss Rehabilitation Research Institute, Korman Building, Suite 213, 1200 West Tabor Road, Philadelphia, PA 19141, USA. Email: fink@shrsys.hslc.org

MossTalk Words® software was developed with partial funding from MossRehab and the McLean Contributionship. Support for the computer lab came from the Albert Einstein Society and the Scholler Foundation. Dissemination of MossTalk Words® was made possible by a grant from the NEC Foundation of America. A special thanks to SB's volunteer, Barbara Ayes, and to speech-language pathologist Jennifer Lowery.

     DOI:10.1080/02687030544000155

Impaired word retrieval is common to most individuals with aphasia and has a variety of underlying causes. Under the widespread assumption that different treatment approaches are called for in, for example, phonologically vs semantically based retrieval deficits or deficits affecting verbs more than nouns, clinicians are challenged to devise individualised treatment programmes with appropriate and relevant stimuli. Computerised stimuli and therapy exercises can facilitate the work of clinicians in this regard. Moreover, computer-based therapy designed for independent or volunteer-assisted usage has the potential to extend the rehabilitation process beyond the all too brief period of formal, clinician-led therapy.

Although computer-based rehabilitation programmes are increasingly available for patients' use at home and in the clinic, there are limited data on their usefulness in these settings. In this paper we first review briefly some relevant single and multiple case studies that use computers in various clinical and home settings to treat word retrieval deficits. In the remainder of the paper we discuss a computerised therapy system, developed in our laboratory, to treat word-level deficits. The system was designed to be used in the clinical setting, as well as by patients working independently. We describe an outcome study that used the system to deliver a hierarchical, multi-modality cueing protocol under clinician-guided and self-guided instruction, and, through the use of mini case studies, exemplify the system's application in the clinical setting and in home usage.

TREATMENT FOR NAMING DISORDERS

There are now numerous experimental studies demonstrating successful treatment of word retrieval impairments in aphasia (for review see Nickels, 2002; Nickels & Best, 1996a, 1996b). Following the seminal work of Howard, Paterson, Franklin, Orchard-Lisle, and Morton (1985a, 1985b), researchers have distinguished between semantic approaches, which aim to strengthen access to word meaning; and phonologic approaches, which aim to improve phonological production. Both approaches have been shown to be beneficial. In the clinical setting, speech-language pathologists typically use a combination of approaches to improve word retrieval. Advances in technology now enable us to implement many of these approaches on the computer. This poses a number of questions. Is this method of administering therapy beneficial? Are patients and therapists able and willing to adopt this new technology? Is it cost effective? In the following section, we begin to address some of these questions.

COMPUTER-ASSISTED NAMING TREATMENTS: WHAT ARE THE BENEFITS?

There is a small, but growing body of literature that reports positive outcomes associated with self- and/or clinician-guided anomia therapy administered via computers. What follows is a brief review of selected experimental studies.

Bruce and Howard (1987) developed a computer-generated treatment, which converted letters to sounds to provide self-generated cues. Five individuals with naming disorders, who were responsive to initial phoneme cues and demonstrated some facility in indicating the first letter of the word they were unable to say, were treated for four sessions. During these sessions patients were trained to use the cueing aid to generate phonemic cues for naming. All patients demonstrated improvement in naming treated and untreated items *with the aid*. One patient improved to the point where she no longer needed the aid.

Best, Howard, Bruce, and Gatehouse (1997) used this same computer-generated cueing procedure with a patient with severe deficits in word retrieval and limited letter knowledge. Treatment was administered once a week for 5 weeks. In spite of the patient's limited letter knowledge, treatment resulted in highly significant and lasting improvement (over 15 months) for both treated and untreated items *without the use of the aid*. Furthermore, these gains surpassed the gains made on previous treatments and were evident in spontaneous speech.

Van Mourick and Van de Standt-Koenderman (1992) developed a computer program called Multicue, which offered patients a variety of cueing options (semantic and phonological) with a goal of enabling patients to integrate successful word-finding strategies to access words. Four chronic aphasic patients were treated with Multicue for 3–6 weeks. Gains were measured by improvement in naming test scores pre- and post-treatment. Two patients showed modest gains and one patient made no gains; however, the fourth patient showed a significant gain. In a follow-up study (Doesborgh, van de Standt-Koenderman, Dippel, van Harskamp, Koudstaal, & Visch-Brink, 2004), 18 individuals with aphasia were randomised to 10–11 hours of Multicue ($n = 8$) or no treatment ($n = 10$). Improvement in naming of untreated items (measured by the Boston Naming Test; Goodglass, Kaplan, & Weintraub, 1983) was significant only for the treated group, indicating a beneficial effect of treatment.

Deloche, Dordain, and Kremins (1993) studied the use of a computer program to improve written naming with two chronic aphasic patients, each with different underlying naming impairments. The therapist determined the cues (word meaning or word form cues) based on the patients' impairment profile. Cues were delivered simultaneously with the picture as a priming technique. Patients responded by typing in the correct answer. The computer automatically provided corrective feedback (the correct letter for copying) after two successive errors. There was no oral training and no auditory feedback. Improvement and varying generalisation patterns were noted for each patient. Patient 1 showed generalisation to untreated items in both the written and oral modality, suggesting that she had learned some phoneme to grapheme conversion skills. Patient 2 showed generalisation to untrained items in the written modality and trained items in the oral modality. Both showed generalisation to handwritten responses and improvement was maintained at 1 year.

Pederson, Vintner, and Olson (2001) investigated the effectiveness of using unsupervised, computerised treatment for three individuals in their home. The computer was programmed with a set of tasks selected for each patient until a criterion was reached. Treatment focused on written naming. Patients progressed through a programme that included semantic tasks (e.g., spoken and printed word to picture matching with semantic foils), phonological tasks (e.g., printed word–picture match with phonological foils), and written tasks (copying, arranging anagrams and writing without assistance). Patient 1 (with impairment to phonological output lexicon) showed improvement on trained words that was maintained. Patient 2 (with semantic deficits) showed statistically significant improvement but only modest clinical improvement (due to the large number of hours spent on training). Patient 3 showed gains primarily on trained items. All patients improved on oral naming even though oral naming was not practised. The patient with the most clear-cut phonological deficit showed the greatest improvement, suggesting to the authors that it is feasible to train phonological deficits using a written approach. A randomised placebo-controlled trial has been initiated with a larger group of patients using this computerised treatment programme.

Laganaro, Di Pietro, and Schnider (2003) investigated the efficacy of using unsupervised computer-assisted treatment (CAT) with four chronic outpatients and seven acute inpatients, a population that had yet to be studied with CAT. Computerised training programmes were selected for each patient based on the nature of their word-finding deficit. For all patients, CAT was used as an adjunct to therapy. All four outpatients showed a significant item-specific effect of CAT. Two of these participants who underwent clinician-aided therapy prior to CAT showed similar effects of treatment regardless of treatment condition (clinician-assisted or computer-assisted). Inpatients showed greater variability: three of the seven patients showed improvement limited to trained items.

Additional evidence that computer-assisted treatment is beneficial and that independent work on the computer can be effective comes from a study by our group (Fink, Brecher, Schwartz, & Robey, 2002a). This study involved a computerised therapy system called MossTalk Words®, which was designed to be used in the clinical setting as well as by patients working independently.

ABOUT MOSSTALK WORDS®

MossTalk Words® (MTW) is a multipurpose software program that implements both standard and psycholinguistically based treatment approaches. The system uses a large, easily customised vocabulary of words and pictures, which can be presented in multiple modalities (auditory, visual). Exercises can be developed and accessed through several interfaces, each designed for a particular user.

The *Standard Interface* consists of three therapy modules (described below) that encompass many of the exercises clinicians typically use with patients and which have been shown to be effective in single subject and small group studies (e.g., Howard et al., 1985a, 1985b; Linebaugh & Lehner, 1977; Thompson, Raymer, & LeGrand, 1991).

- Core-Vocabulary Module: A series of matching and naming exercises for the more severely impaired patient, involving a restricted vocabulary of words with high functional significance (e.g., names of foods, clothing, everyday objects).
- Multiple-Choice Matching Module: A series of exercises for comprehension and vocabulary development in both speech and print. Targets and choice sets can be presented in any combination of speech, print, and picture graphics.
- Cued Naming Module: Multi-modality exercises in single word production using a cueing hierarchy to elicit production.

Within each module there are multiple exercises, organised in a predetermined hierarchy of difficulty. Harder exercises employ lower-frequency vocabulary or, in the case of multiple-choice exercises, more numerous and/or more confusable choices (e.g. semantically related foils).

A high degree of interactivity is achieved through multi-modality cueing and feedback. The Cued Naming module, for example, has four verbal-cue options (first phoneme, sentence completion, definition, and spoken word). The same cues can be presented in the print mode (i.e., first letter, written sentence completion, etc.). In addition to selecting the difficulty level, modality, and vocabulary for a given exercise, the clinician can also select which cues to activate for a given exercise with a particular patient.

The *standard* interface allows clinicians to rapidly select the module and the particular exercise they wish to work on. Unless otherwise specified, the programme selects words at random from the selected vocabulary category (e.g., animals; objects; actions; mixed category). The *customising* interface allows the clinician (or family member) to pre-select the specific items to appear in the exercise. A simpler interface, which we call *assigned exercises*, was designed to enable patients to access pre-selected exercises independently. Performance is automatically tabulated and saved. A summary of the results can be displayed and printed.

FINK ET AL. (2002a)

Using the Cued Naming exercises of MTW, we (Fink et al., 2002a) investigated the effectiveness of a popular clinical intervention—hierarchical cueing—under two conditions of instruction: (1) when instruction was entirely clinician-guided (CG) and (2) when instruction was partially self-guided (PSG). Six chronic aphasic participants with moderate to severe phonologically based naming deficits were enrolled, three in each training condition. In the CG condition, the therapist guided the participant through each of three weekly sessions (selecting the cue, giving feedback). In contrast, PSG participants worked with a therapist once a week, during which the clinician established the participant's cueing hierarchy and guided the participant through the session. For the remaining two sessions, PSG participants worked independently, with instructions to adhere to the cueing procedure established.

The cued naming protocol used in this study was influenced by previous research that used cueing hierarchies in a systematic fashion to improve word retrieval. From Linebaugh and Lehner (1977) we adopted the practice of systematically moving up and down the hierarchy. As in Thompson et al. (1991) and Raymer et al. (1993), our cues were limited to those that were primarily phonological in nature.

Participants saw a picture and were prompted to retrieve and say the word using up to six cues presented in a hierarchy, individually determined for each subject. Participants were treated three times a week until criterion was reached on the 20-item training set or for a maximum of 4 weeks (12 sessions).

Results revealed training-specific acquisition in both conditions: two of three participants from each group made strong gains and maintained them at the 4–6-week follow-up probe; generalisation patterns were variable across participants. Fink et al. (2002a) concluded that chronic aphasic individuals with significant phonologically based deficits can derive benefit from a computerised cued-naming protocol. This lent further support to the claim that computer-assisted treatment can be beneficial and that independent work on the computer can be an effective adjunct to therapy.

In future work, we hope to replicate these findings with a larger number of patients and to evaluate the effectiveness of the Multi-modality Matching module of MTW in the treatment of semantically based anomia. We also aspire to document the software's usefulness in a variety of real-world clinical settings. To this end, we have introduced MTW into the MossRehab outpatient programme and the MossRehab Aphasia Center.

The next section illustrates how this software has been used in our Aphasia Center to help patients improve word retrieval skills and continue the rehabilitation process under varying degrees of professional support and home practice. The case studies discussed below are representative of those we have treated over the past years in two programmes of the Aphasia Center (Fink & Schwartz, 2000). Three patients (AS, SM, and SBI) were enrolled in an outpatient programme designed for people with chronic aphasia; Patient SB was enrolled in our computer lab, a volunteer-supported programme for individuals with chronic aphasia.

TREATING VERB RETRIEVAL AND SENTENCE
CONSTRUCTION WITH MTW: PATIENT AS

We (Fink, Lowery, & Sobel, 2002b) reported on the use of MTW with AS, a 65-year-old right-handed man who suffered a left hemisphere CVA at age 60, resulting in a right hemiplegia and severe non-fluent Broca's aphasia. AS received speech therapy for 6 months immediately post CVA and then participated in a series of research projects aimed at facilitating his language recovery. He was referred to the MossRehab Aphasia Center for additional therapy when he was 5 years post CVA. At that time, despite having made gains in comprehension and single word production, he remained severely agrammatic with marked inability to use verbs in single word or sentence production tasks. Having determined that the verb retrieval and semantics–syntax mapping components of sentence production were both impaired, we implemented a treatment programme that targeted each deficit sequentially.

The treating clinician focused initially on improving verb retrieval. AS had been the subject of our previous MossTalk noun retrieval study (Fink et al., 2002a) where, working in the "partial independent group", he had demonstrated a positive response to learning targeted nouns. His wife was supportive and eager to have him continue to practice MTW at home.

Training consisted of a series of multi-modality matching and cued-naming exercises for verbs. We primarily used printed word-to-picture matching tasks. Prior to each treatment session, a pretest was administered to track improvement on "trained" and "exposed"[1] verbs. AS also practised the computer exercises at home.

Following treatment, performance improved on both trained and exposed verbs (Trained: 35% to 80%; exposed: 27% to 60%). There was no generalisation to untrained/unexposed verbs.

Verb training was followed by a version of mapping therapy, featuring the sentence query approach ("What is the verb", "Which one is doing the verbing"; see Fink, Schwartz, & Myers, 1998; Jones, 1986; Schwartz, Saffran, Fink, Myers, & Martin, 1994). This was supplemented by a sentence anagram task that required AS to order written sentence constituents, which were then used to facilitate oral production. The MTW verb module delivered the picture stimuli and occasional phonological cues, while the clinician delivered the spoken sentence queries. Training sessions consisted of multi-modality matching (written word-to-picture matching), cued naming of each verb, and sentence formulation tasks.

Following this sentence-level therapy, AS's ability to produce S-V utterances improved from 30% to 80% for the trained set. Generalisation in the use of S-V utterances was noted on other untrained picture description tasks (from 12% to 66%). The patient's wife also reported increased use of simple sentences and other grammatical structures at home, which improved AS's ability to convey messages in daily living and social situations.

Prior to discharge, Mr and Mrs S were successfully trained to use the computer program and encouraged to use the probe questions (*who? is doing what? to whom?)* to reinforce the gains made in treatment and to elicit additional information when AS was unable to get his message across.

---

[1] Exposed verbs were not directly trained but were named by the examiner once during the pretest if the patient failed to name an item (Fink, Schwartz, Sobel, & Myers, 1997).

ADDITIONAL CLINICAL REPORTS

In a review of the treatment records for 13 chronic patients with whom we used MTW during the period from November 2001 to May 2003, we found that 11 of the 13 patients who used the programme in treatment showed beneficial effects. Of those who improved, discharge summaries show that 10 patients achieved scores of 80% or higher on items that had undergone training, while one patient improved from 0 to 40%. The two patients whose accuracy scores did not improve following training did show improvement in naming with reduced cueing.

Of particular interest are the positive gains noted with two patients with progressive conditions. Patient SM, diagnosed with primary progressive aphasia, had strong semantic skills but moderate impairment to both phonological retrieval and encoding. Patient SBI showed the reverse pattern: poor semantic processing coupled with strong phonological skills (e.g., in repetition and oral reading); her diagnosis was semantic dementia. For each patient we used a MossTalk programme that aimed to strengthen the impaired function(s). To strengthen SM's impaired phonological function, we used sets of cued naming exercises. To strengthen SBI's poor semantics, we added multi-modality matching (primarily written word to picture).

Therapy outcomes were encouraging for both patients: SM reached a criterion of 80% correct following three treatment sessions for the first set of words practised and 90% correct on the second set after only one treatment session. Even more impressive was her ability to maintain these names at 100% accuracy when they were no longer being trained or practised on a daily basis (i.e., when tested at 1 and 2 weeks post-training). Improved picture naming of untrained/exposed items (presented only for naming during repeated baseline naming measures) was also noted, suggesting that she achieved some benefit from minimal exposure and/or repeated attempts at naming.

SBI, too, learned to name trained items with a high degree of accuracy (achieving 80% or greater accuracy within one to three sessions for each of the three sets). A post-test indicated strong maintenance—SBI was able to name four of five items trained about 3 weeks previously and three of five items that had been trained 2 weeks previously.

COMPUTER LAB: A PROGRAMME FOR EXTENDING THE REHABILITATION PROCESS; PATIENT SB

Although research has shown that individuals with chronic aphasia can continue to make gains with targeted interventions, most are unable to continue treatment in an outpatient facility for an extended period of time. In our experience, the most frequently cited reasons relate to exhaustion of insurance benefits and "plateau in performance". Computer technology can play an important role in extending the rehabilitation process during this "post-therapy" period. The computer lab at the MossRehab Aphasia Center was established to train individuals and families to use technology to continue their rehabilitation programme.

Patient SB, described in detail by Fink et al. (2002b), was our first client and a prime candidate. She was young (45 yrs), motivated, and had a supportive family with high computer literacy. SB was referred to our computer lab 2 years after her stroke. She had exhausted all insurance benefits and, according to the referring clinician, had not demonstrated sufficient gains to warrant continuing treatment. When we first met SB, her language skills were essentially unchanged from that reported in her discharge summary from 2 years previously. Spontaneous speech was limited to well-articulated automatic phrases (e.g., *hello, I love you*), and while able to repeat single words and complete some sentences, she was unable to initiate any verbal responses independently. Auditory comprehension, as measured by the BDAE (Goodglass & Kaplan, 1983) was also severely impaired, although she benefited from context and utilised environmental cues well. Reading and writing were equally impaired: she was able to copy words, but unable to write any words independently. Although prognosis for additional improvement in verbal skills was guarded, SB and her family requested guidance in developing a home programme that would enable her to practise verbal skills more independently. They were particularly interested in training SB to use computer software for drill and practice.

In the computer lab, the supervising speech-language pathologist designed a pro-gramme for SB, monitored her progress, and adjusted the programme as indicated. SB and her husband attended the computer lab once a week, during which time a trained volunteer assisted SB in implementing the programme. In addition, SB worked on her programme independently at home, for approximately 40 minutes a day, 5–6 days a week.

Using MTW, we began with a small functional vocabulary (5–10 words at a time). New vocabulary sets were added as SB improved. Because of SB's severe lexical comprehension impairment, it was deemed important to strengthen both semantic and phonological processing. Therefore, a typical session included word–picture matching tasks followed by cued naming tasks with the same vocabulary. In the word–picture matching tasks, we began with a response field of three and used unrelated foils. As SB improved, we increased the response field and added semantically related foils. In the cued naming task we moved up and down a hierarchy of spoken and written cues to facilitate word production. Over the course of the first 2 years, SB worked on 55 words. Test performance improved for all trained items: uncued naming of the first set of words ($n = 25$) improved from 0 to 70% and the second set of words ($n = 30$) improved from 0 to 40%). In addition, percentile scores on the word discrimination subtest of the BDAE, improved from 22.5 to 40.

In the third year of SB's programme an additional 80 words were gradually added. The treating speech-language pathologist reported that independent naming of these words varied from 40–80% correct. According to her husband and family, SB was initiating some of these and other words at home, and was participating in family conversations and other activities with greater confidence and independence.

Although SB was capable of working independently at home, and her husband was capable of modifying and supervising the computer exercises, SB and her husband continued to attend the computer lab twice a month. They both looked forward to the social interaction that accompanied her practice sessions with her very dedicated volunteer.

MOSSTALK WORDS®: FURTHER EVALUATION

In the summer of 1999, MossRehab's outpatient aphasia programmes were provided with freestanding and laptop computers equipped to run an experimental version of MossTalk Words®, and clinicians were trained to use the system. Between September 1999 and May 2000 we conducted a small-scale impact study (Sobel, Fink, & Schwartz, 2000) the main purpose of which was to obtain use and satisfaction data (e.g., how often, and with what types of patients, therapists utilise the system; how extensively patients use it for independent practice; and how clinicians and patients respond to it). The following is a brief summary of what we found.

Use and satisfaction

- Clinicians elected to use MossTalk with most of their patients (23/29 or 79%). The primary reason cited for deciding not to use the programme with a given patient was the limitations in the types of exercises available, rather than the quality or suitability of the exercises.
- Patients gave high satisfaction ratings in the ease of use, enjoyment, and perceived effectiveness dimensions.
- Clinicians also gave high satisfaction ratings for ease of use and reported that, although there was extra time spent early in therapy in learning the system, they did save time later in therapy. Time gained was attributed to efficient selection and preparation of therapy materials.

Independence

- Clinicians identified 10 out of 23 patients as good candidates for using the system at home; of those, six patients actually used the programme outside therapy.[2]
- The primary impediment to recommending home use was that the patient needed help with the hardware or software, and that this help would not be available in the home. A second reason was that the MossTalk exercises were not what the patient needed to practise at home.

Economic impact

To assess the financial impact of using software in treatment, Sobel and colleagues (2000) looked at two factors: (1) support costs and (2) potential added revenue.

- On average, support costs (time for training and subsequent technical support) were minimal and concentrated in the early weeks, when the software was first introduced.
- To assess the potential to bring in added revenue, clinicians were asked: "Would your treatment of this patient have lent itself to a '2-on-1' (shared clinician time between two patients) model?" Clinicians did not find their patients (or their programme scheduling systems and space requirements) well suited to a 2-on-1 model. Although this model is routinely practised in PT and OT, it is a new model for speech-language pathologists and the availability of this software did not overcome a general reluctance to move in that direction.

WHAT HAVE WE LEARNED FROM MOSSTALK WORDS®?

Therapeutic benefit

Our research (Fink et al., 2002a) lends further support to the benefits of using computer-assisted treatment as an adjunct to one-on-one speech/language therapy. With minimal clinician guidance, our participants were able to learn to use the cued naming program and practise independently with positive outcomes.

---

[2] Home usage required that patients rent a laptop computer for a fee for $75.00 per month and a one-time refundable deposit of $250.00. Five of the ten patients declined due to financial reasons, even when the rental fee was waived and a reduced refundable deposit was offered. Four accepted the rental offer and two others used the software independently in the clinic for extra practice.

Our clinical experience provides evidence that when combined with semantic tasks from the multi-modality matching module, the benefits of cued naming extend to a wider patient population, including individuals with moderate semantically based impairments, and individuals with primary progressive aphasia and semantic dementia. We have not found the computerised treatment protocols beneficial to individuals with severe lexical comprehension impairments (e.g., Wernicke's aphasia), individuals who perseverate, or those with additional, marked cognitive deficits.

Our computer lab experience (e.g., with Patient SB) suggests that intensive home practice, coupled with professional guidance and the support of a trained volunteer, can be a cost-effective way to continue the rehabilitation process for patients with severe impairments and others.

Use and satisfaction

Our research adds to the literature that supports the independent use of a computer to supplement therapy. We have found that many of our patients are capable of working independently or with minimal assistance to achieve their goals.

User-friendly interfaces that allow for easy customising and access are crucial for promoting independent use, for clinicians as well as patients. For a program to be maximally useful across settings and patients, it should incorporate varied interfaces for clinicians and patients, and stimulus files with both standard and customisable exercises at multiple levels of difficulty.

The enthusiasm expressed by the clinicians and clients was high, and clinical use was limited only because the types of exercises available.

Obstacles to overcome

Breaking the digital divide.   There is a large gap between those who are capable of using the program outside therapy and those who actually do so. For the population treated in our facility, computers still represent an unfamiliar and intimidating technology. Moreover, access to this technology in the home remains limited, and we need to explore ways to make computers and software accessible to all who would benefit. Based on our computer lab experience, it appears that trained volunteers, under the supervision of a certified Speech-language pathologist, can provide the support that is all too frequently missing in the home. Whether this could successfully be extended to the home environment is an empirical question.

Financial.   We did not find that the use of computers brought in additional revenue or saved money in a traditional outpatient clinical setting. Furthermore, the cost of purchasing and maintaining computers places an additional burden on financially strapped programmes. Perhaps the value of computer-assisted naming therapy lies in alternative treatment delivery models, such as the model developed in our computer lab, or in Internet-delivered therapy (Mortley, Wade, & Enderby, 2004). By using a computer to administer those therapy tasks that can be automated, the speech-language pathologist's role shifts to other tasks that cannot as yet be provided by a computer.

Clinical time constraints.   There is a learning curve in becoming facile with new technology. Once clinicians learn the software, however, it actually saves them time and they are more motivated to incorporate technology into their programmes.

FUTURE DIRECTIONS

We hope in the future to replicate the use and satisfaction study in a facility with a different demographic base, preferably one that has a higher income and education level than that served by MossRehab. This will tell us whether less disadvantaged populations have greater access and comfort level with independent home use of computers. Other important questions for future study include: What is the optimal balance of clinician- vs self-guided practice? Does the extra practice afforded to independent users improve therapeutic effects? Who benefits from cued naming vs multi-modality matching?

We have made strides towards further evaluation of MossTalk Words®. This is being done through a grant funded by NEC Foundation of America, which supports the dissemination of MossTalk Words® to a national network of researchers and clinicians interested in evaluating the software.[3] To date, four additional small-scale studies are in various stages of completion. One of these studies (Raymer, Kohen, & Saffell, 2004), used the Multi-modality Matching Module with individuals with severe semantically based anomias, and found increases in comprehension and naming for the two individuals who completed the study—additional participants are being run. Data collected from this and the other ongoing studies could potentially lead to a large-scale clinical trial.

REFERENCES

Best, W., Howard, D., Bruce, C., & Gatehouse, C. (1997). Cueing the words: A single case study of treatments for anomia. *Neuropsychological Rehabilitation, 7*, 105–141.

Bruce, C., & Howard, D. (1987). Computer-generated phoneme cues: An effective aid for naming in aphasia. *British Journal of Disorders of Communication, 22*, 191–202.

Deloche, G., Dordain, M., & Kremins, H. (1993). Rehabilitation of confrontation naming in aphasia: Relations between oral and written modalities. *Aphasiology, 7*, 201–216.

Doesborgh, S. J., van de Standt-Koenderman, M. W., Dippel, D. W., van Harskamp, F., Koudstaal, P. J., & Visch-Brink, E. G. (2004). Cues on request: The efficacy of Multicue, a computer program for word-finding therapy. *Aphasiology, 18*, 213–222.

Fink, R. B., Brecher, A. R., Montgomery, M., & Schwartz, M. F.(2001). *MossTalk Words* [computer software manual]. Philadelphia: Albert Einstein Healthcare Network.

Fink, R. B., Brecher, A., Schwartz, M. F., & Robey, R. R. (2002a). A computer implemented protocol for treatment of naming disorders: Evaluation of clinician-guided and partially self-guided instruction. *Aphasiology, 16*, 1061–1086.

Fink, R. B., Lowery, J., & Sobel, P. (2002b). Clinical narrative. *Perspectives on Neurophysiology and Neurogenic Speech and Language Disorders, American Speech-Language Hearing Association Newsletter: Special Interest Division, 2, 12*(3), 25–29.

Fink, R. B., & Schwartz, M. F. (2000). MossRehab Aphasia Center: A collaborative model for long-term rehabilitation. *Topics in Stroke Rehabilitation, 7*(2), 32–43.

Fink, R. B., Schwartz, M. F., & Myers, J. L. (1998). Investigations of the sentence query approach to mapping therapy. *Brain & Language (Academy of Aphasia Conference Proceedings), 65*(1), 203–207.

Fink, R. B., Schwartz, M. F., Sobel, P. R., Meyers, J. L. (1997). Effects of multilevel training on verb retrieval: Is more always better? *Brain and Language (Academy of Aphasia Conference Proceedings), 60*(1), 41–44.

Goodglass, H., & Kaplan, E. (1983). *The assessment of aphasia and related disorders* (2nd ed.). Philadelphia: Lea & Febiger.

Goodglass, H., Kaplan, E., & Weintraub, S. (1983). *The Boston Naming Test.* Philadelphia: Lea & Febiger.

Jones, E. V. (1986). Building the foundations for sentence production in a non-fluent aphasic. *British Journal of Disorders of Communication, 21*, 63–82.

Howard, D., Patterson, K., Franklin, S., Orchard-Lisle, V., & Morton, J. (1985a). The facilitation of picture naming in aphasia. *Cognitive Neuropsychology, 2*, 49–80.

---

[3] Additional information about this project is available at http://www.ncrrn.org and http://www.nec.com

Howard, D., Patterson, K., Franklin, S., Orchard-Lisle, V., & Morton, J. (1985b). Treatment of word retrieval deficits in aphasia: A comparison of two therapy methods. *Brain, 108*, 817–829.

Laganaro, M., Di Pietro, M., & Schnider, A. (2003). Computerised treatment of anomia in chronic and acute aphasia: An exploratory study. *Aphasiology, 17*, 707–721.

Linebaugh, C., & Lehner, L. (1977). Cueing hierarchies and word retrieval: A treatment programme. In R. H. Brookshire (Ed.), *Clinical Aphasiology: Conference proceedings* (pp.19–31). Minneapolis, MN: BRK Publishers.

Mortley, J.,Wade, J., & Enderby, P. (2004). Superhighways to promoting client–therapist partnership? Using the Internet to deliver word-retrieval computer therapy, monitored remotely with minimal speech and language therapy input. *Aphasiology, 18*, 213–222.

Nickels, L. (2002). Therapy for naming disorders: Revisiting, revising, and reviewing. *Aphasiology, 16*, 935–980.

Nickels, L., & Best, W. (1996a). Therapy for naming disorders (Part 1): Principles, puzzles and progress. *Aphasiology, 10*, 21–47.

Nickels, L., & Best, W. (1996b). Therapy for naming disorders (Part 2): Specifics, surprises and suggestions. *Aphasiology, 10*, 109–136.

Pederson, P. M., Vintner, K., & Olson, T. S. (2001). Improvement of oral naming by unsupervised computerised rehabilitation. *Aphasiology, 15*, 151–169.

Raymer, A. M., Kohen, F., & Saffell, D. (2004). *Computerised training for lexical processing impairments in aphasia.* Poster presented at the ASHA Convention, Philadelphia, PA, November.

Schwartz, M. F., Saffran, E. M., Fink, R. B., Myers, J. L., & Martin, N. (1994). Mapping therapy: A treatment programme for agrammatism. *Aphasiology, 8*, 19–54.

Sobel, P., Fink, R. B., & Schwartz, M. F. (2000). *The impact of computer-assisted aphasia therapy in the outpatient aphasia clinical setting* [Report to McLean Contributionship]. Philadelphia: Moss Rehabilitation Research Institute, Albert Einstein Healthcare Network.

Thompson, C. K., Raymer, A. M., & Le Grand, H. R. (1991). The effects of phonologically based treatment on aphasic naming deficits: A model-driven approach. In T. E. Prescott (Ed.), *Clinical aphasiology* (pp. 239–261). Texas: ProEd Inc.

Van Mourick, M., & Van de Standt-Koenderman, W. M. (1992). Multicue. *Aphasiology, 6*, 179–183.

APHASIOLOGY, 2005, 19 (10/11), 955–964

Computer-mediated tools for the investigation and rehabilitation of auditory and phonological processing in aphasia

Gerry A. Stefanatos and Arthur Gershkoff

Albert Einstein Medical Center, Philadelphia, PA, USA

Sean Madigan

University of Delaware, Wilmington, DE, USA

Background: Advances in technology have enhanced our ability to use computers to manipulate the spectrotemporal characteristics of speech waveforms in ways that can influence the processing of linguistically important features. These modifications are important in patients with auditory/phonetic processing disorders.

Aims: We present some preliminary data detailing the effect of modifying the spectro-temporal structure of speech on the ability to discriminate consonant-vowel syllables and comprehend spoken words and sentences in a case of Pure Word Deafness (PWD).

Methods & Procedures: We documented severe phonemic processing deficits in a patient with PWD resulting from a unilateral left temporal lesion. Her ability to distinguish between stop consonants was severely impaired while her perception of vowels was relatively spared. This pattern suggested problems with online perceptual elaboration of short-term acoustic features such as rapid formant frequency transitions. We digitally synthesised consonant-vowels with normal (40 millisecond) and extended (80 millisecond) formant frequency transitions and examined her ability to discriminate these stimuli when presented in rapid sequence. In addition, we temporally expanded natural words and sentences by 1.5 and 2 times their original duration (without altering voice pitch) and examined the effects of these manipulations on her auditory comprehension.

Outcomes & Results: Altering the temporal parameters of speech had varied effects on decoding auditory linguistic information. Temporal expansion of sentences produced a small but noteworthy increase in performance on an auditory language comprehension task. Extension of brief formant transitions had no substantial effect on phonemic discrimination of rapidly presented CV pairs.

Conclusions: These findings illustrate that temporal conditioning of auditory stimuli can potentially enhance the ability of patients with PWD to comprehend speech. The implications of the findings for aphasia therapy are discussed.

Technological and methodological advances in recent years have enhanced our ability to utilise computers as effective clinical tools for the treatment of aphasia. A number of sophisticated applications have been developed that administer therapeutic tasks according to prescribed algorithms, collect responses, and correspondingly adjust task

---

Address correspondence to: Gerry A. Stefanatos, Moss Rehabilitation Research Institute, Albert Einstein Medical Center, 1200 W. Tabor Road, Philadelphia, PA 19027, USA. Email: gstefana@einstein.edu

Presented at the Aphasia Therapy Workshop: Current Approaches to Aphasia Therapy, Principles and Applications, 22–23 October 2003, Vienna, Austria.

parameters in relation to designated contingencies (Crerar, 1996; Doesborgh, van de Sandt-Koenderman, Dippel, van Harskamp, Koudstaal, & Visch-Brink, 2004; Fink, Brecher, Montgomery, & Schwartz, 2001; Katz & Wertz, 1992; Linebarger, Schwartz, Romania, Kohn, & Stephens, 2000; Stachowiak, 1993). This capacity to dynamically administer and seamlessly monitor progress on therapeutic exercises underlies the potential of computers to augment the operational efficiency of treatment protocols and provide opportunities for extension of clinician-initiated therapeutic activities in a cost-effective manner. Increasingly refined approaches to program design as well as greater accessibility and utilisation of the Internet (Egan, Worrall, & Oxenham, 2004; Mortley, Wade, & Enderby, 2004) will ensure a growing role for applications of information technology to the treatment of aphasia.

An application of computer technology to aphasia therapy that has received relatively little attention concerns its potential utilisation in conditioning acoustic stimuli used in therapeutic activities. Advances in digital sound processing, combined with increases in the computational power of personal computers, have enhanced the capacity of users to analyse the acoustic parameters of speech samples and modify those acoustic features in natural or synthesised samples that are important to verbal comprehension. This capability provides unprecedented opportunities for increasing the salience of linguistically important stimulus features (e.g., formant transitions) that could potentially augment the proficiency with which individuals with aphasia can decode auditory input. This general approach has been adopted in efforts to remediate developmental language disorders (Nagarajan et al., 1998), and some success has been observed in applying these techniques to adults with acquired aphasia (Dronkers, Husted, & Deutsch, 1999; Louis, Espesser, Rey, Daffaure, Di Cristo, & Habib, 2001). We will describe here our recent attempts to circumvent deficiencies in auditory perceptual analysis observed in a patient with pure word deafness (PWD) by modifying the spectrotemporal structure of speech.

PWD is a rare neurological syndrome characterised by severe difficulties in understanding and reproducing spoken language (Kussmaul, 1877; Lichtheim, 1885). The deficiencies in decoding language commonly occur at an early stage of analysis that markedly impairs the processing of speech sounds, words, phrases, and sentences, but leaves nonverbal sound recognition and identification relatively preserved. The fundamental nature of the speech-processing disturbance that characterises PWD has not been firmly established, nor is it clear that the same mechanism is operative in all cases. However, in most cases, there is substantial evidence to suggest that disordered auditory comprehension results from functional compromise of mechanisms involved in the temporal analysis of speech (Stefanatos, Gershkoff, & Madigan, 2005; Wang, Peach, Xu, Schneck, & Manry, 2000).

Similar but less severe problems have been also described in patients with acquired aphasia (Gow & Caplan, 1996; Tallal & Newcombe, 1978; Tyler, 1992). Since short-term transitional acoustic features in speech are important cues to the specification of linguistic content (Liberman, Cooper, Shankweiler, & Studdert-Kennedy, 1967; Remez, Rubin, Pisoni, & Carrell, 1981), it has been argued that deficiencies in the rapid appreciation of the temporal structure of speech also contribute to the difficulties individuals with aphasia experience with language comprehension (Divenyi & Robinson, 1989; Tallal & Newcombe, 1978). While there is no consensus on the relationship between auditory processing problems and language comprehension in aphasia (Blumstein, 2001; Saygin, Dick, Wilson, Dronkers, & Bates, 2003; Tallal & Newcombe, 1978; Varney, 1984), the contribution of auditory factors to impaired comprehension in PWD is widely acknowledged because higher-order linguistic processes in pure cases are commonly spared (Buchman, Garron, Trost-Cardamone, Wichter, & Schwartz, 1986; Saffran, Marin, & Yeni-Komshian, 1976; Stefanatos et al., 2005; Wang et al., 2000).

Interestingly, there is evidence that the comprehension of speech in individuals with PWD (Albert & Bear, 1974; Yaqub, Gascon, Al-Nosha, & Whitaker, 1988) and those with aphasia (Blumstein, Katz, Goodglass, Shrier, & Dworetsky, 1985; Gardner, Albert, & Weintraub, 1975) may be improved by slowing the rate at which speech is presented. Early approaches to slowing speech rate simply involved increasing inter-word intervals. However, this does not significantly alter the temporal microstructure of rapidly occurring, linguistically important acoustic cues in speech. Tallal and Newcombe (1978) were among the first to use computer-generated stop consonants to study the effects of temporal manipulations of speech in patients with acquired aphasia. They found that patients who had difficulty in discriminating stop consonants with typical formant transition durations (40 milliseconds) performed significantly better when the duration of these transitions was extended (80 milliseconds). Dronkers et al. (1999) reported that a structured therapy based on this form of acoustic manipulation was successful in improving moderate to severe auditory comprehension deficits in both acute and chronic aphasia with left temporoparietal lesions, although patients with large fronto/temporal/parietal lesions did not demonstrate significant gains. Louis et al. (2001) observed that therapy emphasising auditory temporal feature analysis during phonological processing improved performance on trained tasks in three patients with progressive aphasia, and generalised to other tasks such as nonword repetition and reading. There is little information on the efficacy of this approach in patients with PWD who commonly have severe difficulties with the temporal analysis of speech. We therefore examined the performance of a patient with PWD secondary to a discrete left temporal lesion on two tasks in which we extended the temporal microstructure of speech.

CASE REPORT

NH is a 43-year-old right-handed Caucasian female diagnosed with a subarachnoid haemorrhage secondary to a ruptured middle left cerebral artery aneurysm. The bleed was identified on a Computed Tomographic (CT) scan following her emergency admission to a university hospital due to severe headache and loss of consciousness. She subsequently underwent endovascular treatment of the aneurysm with implantation of Guglielmi Detachable Coils. The procedure was completed without complication and she made a full recovery from the operation. However, postoperatively she demonstrated profound difficulties in understanding spoken language. She reacted to verbal communications with a quizzical look and required numerous repetitions before she understood simple questions. Despite her difficulties, she was attentive to these communications and attempted to facilitate her comprehension by reading lips and utilising contextual cues. In contrast to her profound receptive impairment, she demonstrated normal oromotor function and her speech was fluent. Early in her postoperative course, she demonstrated word-finding difficulties, produced phonemic paraphasias, and had difficulty reading, but these symptoms resolved in the first couple of weeks of her recovery.

An evaluation several weeks later with the Western Aphasia Battery (Kertesz, 1982) revealed persisting severe problems with speech repetition and auditory comprehension. By contrast, reading comprehension was within normal limits for her age and educational background. She had no difficulty with naming and spoke in fluent utterances at a low volume. She produced rare phonemic paraphasias, likely related to poor self-monitoring. She obtained an aphasia quotient of 69.7. On the Token Test, a non-redundant measure of auditory comprehension, NH scored at the 1st percentile in comparison with individuals her age. She also performed very poorly on measures of phonemic discrimination. On Benton's Phoneme Discrimination Test, she correctly discriminated only 18 of 30 items. A score less than 21 is below the lowest performance of the normative group and is considered "defective". A more extensive description of her neuropsychological findings can be found in Stefanatos et al. (2005).

Nonverbal cognitive ability assessed with the General Assessment of Mental Abilities revealed a nonverbal IQ of 87, which placed her in the upper end of the low average range. Hearing thresholds were within normal limits for the left ear and slightly raised (30 db) at higher frequencies (4 and 8 kHz) in the right ear. An MRI scan revealed encephalomalacia and gliosis involving the dorsal surface of the left temporal lobe. This included the transverse temporal gyrus, the planum temporale, and the planum polare, extending from the dorsal aspect of the superior temporal gyrus to the insula. At times, adjacent intrasylvian structures on the ventral surface of the frontoparietal operculum were also involved. Homologous areas of the right temporal and inferior frontal region appeared intact.

COMPUTER-MEDIATED ASSESSMENT OF SPEECH PERCEPTION

NH's perception of speech and nonspeech sounds was assessed in three parallel tasks that examined her discrimination of CV syllables, isolated vowels, and complex tones. Each task included six tokens that were contrasted in all possible combinations. Stimuli were digitally synthesised with Praat 4.1 (Boersma, 2003), which allowed for precise control over acoustic parameters, timing onset/offset, and frequency characteristics. All stimuli were matched for duration (250 milliseconds) and root mean square amplitude. Following digital to analogue conversion using a high-performance Roland ED UA-5 external amplifier/soundcard, the signal passed along shielded cabling to a custom-built attenuator and was transduced by Sennheiser HD 240 stereo headphones. Stimulus presentation and response monitoring was controlled using E-Prime software (Psychology Software Tools, 2001). NH was required to indicate whether the items of a stimulus pair were the "same" or "different" by a button-press response. The inter-stimulus interval (ISI) within a stimulus pair was 800 milliseconds while the response window was 2000 milliseconds.

Six vowels—\i\, \ɪ\, \ɛ\, \ae\, \ɑ\, \u\—were synthesised utilising parameters for formant frequencies adapted from Peterson and Barney (1952). Formant frequencies for the four-formant vowels are provided in Table 1. A nonverbal analogue of this task comprised six complex tones, each generated to be comparable to one of the six vowels. Individual complex tones consisted of four frequency components corresponding to the centre formant frequencies of the corresponding vowel. Finally, six CV syllables were

TABLE 1

Vowel	As in	F1	F2	F3	F4
\i\	S(ee)	270	2290	3010	3600
\ɪ\	S(i)t	390	1990	2550	3600
\ɛ\	S(e)t	530	1840	2480	3600
\ae\	S(a)t	660	1720	2410	4000
\ɑ\	R(o)t	730	1090	2440	3500
\u\	B(oo)t	300	870	2240	3200

synthesised by pairing the stop consonants—\b\, \d\, \g\, \k\, \p\, \t\—with the synthesised vowel \ɑ\. The consonantal burst appropriate to each CV was sampled from natural productions of each consonant by a male speaker and inserted at the onset of each CV.

NH was able to correctly discriminate complex tone contrasts on 90% of trials. She demonstrated comparable levels of performance (84% correct) in her ability to identify vowel contrasts. Primary cues for vowel discrimination are the frequency of the first formant (F1), which is related to the height of the tongue, and the relative spacing between F1 and F2, which is related to the "backness" of the tongue during articulation (Delattre, Lieberman, Cooper, & Gerstman, 1952). In natural speech, these cues maintain a relatively steady state for 100–150 milliseconds. Errors were produced on acoustically similar contrasts such as \ɪ\ vs. \ɛ\ and \ɛ\ vs. \ae\. By contrast, on the CV discrimination task, NH correctly discriminated only 69% of the trials. The perception of consonants necessitates successful online perceptual elaboration of short-term acoustic features in the speech signal (Fant, 1973) such as the rate, duration, and direction of rapid (20–50 milliseconds) formant frequency transitions (Delattre, Liberman, & Cooper, 1976; Diehl, 1981; Keating & Blumstein, 1978; Liberman et al., 1967). NH's poor performance on this measure suggested deficiencies in the rapid temporal processing of short-term spectrotemporal features. This pattern of performance is consistent with previous studies in suggesting dissociation between consonant and vowel perception in individuals with PWD (Auerbach, Allard, Naeser, Alexander, & Albert, 1982; Miceli, 1982; Praamstra, Hagoort, Maassen, & Crul, 1991; Saffran et al., 1976). Similar dissociations have also been observed in aphasia (Gow & Caplan, 1996).

PERCEPTION OF STOP CONSONANTS WITH STANDARD AND EXTENDED FORMANT TRANSITIONS

Given these findings, we manipulated the short-term spectrotemporal features in a pair of stop consonants, based on the work of Tallal and her colleagues (Tallal, 1990; Tallal & Piercy, 1974, 1975). In contrast to the task typically employed in these studies, which requires a serial motor response, we developed a modified temporal processing task that required NH make same/different judgements when presented with a pair of synthesised speech stimuli at several inter-stimulus intervals (10, 20, 40, 80, 100, and 120 ms). Three different conditions included: (1) CVs (/ba/, /da/) with 40ms formant transitions, (2) CVs (/ba/, /da/) with extended 80 ms formant transitions, and (3) vowels (/a/, /ae/). We have previously found that a group of subjects with nonfluent aphasia ($N = 13$) performed worse on this task at small ISIs (20, 40, and 80 milliseconds) compared to normal controls who performed near ceiling in all conditions. On the CV tasks, individuals with aphasia performed significantly better with the extended (80-millisecond) formant transitions compared to their performance with the 40-millisecond transitions. On this task, NH performed above chance only on the vowel condition (75%). Her performance on discrimination of CV syllables cued by 40-millisecond formant transitions was at chance (54%) and, contrary to expectations, her performance with longer formant transitions was no better (46%). This indicates that extending formant transitions to double their typical duration was not sufficient to augment her discrimination on this task. Based on additional evidence (Stefanatos et al., 2005), the extended formant transitions in these CV's remained too brief to adequately resolve.

COMPREHENSION OF NATURAL AND TEMPORALLY EXPANDED SENTENCES

We then utilised a procedure that temporally extended the duration of entire natural sentences. We recorded a male speaker producing 32 utterances adapted from the Test of Recognition of Grammar (TROG, Bishop, 1989) at a natural rate of production. Item complexity ranged from single words to simple canonical, base-generated sentences (i.e., subject-verb-object). From the corresponding digital sound files, three stimulus sets were developed corresponding to different rates of presentation.

In one condition, stimuli were delivered at their natural rate of production (1 ×). In two additional conditions, they were temporally stretched to 1.5 times (1.5 ×) and double their original duration (2 ×). The expansion process utilised a pitch-synchronous overlap-and-add algorithm that lengthens the duration of a sample while maintaining the original fundamental frequency. This algorithm employs a short-term Fourier transform that computes variations in the fundamental frequency and formant trajectory over time. Then, for each epoch, the fundamental frequency and formant centre frequency are recomputed, stretching the epoch and interpolating (smoothing) variations between adjacent points. An example of the spectrotemporal of a natural sentence is depicted in Figure 1 along with the corresponding spectrogram from a transformed sentence, expanded to 1.5 times the original duration.

After listening to each sentence over headphones, NH was asked to demonstrate her comprehension by pointing to one of four pictures corresponding to the test utterance. She was assessed on three occasions separated by a few weeks to reduce familiarity with the stimuli. In addition, subject and object were varied between sessions. As can be seen in Figure 2, NH performed best during the 1.5 × condition (28/32). Performance at the 1 × (25/32) and 2 × rate (24/32) was nearly identical.

DISCUSSION

The present study represents pilot work that examined the application of computer-based tools to an investigation of the nature and potential treatment of phonological processing deficits in a patient with PWD resulting from a unilateral temporal lesion. Extending the duration of formant frequency changes did not appear to have an effect on NH's ability to discriminate rapidly presented minimally different stop consonants. These results differ from those of Tallal and Newcombe (1978), who demonstrated that individuals with aphasia who performed poorly on the discrimination of computer-generated stop consonants performed significantly better when formant transitions were extended in time. Given the severity of the phonemic perception deficit in NH, this manipulation alone may be insufficient to result in immediate changes in performance. Evidence described elsewhere (Stefanatos et al., 2005) suggests that longer transition durations (200+ milliseconds) were required for this patient to accurately distinguish up-going from down-going modulations in an isolated formant. We have not yet examined whether training may help this patient resolve shorter duration transitions. It is unclear whether acoustic alterations, in addition to extended formant durations, are required to overcome the substantial temporal processing problems she demonstrates. These questions are the focus of future investigations.

Anecdotal reports have suggested that slowing the rate of presentation of speech enhances sentence comprehension in patients with PWD (Albert & Bear, 1974; Yaqub et al., 1988). We therefore expanded entire sentences, stretching multiple short-term acoustic features that may be important for the perception of consonants. This included

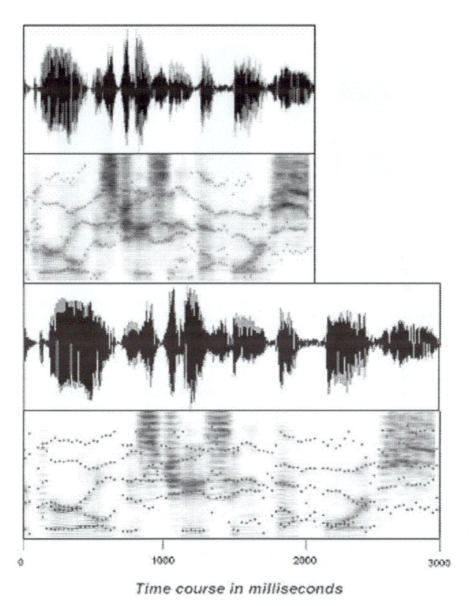

Time course in milliseconds

Figure 1.   Depiction of the temporal lengthening of a digital sound file "The girl is chasing the horse" using PRAAT 4.1 software. The upper spectrogram depicts the spectrotemporal characteristic of the naturally spoken sentence and the lower image depicts the effect of temporally stretching the sentence 1.5 times the normal duration. The black dots mark the centre of the formant frequencies. Note that this extends the duration of formant transitions as well as other acoustic features.

the duration of brief consonantal noise bursts, formant frequency transitions, vowel duration, and the duration of silent intervals. This appeared to have a positive effect on comprehension. However, there were rate dependencies in this effect such that excessive expansion resulted in a decrease in performance. In future studies, we propose to identify and isolate those manipulations that may optimally condition speech for patients with acoustic-phonetic deficits by independently varying specific parameters.

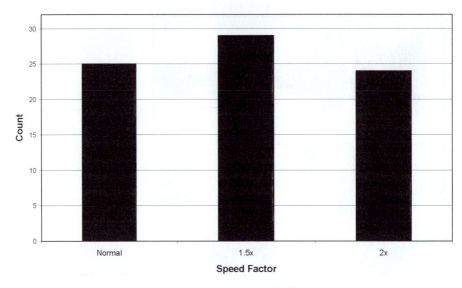

Figure 2. NH's performance on a task that measured correct identification of pictures based on auditory-only presentation of words and sentences. These utterances were lengthened to 1.5 and 2.0 times the normal rate of speech. Note the increase of accuracy at the 1.5 times normal condition.

The approach outlined here may have broader relevance to aphasia, since approximately 18% of individuals with aphasia demonstrate similar but less severe disturbances of phonemic processing (Varney, Damasio, & Adler, 1989). Individuals with aphasia appear to have most difficulty in discriminating phonemes differing only in their place of articulation (Miceli, Caltagirone, Gainotti, & Payer-Rigo, 1978; Oscar-Berman, Zurif, & Blumstein, 1975; Tyler, 1992) relative to discriminations based on voice onset time. Place contrasts are more context dependent and contingent upon the ability to track rapid formant frequency transitions. These difficulties are not restricted to Wernicke's aphasia, but have also been described in other aphasic syndromes (Basso, Casati, & Vignolo, 1977; Blumstein, Baker, & Goodglass, 1977; Miceli et al., 1978).

Commercially available computer-based remediation programs, such as Fast ForWord (Dronkers et al., 1999; Merzenich, Jenkins, Johnston, Schreiner, Miller, & Tallal, 1996; Tallal et al., 1996) utilise the general approach outlined here within well-considered protocols based on principles of perceptual learning. However, such packages do not allow users to independently manipulate specific acoustic variables or provide the capacity to individualise the stimuli (e.g., use familiar voices or local accents). Several programs are available to allow clinicians and researchers to tailor stimuli to the individual patient. Given the high degree of symptom and aetiological variability across patients, this flexibility may be important.

In summary, these preliminary findings in a person with PWD suggest that conditioning auditory stimuli has a significant and hitherto underestimated role in the treatment of auditory-phonetic disorders. These manipulations may serve to optimise the starting point from which to promote neuroplastic changes in perceptual learning paradigms. Clearly, further work is required to systematically investigate the different manipulations that may best augment processing in patients auditory processing problems secondary to cortical lesions. Based on these investigations, it may eventually be possible to develop a processing prosthetic device that could condition speech in real time.

REFERENCES

Albert, M. L., & Bear, D. (1974). Time to understand. A case study of word deafness with reference to the role of time in auditory comprehension. *Brain, 97*(2), 373–384.

Auerbach, M. L., Allard, T., Naeser, M., Alexander, M. P., & Albert, M. L. (1982). Pure word deafness. Analysis of a case with bilateral lesions and a defect at the prephoneme level. *Brain, 105,* 271–300.

Basso, A., Casati, G., & Vignolo, L. A. (1977). Phonemic identification defect in aphasia. *Cortex, 13*(1), 85–95.

Bishop, D. V. M. (1989). *Test for the Reception of Grammar.* Abingdon, UK: Thomas Leach.

Blumstein, S. E. (1994). Impairments of speech production and speech perception in aphasia. *Philosophical Transactions of the Royal Society, London B, Biological Science, 346*(1315), 29–36.

Blumstein, S. E. (2001). Deficits of speech production and speech perception in aphasia. In R. S. Berndt (Ed.), *Language and aphasia. Handbook of neuropsychology* (2nd ed., Vol. 3, pp. 95–113). Amsterdam: Elsevier.

Blumstein, S. E., Baker, E., & Goodglass, H. (1977). Phonological factors in auditory comprehension in aphasia. *Neuropsychologia, 15,* 19–30.

Blumstein, S. E., Katz, B., Goodglass, H., Shrier, R., & Dworetsky, B. (1985). The effects of slowed speech on auditory comprehension in aphasia. *Brain and Language, 24*(2), 246–265.

Boersma, P. (2003). *PRAAT 4.1.* Amsterdam: University of Amsterdam.

Buchman, A. S., Garron, D. C., Trost-Cardamone, J. E., Wichter, M. D., & Schwartz, M. (1986). Word deafness: One hundred years later. *Journal of Neurology, Neurosurgery and Psychiatry, 49*(5), 489–499.

Crerar, M., Ellis, A., & Dean, E. (1996). Remediation of sentence processing deficits in aphasia using a computer-based microworld. *Brain and Language, 52,* 229–275.

Delattre, P., Lieberman, A., Cooper, F., & Gerstman, L. (1952). An experimental study of the acoustic determinants of vowel color. *Word, 8,* 195.

Delattre, P. C., Liberman, A. M., & Cooper, F. S. (1976). *Acoustic loci and transitional cues for consonants. Acoustic Phonetics.* Cambridge: Cambridge University Press.

Diehl, R. L. (1981). Feature detectors for speech: A critical reappraisal. *Psychological Bulletin, 89*(1), 1–18.

Divenyi, P. L., & Robinson, A. J. (1989). Nonlinguistic auditory capabilities in aphasia. *Brain and Language, 37*(2), 290–326.

Doesborgh, S., van de Sandt-Koenderman, M., Dippel, D., van Harskamp, F., Koudstaal, P., & Visch-Brink, E. (2004). Cues on request: The efficacy of Multicue, a computer program for wordfinding therapy. *Aphasiology, 18*(3), 213–222.

Dronkers, N., Husted, D. A., & Deutsch, G. (1999). Lesion site as a predictor of improvement after "Fast ForWord" treatment in adult aphasic patients. *Brain and Language, 69,* 450–452.

Egan, J., Worrall, L., & Oxenham, D. (2004). Accessible Internet training package helps people with aphasia cross the digital divide. *Aphasiology, 18*(3), 265–280.

Fant, G. (1973). *Stops in CV syllables, in speech sounds and features* (pp. 110–139). Cambridge, MA: MIT Press.

Fink, R. B., Brecher, A., Montgomery, M., & Schwartz, M. F. (2001). *MossTalk Words* [computer software manual]. Philadelphia: Albert Einstein Healthcare Networks.

Gardner, H., Albert, M. L., & Weintraub, S. (1975). Comprehending a word: The influence of speed and redundancy on auditory comprehension in aphasia. *Cortex, 11*(2), 155–162.

Gow, D. W. Jr., & Caplan, D. (1996). An examination of impaired acoustic-phonetic processing in aphasia. *Brain and Language, 52*(2), 386–407.

Katz, R., & Wertz, R. (1992). *Microaphasiology and the computerized clinician* (Vol. 21). New York: College-Hill Publications, Little Brown & Co.

Keating, P., & Blumstein, S. E. (1978). Effects of transition length on the perception of stop consonants. *Journal of the Acoustical Society of America, 64*(1), 57–64.

Kertesz, A. (1982). *The Western Aphasia Battery.* New York: Grune & Stratton.

Kussmaul, A. (1877). Disturbances of speech. In H. von Ziemssien (Ed.), *Cyclopedia of the practice of medicine* (pp. 581–875). New York: William Wood & Company.

Liberman, A. M., Cooper, F. S., Shankweiler, D. P., & Studdert-Kennedy, M. (1967). Perception of the speech code. *Psychological Review, 74*(6), 431–461.

Lichtheim, C. (1885). On aphasia. *Brain, 7,* 433–484.

Linebarger, M. C., Schwartz, M. F., Romania, J. R., Kohn, S. E., & Stephens, D. L. (2000). Grammatical encoding in aphasia: Evidence from a "processing prosthesis". *Brain and Language, 75*(3), 416–427.

Louis, M., Espesser, R., Rey, V., Daffaure, V., Di Cristo, A., & Habib, M. (2001). Intensive training of phonological skills in progressive aphasia: A model of brain plasticity in neurodegenerative disease. *Brain and Cognition, 46*(1/2), 197–201.

Merzenich, M. M., Jenkins, W. M., Johnston, P., Schreiner, C., Miller, S. L., & Tallal, P. (1996). Temporal processing deficits of language-learning impaired children ameliorated by training. *Science, 271*(5245), 77–81.

Miceli, G. (1982). The processing of speech sounds in a patient with cortical auditory disorder. *Neuropsychologia, 20,* 5–20.

Miceli, G., Caltagirone, C., Gainotti, C., & Payer-Rigo, P. (1978). Discrimination of voice versus place contrasts in aphasia. *Brain and Language, 6,* 47–51.

Mortley, J., Wade, J., & Enderby, P. (2004). Superhighway to promoting a client-therapist partnership? Using the Internet to deliver word-retrieval computer therapy, monitored remotely with minimal speech and language therapy input. *Aphasiology, 18*(3), 193–211.

Nagarajan, S. S., Wang, X., Merzenich, M. M., Schreiner, C. E., Johnston, P., Jenkins, W. M. et al. (1998). Speech modifications algorithms used for training language learning-impaired children. *IEEE Transactions on Rehabilitation Engineering, 6*(3), 257–268.

Oscar-Berman, M., Zurif, E. B., & Blumstein, S. (1975). Effects of unilateral brain damage on the processing of speech sounds. *Brain and Language, 2*(3), 345–355.

Peterson, G., & Barney, H. (1952). Control methods used in a study of the vowels. *Journal of the Acoustical Society of America, 24,* 175–184.

Praamstra, P., Hagoort, P., Maassen, B., & Crul, T. (1991). Word deafness and auditory cortical function. A case history and hypothesis. *Brain, 114*(Pt 3), 1197–1225.

Psychology Software Tools, I. (2001). *E-Prime (Version 1.0.20.2).* Pittsburgh, PA: Psychology Software Tools.

Remez, R. E., Rubin, P. E., Pisoni, D. B., & Carrell, T. D. (1981). Speech perception without traditional speech cues. *Science, 212*(4497), 947–949.

Saffran, E. M., Marin, O. S., & Yeni-Komshian, G. H. (1976). An analysis of speech perception in word deafness. *Brain and Language, 3*(2), 209–228.

Saygin, A. P., Dick, F., Wilson, S. M., Dronkers, N. F., & Bates, E. (2003). Neural resources for processing language and environmental sounds: Evidence from aphasia. *Brain, 126*(Pt 4), 928–945.

Stachowiak, F. J. (1993). Computer-based aphasia therapy with the Lingware/STACH system. Tübingen: Gunter Narr Verlag.

Stefanatos, G. A., Gershkoff, A., & Madigan, S. (2005). On pure word deafness, temporal windows and the left hemisphere. *Journal of the International Neuropsychological Society, 11,* 456–470.

Tallal, P. (1990). Fine-grained discrimination deficits in language-learning impaired children are specific neither to the auditory modality nor to speech perception. *Journal of Speech and Hearing Research, 33*(3), 616–619.

Tallal, P., Miller, S. L., Bedi, G., Byma, G., Wang, X. Q., Nagarajan, S. S. et al. (1996). Language comprehension in language-learning impaired children improved with acoustically modified speech. *Science, 271*(5245), 81–84.

Tallal, P., & Newcombe, F. (1978). Impairment of auditory perception and language comprehension in dysphasia. *Brain and Language, 5*(1), 13–34.

Tallal, P., & Piercy, M. (1974). Developmental aphasia: Rate of auditory processing and selective impairment of consonant perception. *Neuropsychologia, 12*(1), 83–93.

Tallal, P., & Piercy, M. (1975). Developmental aphasia: The perception of brief vowels and extended stop consonants. *Neuropsychologia, 13*(1), 69–74.

Tyler, L. K. (1992). Spoken language comprehension: An experimental approach to disordered and normal processing. Cambridge, MA: MIT Press.

Varney, N. R. (1984). The prognostic significance of sound recognition in receptive aphasia. *Archives of Neurology, 41*(2), 181–182.

Varney, N. R., Damasio, H., & Adler, S. (1989). The role of individual difference in determining the nature of comprehension defects in aphasia. *Cortex, 25*(1), 47–55.

Wang, E., Peach, R. K., Xu, Y., Schneck, M., & Manry, C. II (2000). Perception of dynamic acoustic patterns by an individual with unilateral verbal auditory agnosia. *Brain and Language, 73,* 442–455.

Yaqub, B. A., Gascon, G. G., Al-Nosha, M. and Whitaker, H. (1988). Pure word deafness (acquired verbal auditory agnosia) in an Arabic speaking patient. *Brain, 111*(Pt 2), 457–466.

APHASIOLOGY, 2005, 19 (10/11), 965–974

Comparing the outcomes of intensive and non-intensive context-based aphasia treatment

Jacqueline J. Hinckley

University of South Florida, Tampa, FL, USA

Thomas H. Carr

Michigan State University, East Lansing, MI, USA

Background: Intensive rates of treatment have been shown to have positive outcomes but have rarely been directly compared with non-intensive treatment. Certain types of treatment may be more effective at intensive rates than others.

Aims: The purpose of this study was to compare intensive and non-intensive rates of one particular, highly specified type of treatment termed "context-based treatment".

Methods & Procedures: Thirteen adults with moderately severe aphasia were assigned to either intensive or non-intensive treatment. A battery of assessments was designed to measure the effectiveness of the treatment and the transfer of the treatment to more and less similar contexts.

Outcomes & Results: There was no advantage of intensive treatment for achieving mastery of the trained context, or in transferring those skills to similar environments, or challenging environments.

Conclusions: If replicated, the results could suggest that context-based treatment may be a treatment type of choice when treatment time is limited.

For any aphasia treatment, it is critical to know the appropriate dosage in terms of total amount and rate of treatment. Unfortunately, this is an issue that has received little clinical research attention.

An intensive rate of treatment can be defined as more treatment provided over a shorter amount of time (Hinckley & Craig, 1998). Robey's (1998) meta-analysis suggested that more treatment was associated with better outcomes, and several empirical studies have demonstrated positive outcomes of intensive rate (e.g. Mackenzie, 1991; Poeck, Huber, & Willmes, 1989; Pulvermuller et al., 2001; Wertz et al., 1986; see Bhogal, Teasell, Foley, & Speechley, 2003, for a recent review). Few studies, however, have been designed to directly compare intensive and non-intensive rates of treatment. In two such studies, positive outcomes of the intensive treatment were reported, but the treatment was not well specified in the published report (Denes, Perazzolo, Piani, & Piccione, 1996; Hinckley & Craig, 1998). Without knowing exactly what activities

Address correspondence to: Jacqueline J. Hinckley PhD, Communication Sciences and Disorders, University of South Florida, 4202 E. Fowler Ave., PCD1017, Tampa, FL 33620, USA.
Email: jhinckle@chuma1.cas.usf.edu

This project was supported in part by a grant from the James S. McDonnell Foundation, JSMF 97-44, Pilot Studies in Cognitive Rehabilitation Research, and by a Research and Creative Scholarship Grant from the University of South Florida.

comprised the treatment, it is not possible to replicate the treatment or to determine whether the positive outcomes might generalise or are limited to the particular combination of activities used in that study.

The idea that intensive treatment may be more efficient for certain treatment types can be linked to the literature on massed versus distributed training. Massed training refers to training in which there are no breaks between practice items. There are breaks of hours or even days between practice trials in training that is described as distributed (Donovan & Radosevich, 1999). Meta-analysis of skill training among non-impaired populations suggests that distributed practice is generally better, except when the task to be learned is particularly complex or when the likelihood of errors or forgetting is high (Donovan & Radosevich, 1999).

Thus, if one assumes that intensive rates correspond more to massed training whereas non-intensive rates correspond more to distributed training, then one should expect that intensive treatment would be effective for some but not all language tasks (more effective for more complex tasks, for example) and with some aphasic populations more than others (more effective when forgetting is a more significant component of the patient's deficits). This hypothesis from the skill-training literature underscores the need in aphasiology to specify the treatment and investigate various types of treatments at intensive and non-intensive rates. The present study compared intensive and non-intensive rates of a particular treatment type, referred to as context-based treatment, among adults with non-fluent aphasia. Context-based treatment is consistent with the current emphasis in the field on functional outcomes. We selected participants with non-fluent aphasia because their relatively preserved auditory comprehension would facilitate ability to follow task instructions.

METHOD

Design

Participants were assigned to either intensive or non-intensive context-based treatment in a between-groups pre–post test design.

Participants

Participants had a moderate-to-severe non-fluent-type aphasia as determined by interpretation of scores on the *Boston Diagnostic Aphasia Examination* (BDAE; Goodglass & Kaplan, 1983)[1] or the *Western Aphasia Battery* (Kertesz, 1982) due to a single left hemispheric CVA. They also had sufficient physical and cognitive endurance to participate in an intensive treatment regimen. All participants were monolingual speakers of English who were premorbidly right-handed. None reported a history of other neurologic disease, psychiatric diagnosis, or substance abuse. Participants were at least 3 months post-onset of stroke and aphasia.

A total of 13 adults with aphasia met these criteria and were assigned to either intensive or non-intensive treatment. Of these, 12 were diagnosed with Broca's aphasia, and one with transcortical motor aphasia. All of the participants were rated between 1 and 3 on the 6-point Severity Rating Scale of the *BDAE*. Socioeconomic status was estimated

---

[1] The second edition of the Boston Diagnostic Aphasia Examination was used because the third edition was not available at the time that the study began.

TABLE 1
Means, SD, and ranges (in parentheses) for descriptors of
the two groups

	Intensive (n = 8)	Non-intensive (n = 5)
Age (years)	47	55
	17.0	11.3
	(19–63)	(42–72)
Time post-onset (months)	27	40
	18.3	33.6
	(6–58)	(14–99)
Aphasia severity[a]	2.5	2.2
	0.7	0.8
	(1–3)	(1–3)
Socioeconomic status[b]	2.5	2.0
	0.9	0.8
	(2.4)	(1–3)

[a] Based on the Severity Rating Scale of the *BDAE*.
[b] On a 5-point scale, where 1 = higher professionals and business owners, and 5 = menial workers.

using the Four Factor Index (Hollingshead, 1975), which is weighted on education and occupation.

The two groups were comparable for age, time post-onset, socioeconomic status, and aphasia severity. The means, standard deviations, and ranges of these descriptors for the two groups are provided in Table 1.

Both groups demonstrated relatively preserved cognitive abilities as evidenced by their performance on tasks associated with the Global Aphasia Neuropsychological Battery (van Mourik, Verschaeve, Boon, Paquier, & van Harskamp, 1992). Scores for all participants in both groups were high for a visual cancellation task (range = 97–100%), and for the object recognition subtest of the Rivermead Behavioral Memory Test (Wilson, Cockburn, & Baddeley, 1985) (range = 71–100%). Performances were more variable across participants on the Ravens Coloured Progressive Matrices (Raven, Court, & Raven, 1979) (range = 41–100%). On the Wisconsin Card Sort (Grant & Berg, 1993), most participants were able to learn three to four categories, but one participant could not learn any categories and one participant learned only one category (range = 0–6 categories learned).

Treatment

The context-based treatment was based on principles of whole-task training and ecological validity, as described in previous work (Hinckley, Patterson, & Carr, 2001). It is task specific and employs a problem-solving approach to develop compensatory strategies to achieve personally relevant goals and tasks. The goal of context-based treatment is to attain communication adequacy based on the receipt of an intended message or the completion of the targeted communication task. Activities include role-plays, self-generation of strategies, and context-specific cues. The principles of context-based treatment were adhered to for all treatment activities in both the intensive and non-intensive groups.

Treatment consistent with these guidelines was provided to both groups at different rates. Participants in the non-intensive group received 4 hours of individual treatment weekly. The participants in the intensive group received 20 hours of individual treatment and 5 hours of group treatment weekly. Participants in both groups were trained on the catalogue-ordering task, described below. The catalogue-ordering task was used as a criterion task, and participants were administered a treatment probe at the beginning of each treatment session, and then practised the catalogue-ordering role-play three times. The remainder of the treatment session time was used to target additional tasks besides catalogue ordering. Other tasks were determined individually for each participant based on personal relevance, and included tasks such as: calling a friend on the phone, using a communication notebook in a conversation, planning a vacation and contacting a travel agent, or calling a taxi. Regardless of activity—catalogue ordering or calling a taxi—all steps of the task were presented in sequence, and treatment comprised repeating the entire sequence with cueing to develop self-generated or personally relevant strategies for completing the task. The strategies could include using a communication notebook, self-cueing with a first letter written cue, circumlocution, or another strategy.

Participants in both groups were trained on ordering clothing items from a catalogue over a telephone. A script was generated from actual catalogue-ordering transcripts and was used in both the treatment and the catalogue-ordering assessment task (which was part of the pre-post assessment battery described below).

During training of the catalogue-ordering task, the participant was presented with the first item on the script (e.g., ''Thank you for calling. May I help you?''). After the participant's initial response, the clinician worked out successful compensatory strategies or techniques for the client to use in order to respond appropriately to the script item. A ''good'' response was judged to be one that carried the critical information in any form, using any self-cue techniques that could reliably be used in the targeted environment. Details for the catalogue-ordering task can be found in Hinckley et al. (2001).

The same general training techniques were applied to other tasks in addition to the catalogue ordering in the two treatment groups. For example, a client's treatment may have targeted calling for a taxi. In that case, a role-play of calling for a taxi was implemented during the treatment, and the typical sequence of items required to complete the task was presented in the same order at each session. In this way, the context-based treatment adhered to basic principles of whole-task training.

Treatment probes consisted of half of the training script items for the catalogue-ordering task and were administered daily at the beginning of each treatment session. During probe administration, the clinician provided no cues or other assistance. Role-play practice with the use of individualised compensatory strategies continued until the participant achieved 90% accuracy on three consecutive probes.

In order to ensure that treatment was consistently provided, a direct observation measure of treatment integrity was calculated. Two independent raters viewed videotaped samples of 10% of the treatment sessions, selected randomly from among all participants and early and later phases of treatment. Critical elements of the context-based training were rated as being present or not present (these critical elements are listed in Table 2). There was 85% agreement between the two raters that all critical elements of the context-based treatment were present in every rated session.

TABLE 2
Critical elements of the context-based treatment administered to both intensively and non-intensively treated groups

1. Establish compensatory strategies based on the participant's strengths to achieve targeted task.
2. Use various means, including a variety of modalities, to achieve goal/task.
3. Centred on problem solving. Problem-solving feedback interspersed within targeted task.
4. Role-play of functional task such as calling for a taxi, contacting a travel agent, or ordering something from a catalogue.
5. Performance evaluation based on communication adequacy, determined by listener receiving message.

These elements guided the development of treatment activities, and were judged as present or absent in the determination of treatment integrity.

Pre- and post-assessment measures

Four assessment tools were selected to serve as pre- and post-assessment measures. These tools were selected because they were likely to be relevant to the treatment, and because they measure near and far transfer from the criterion training task that was common to both intensively and non-intensively treated groups.

The criterion task itself, a role-play based on ordering items from a catalogue, was used as the first pre- and post-test measure. The catalogue-ordering task was developed from actual catalogue-ordering phone scripts, and therefore is a highly valid representation of catalogue ordering. In this task, the participant is randomly assigned a clothing item, colour, and size to order, and is given a scripted credit card number to use. The task is completed in two versions. The first version simulates ordering items over the phone, and the second version simulates completing a mail-order form. Treatment should most obviously improve the oral/phone version of the task. The written/mail-order version of the task is administered at pre- and post-testing to assess transfer from the oral-based treatment to written abilities requiring similar vocabulary and contextual information.

The examiner and participant role-play the catalogue-ordering task in two different sets of conditions. In the first condition, the task is completed in a quiet environment, similar to the treatment context. In the second condition, a concurrent tone detection task is added to catalogue ordering. Participants hear an occasional computer-generated tone while completing the two versions of catalogue ordering, and press a foot pedal in response to each tone presentation. This condition simulates real-life environments in which there are interruptions and noisy backgrounds, and was administered to assess robustness and durability of the treatment to challenging environments.

A standardised assessment, the *Communicative Abilities in Daily Living* task (CADL-2; Holland, Fromm, & Frattali, 1999) was administered before and after the treatment to all participants. This assessment measures the individual's ability to communicate in role-plays and other simulated everyday environments, such as the doctor's office or shopping. Many strategies and information similar to that practised on catalogue-ordering (e.g., personal information) and other targeted functional tasks are needed for successful completion of CADL-2 items. In this way the CADL-2 is a somewhat more distant measure of transfer of trained skill than the catalogue-ordering task (in quiet conditions or with the concurrent task).

Selected subtests from the *Psycholinguistic Assessment of Language Processing in Aphasia* (PALPA; Kay, Lesser, & Coltheart, 1992) were also administered. All participants, consistent with their relatively good comprehension abilities, performed comprehension measures such as auditory and visual word–picture matching at a high level. Thus, pre- and post-scores for those subtests are not reported since a potential ceiling effect precluded the detection of any change on these measures. The Picture Naming subtest (subtest 53) was administered and provided a measure of both oral and written naming abilities. This task might be considered "de-contextualised" and represents the farthest form of transfer measured in this study.

RESULTS

There were no statistically significant differences between the two groups on any of the pre-test measures. Means, standard deviations, and ranges are listed in Table 3.

Pre-test scores were subtracted from post-test scores to generate difference scores. Means, standard deviations, and ranges of difference scores for both groups are given in

TABLE 3
Means, SD, and ranges (in parentheses) for pre-test and difference scores for the two groups

| | Pre-test scores | | Difference score | |
	Intensive (n = 8)	Non-intensive (n = 5)	Intensive (n = 8)	Non-intensive (n = 5)
Catalogue-ordering task				
Oral – quiet	54.1	43.8	+29.6	+45.0
	22.3	25.1	14.9	21.5
	(27–90)	(11–69)	(10–54)	(16–70)
Oral – concurrent	55.7	52.0	+23.3	+24.0
	26.5	22.2	17.1	16.7
	(31–100)	(22–80)	(0–50)	(9–47)
Written – quiet	71.1	73.0	+4.1	+14.2
	20.8	14.0	15.0	20.6
	(36–94)	(52–81)	(−12–33)	(−6–43)
Written – concurrent	59.4	70.7	+19.1	+15.0
	29.8	11.2	23.3	18.1
	(19–94)	(59–86)	(−12–55)	(−11–31)
CADL-2	87.9	83.8	+0.4	+4.8
	5.6	6.9	4.3	1.6
	(77–93)	(76–95)	(−5–7)	(3–7)
PALPA				
Oral naming	68.8	54.7	+10.0	+8.0
	34.8	41.6	13.9	7.0
	(0–98)	(0–93)	(−3–37)	(0–18)
Written naming	53.1	35.2	+7.1	−6.0
	38.8	41.7	8.7	7.3
	(0–98)	(0–98)	(−5–18)	(−17–0)

Difference scores were calculated by subtracting pre-test scores from the post-test scores.

Table 3. Both the intensively treated group ($t = -5.68$, $p < .05$) and the non-intensively treated group ($t = -3.45$; $p < .05$) made significant improvement on the oral/phone version of the catalogue-ordering task in quiet conditions. This was expected since this was a direct test of a training task (catalogue ordering) and condition (quiet) common to both groups. There was transfer as evidenced by statistically significant improvement in the catalogue-ordering performance with the concurrent task in the intensively treated ($t = -3.2$; $p < .05$) and non-intensively treated groups ($t = -2.85$; $p < .05$). Both groups also improved on the untrained written/mail-order version of the catalogue-ordering task in quiet conditions (intensive M = +4.1; non-intensive M = +14.2) and in the concurrent task condition (intensive M = +19.1; non-intensive M = +15.0) but these differences were not statistically significant.

The intensive group demonstrated essentially no change on the CADL-2, but the non-intensive group showed a significant difference between pre- and post-test scores ($t = -2.85$; $p < .05$).

A similar amount of improvement was made on the oral naming assessment (intensive M = +10.0; non-intensive M = +8.0), a kind of task (picture naming) that was not directly trained in either of the two treatment groups. On the written naming task, the intensive group performed better on average (M = +7.1 percentage points) than the participants in the non-intensive group (M= −6.0 percentage points), but this difference was statistically important. The non-intensive group's decrease was the only negative change observed in the study.

Performance on each of the measures was compared between the two groups to investigate potential differences between intensive and non-intensive treatment. There were no statistically significant differences between the two groups for accuracy on the oral/phone version of the catalogue-ordering task in quiet conditions ($F = 2.3$, $p > .05$), the oral/phone version of the catalogue-ordering task with the concurrent task ($F = 0.006$, $p > .05$), the written/mail order version of catalogue ordering in quiet conditions ($F = 0.89$, $p > .05$), or for the written/mail order version of catalogue ordering with the concurrent task ($F = 0.93$, $p > .05$).

There was a statistically significant difference between the two groups for pre–post difference scores on the CADL-2 ($F = 4.78$, $p < .05$). Specifically, the non-intensive group improved more (M = +4.8 percentage points) than the intensive group (M = +0.4 percentage points).

There were no significant differences between the intensive and non-intensive groups on the oral naming subtest of the PALPA ($F = 0.08$, $p > .05$). There was a statistically significant difference between the two groups on the written naming subtest of the PALPA ($F = 7.78$, $p < .05$). In this case, participants in the intensive treatment group performed generally better (M = +7.1 percentage points) than the participants in the non-intensive group (M= −6.0 percentage points).

DISCUSSION

Intensive and non-intensive treatment using an approach focused on the development of individualised strategies for the achievement of communication goals in realistic contexts (termed "context-based treatment") resulted in a similar pattern of improvements across some of the pre–post test measures. Specifically, participants in both groups performed similarly in catalogue-ordering transfer tasks and oral naming testing. This seems to suggest that context-based treatment, regardless of intensity, yielded improvement in tasks highly similar to the trained task (e.g., the written/mail-order catalogue-ordering task) and highly similar tasks in challenging environments (catalogue ordering with the concurrent task). There also seemed to be a general improvement on oral picture naming for both groups, regardless of intensity of treatment. Perhaps even non-intensive treatment is sufficient to produce transfer to a decontextualised task (oral picture naming) when the task targets the same modality as the context-based treatment (oral language).

The intensively trained group made significantly more improvement on the written picture-naming test than the non-intensively trained group. A significant advantage for the intensively trained group on written naming may suggest that the additional treatment across a wider variety of contexts facilitated transfer of language abilities to other modalities, specifically written picture naming. This may be an extension of the transfer to written/mail-order improvements observed in both groups. Intensive treatment may produce additional improvements in a language modality beyond the confines of a context that is highly similar to those trained. So, the non-intensive treatment may be sufficient to produce transfer in a non- or little-trained modality (writing) to a highly similar context (written/mail order task). But intensive treatment may be required to improve writing abilities to a level detectable on a task that is highly decontextualised (written picture naming).

The non-intensively trained group made significantly more improvement on the CADL-2 than the intensively treated group. The difference between the two groups on the CADL-2 must be treated with caution. Since the mean CADL-2 score for both groups was relatively high, there may have been a ceiling effect on this measure that should temper our interpretation of this significant difference. Alternatively, the non-intensively treated group may have demonstrated flexibility in the application of the targeted communication strategies that might be lost over the course of additional treatment.

Whole-task training of complex tasks requires learning organisational aspects of the task early in training. This heavy organisational load makes initial learning slower and more difficult, but a high level of performance can be achieved quickly once the organisation of the task is mastered. For complex tasks, whole-task training may achieve the biggest gains early on in training time, and as training continues there are fewer obvious gains. So, more training becomes frustrating to the participant and has a negative effect (Mattoon, 1994). Thus, context-based treatment, or similar treatment based on principles of whole-task training, may achieve its initial effect early, and from there on there are diminishing returns of the treatment time invested.

The initial organisational load of whole-task training may be reliant on certain executive functions, and suggests that executive function in aphasia may be an important indicator of amount of context-based treatment required to achieve a criterion. The more impaired the executive function as measured by tasks like the Wisconsin Card Sort (Grant & Berg, 1983), the more context-based treatment time may be required (Hinckley et al., 2001).

The notable conclusion from this study is that intensive context-based treatment did not result in more improvement in the trained tasks, in similar tasks in untrained conditions, or in tasks that were role-plays of other contexts that incorporated similar skills or strategies. Thus, if the treatment and the desired outcomes are context specific, there is no advantage to increasing treatment from 4 hours weekly (non-intensive in this study) to 20–25 hours weekly (intensive). This observation is consistent with the conclusion that distributed practice is generally more effective (Donovan & Radosevich, 1999).

There was evidence, however, of additional generalised improvements in language modalities that were not primarily targeted (writing) when the treatment was intensive.

This could be interpreted as being consistent with the general finding that more treatment yields better outcomes (e.g., Robey, 1998).

The mean number of minutes required to achieve criterion in the catalogue-ordering task was 233 minutes, with a minimum of 29 minutes and a maximum of 597 minutes, across both groups. So, for adults with moderately severe aphasia, treatment that is focused on a specific task may take from 1 to 10 hours of treatment. Once a stable level of high performance is achieved, skills may transfer to tasks that are similar to the trained task and incorporate similar vocabulary or strategies. In this study, improved performance was also durable enough to persist under challenging conditions, such as the concurrent tone detection task.

The observation that relatively few hours of treatment are required to achieve improvement in a set of specific tasks like catalogue ordering does not undermine or contradict the potential benefits of more intensive treatment. It may be that other types of treatment, like stimulation-facilitation or constraint-induced treatment, are effective at intensive rates and produce different types of outcomes, whereas treatment similar in principle to context-based treatment can achieve its effect in fewer hours. Indeed, situation-specific treatment that was focused on being able to call emergency numbers was achieved in about 10 hours of treatment as well (Hopper & Holland, 1998).

The results of the current study will need to be replicated before broader conclusions can be drawn. If indeed context-based treatment is sufficiently effective at 10 hours of treatment or less, then context-specific treatment might be a treatment type of choice when only a brief course of treatment is possible.

REFERENCES

Bhogal, S. K., Teasell, R. W., Foley, N. C., & Speechley, M. R. (2003). Rehabilitation of aphasia: More is better. *Topics in Stroke Rehabilitation, 10*, 66–76.

Denes, G., Perazzolo, C., Piani, A., & Piccione, F. (1996). Intensive versus regular speech therapy in global aphasia: A controlled study. *Aphasiology, 10*, 385–394.

Donovan, J. J., & Radosevich, D. J. (1999). A meta-analytic review of the distribution of practice effect: Now you see it, now you don't. *Journal of Applied Psychology, 84*, 795–805.

Goodglass, H., & Kaplan, E. (1983). *Boston Diagnostic Aphasia Examination.* Philadelphia: Lea & Febiger.

Grant, D. A., & Berg, E. A. (1993). *Wisconsin Card Sorting Test.* Los Angeles, CA: Western Psychological Services.

Hinckley, J. J., & Craig, H. K. (1998). Influence of rate of treatment on the naming abilities of adults with chronic aphasia. *Aphasiology, 12*, 989–1006

Hinckley, J. J., Patterson, J. P., & Carr, T. H. (2001). Differential effects of context- and skill-based treatment approaches: Preliminary findings. *Aphasiology, 15*(5), 463–476.

Holland, A., Fratalli, C., & Fromm, D. (1999). *Communication Activities of Daily Living* (2nd ed.). Austin, TX: Pro-Ed.

Hollingshead, A. B. (1975). *Four factor index of social status.* [Working paper]. Unpublished.

Hopper, T., & Holland, A. L. (1998). Situation-specific treatment for adults with aphasia: An example. *Aphasiology, 12*(10), 933–944.

Kay, J., Lesser, R., & Coltheart, M. (1992). *Psycholinguistic Assessments of Language Processing in Aphasia.* Hove, UK: Psychology Press.

Kertesz, A. (1982). *Western Aphasia Battery.* New York: Grune & Stratton.

Mackenzie, C. (1991). Four weeks of intensive aphasia treatment and four weeks of no treatment. *Aphasiology, 5*, 435–437.

Mattoon, J. S. (1994). Instructional control and part/whole-task training: A review of the literature and an experimental comparison of strategies applied to instructional simulation. (Final Tech. Rep. No. AL/HR-TR-1994-0041). Armstrong Laboratory, USA.

Poeck, K., Huber, W., & Willmes, K. (1989). Outcome of intensive language treatment in aphasia. *Journal of Speech and Hearing Disorders*, *54*, 471–479.

Pulvermuller, F., Neininger, B., Elbert, T., Mohr, B., Rockstsorn, B., Koebbel, P. et al. (2001). Constraint-induced therapy of aphasia after stroke. *Stroke*, *32*, 1621–1626.

Raven, J. C., Court, J. H., & Raven, J. (1979). *Manual for Raven's Progressive Matrices and Vocabulary Scales*. London: Lewis & Co.

Robey, R. R. (1998). A meta-analysis of clinical outcomes in the treatment of aphasia. *Journal of Speech, Language, and Hearing Research*, *41*, 172–187.

van Mourik, M., Verschaeve, M., Boon, P., Paquier, P., & van Harskamp, F. (1992). Cognition in global aphasia: Indicators for therapy. *Aphasiology*, *6*, 491–499.

Wertz, R. T., Weiss, D. G., Aten, J. L., Brookshire, R. H., Garcia-Bu-Bunuel, L., Holland, A. L. et al. (1986). Comparison of clinic, home, and deferred language treatment for aphasia. Verterans Administration Cooperative Study. *Archives of Neurology*, *43*, 653–658.

Wilson, B., Cockburn, J., & Baddeley, A. (1985). *Rivermead Behavioural Memory Test*. Los Angeles, CA: Western Psychological Services.

APHASIOLOGY, 2005, 19 (10/11), 975–984

How intensive/prolonged should an intensive/prolonged treatment be?

Anna Basso

Institute of Neurological Sciences, Milan University, Italy

Background: The issue of efficacy of aphasia therapy has long been debated and there is now convincing evidence that treatment is effective. More focused questions on aphasia therapy have also been addressed, although less frequently. This paper reviews the literature on the effect of intensity and duration of treatment.
Aims: Data in the literature on intensity and duration of treatment are reviewed.
Main Contribution: Positive and negative studies on treated and untreated patients are reconsidered and the length of treatments in the two groups is compared. Studies directly tackling the question of intensity/duration of therapy are briefly reported as well as the results of a meta-analysis. Improvement in three pairs of matched subjects, all treated for very long periods of time but with different intensity, is compared.
Conclusions: Results clearly indicate that the number of therapy sessions is an important factor in recovery. Results of the meta-analysis support this conclusion. There are also indications that when therapy is protracted for many months or even years with a very strict regimen (2–4 hours daily), aphasic subjects show clear improvement in their daily use of language and communicative competence.

In an Editorial Comment on a recent paper by Bhogal, Teasell, and Speechley (2003), Martin Albert wrote "Medical education, it seems to me, has failed the patient with aphasia. Aphasia therapy works. Why isn't the message getting out?" (Albert, 2003, p. 992). It is so difficult for this message to "get out" that Wertz (2003, p. 259) has compared the efforts of clinicians working in aphasia efficacy studies to those of Sisyphus: "In Greek mythology, Sisyphus was sent to Hades and condemned to roll a huge stone up a hill, only to have it roll down when he reached the top. [...] If you have conducted aphasia treatment studies, you may identify with Sisyphus."

I agree. I identify with Sisyphus. Over and over again I am asked to demonstrate that aphasia therapy works, and each time I feel that I have to apologise for being involved in aphasia treatment.

A nice example of how a positive study on aphasia treatment is received by the scientific community is well described by Wertz (2003), who reports an exchange of opinions between Pedersen and colleagues (Pedersen, Jorgensonen, Nakayama, Raashou, & Olsen, 1995, 1996) and himself. In their paper, Pedersen et al. (1995) cited eight aphasia efficacy studies; three studies compared treatment by speech therapists and volunteers (David, Enderby, & Bainton, 1982; Hartman & Landau, 1987; Meikle et al., 1979), three compared treated and untreated subjects (Basso, Capitani, & Vignolo, 1979;

Address correspondence to: Anna Basso, Institute of Neurological Sciences (Neurology), Via F. Sforza 35, 20122 Milan, Italy. Email: anna.basso@fastwebnet.it

http://www.tandf.co.uk/journals/pp/02687038.html   DOI:10.1080/02687030544000182

Shewan & Kertesz, 1984; Wertz et al., 1986), and one study compared rate of improvement in the experimental subjects with rate of improvement in untreated subjects as evaluated in a previous study (Poeck, Huber, & Willmes, 1989). A significant effect of treatment was found in four studies, and no difference was found in the three studies that compared groups treated by speech therapists and by volunteers. In the last study cited by Pedersen et al. (Lincoln, McGuirk, Mulley, Lendrem, Jones, & Mitchell, 1984) and in their own study, treatment was not found to be effective. Pedersen et al. (1995, p. 665) commented, ''. . . it could be noted that the result is in line with the majority of previous studies . . .''. Wertz (1996, p. 130) replied, ''Three of the studies Pedersen and colleagues cite are inappropriate, because they did not examine the efficacy of treatment. Four studies indicate treatment for aphasia is efficacious. And, one study indicates treatment for aphasia is not efficacious. How Pedersen and colleagues could conclude that their '. . . result is in line with the majority of previous studies . . .' is amazing.'' Pedersen et al. (1996) responded: ''We will maintain that this statement is an accurate description of the treatment studies that we have listed [. . .]. It is only when no difference is found that it is possible to draw a valid conclusion from a comparison with no treatment'' (p. 130).

I will not discuss such a bold assertion, nor will I report for the hundredth time data on aphasia therapy efficacy. I take it for granted that ''aphasia therapy works'', as argued by Albert (2003). However, to say that aphasia therapy is efficacious does not mean that anything performed by a speech pathologist under the umbrella name of aphasia therapy can enhance recovery. There are some requirements that must be observed for something to be considered an aphasia treatment, the most important of which refers to the content of treatment, which must be rational, properly selected, and tailored to the specific aphasic subject's deficits. In this paper I consider a rather peripheral aspect of treatment, which is, in my opinion, an important determinant of recovery in well-conducted treatment and which can perhaps explain some conflicting results in aphasia therapy studies.

Studies on the efficacy of aphasia therapy have been conducted since aphasia therapy began to be carried out on a large scale. The methodology chosen varies. The first studies were based on the analysis of treated subjects only and they all reported positive results. These studies are useless for the demonstration of aphasia therapy efficacy because they fail to take into consideration the effect of spontaneous recovery. Furthermore, subjects were evaluated clinically and evaluation of improvement was subjective.

Successively, treated and untreated subjects were compared. Results of this group of studies are conflicting because aphasia therapy has been found to be efficacious in some but not in all studies. Vignolo (1964), Levita (1978), Pickersgill and Lincoln (1983), and Lincoln et al. (1984) did not find a significant difference in the level of recovery between treated and untreated subjects. On the other hand, positive results have been reported by Hagen (1973), Basso, Faglioni, and Vignolo (1975), Gloning, Trappl, Heiss, and Quatember (1976), Basso et al. (1979), Shewan and Kertesz (1984), Poeck et al. (1989), and Mazzoni, Vista, Avila, Bianchi, and Moretti (1995).

The studies are heterogeneous and all suffer from some methodological weaknesses that will not be considered in detail here because the topic is outside the scope of the present paper. However, two criticisms will be commented on because they have been considered important enough to undermine the scientific validity of the studies. The first one is that, except in the Lincoln et al. study (1984), in no case were subjects randomly allocated to the treated and untreated groups. Random allocation of subjects guarantees that the groups are comparable, but in the behavioural sciences ethical reasons often prevent random allocation of subjects and make it difficult to create a perfectly comparable no-treatment group.

The second criticism, valid for all studies, is that they do not take into account the fact that the treated and untreated groups do not differ only in respect to presence/absence of therapy; untreated subjects are offered fewer conversational opportunities than treated subjects. The difference in amount of recovery between treated and untreated subjects may therefore be due to the amount of attention and conversational opportunities the treated subjects receive from speech pathologists, and not to the specific treatment delivered. This second criticism is rather unconvincing since the amount of attention and conversational opportunities offered at home to each aphasic individual varies widely between subjects, and it is unlikely that the 2 or 3 hours a week the treated subjects spend with the therapist make a difference.

Robey (1998) performed an extensive search of aphasia treatment literature to collect data for a meta-analysis. He agrees that the literature on aphasia treatment is far from experimentally sound, and that the value of this literature is constrained because many studies have chosen to test such general hypotheses as whether "heterogeneous patients improve with the administration of heterogeneous treatments provided on heterogeneous schedules in heterogeneous contexts" (p. 183). However, based on the results of a meta-analysis on 55 efficacy studies he argues that two conclusions are warranted: (1) treatment is effective and (2) "Further studies to reinforce the general conclusion would waste resources required to test more focused hypotheses" (p. 183).

I take up Robey's suggestion and move on to a more focused question: whether or not the duration of treatment is an important factor in recovery. Duration of treatment is the focus of the present paper. I first consider whether differences in the duration of treatment can explain the conflicting results of the research that compared treated and untreated subjects. Studies that directly tackled the problem of the intensity/duration of aphasia therapy and results of a meta-analysis are then reported. Finally, results are summarised of research that compared three pairs of similar subjects with respect to the variables known to influence recovery but with different amounts of treatment.

INTENSITY AND DURATION OF TREATMENT

Duration of treatment varied widely in the above reported studies, which compared treated and untreated subjects. Treatment lasted from a minimum of 40 days to a maximum of 24 weeks in the four studies that did not find a significant effect of therapy; it lasted from a minimum of 6 weeks to a maximum of 6 months in the studies that found a significant difference. More importantly, the number of sessions ranged from a minimum of 40 (lasting 20 minutes each) to a maximum of 48 (mean = 42) in three negative studies (number of sessions is not reported in the Pickersgill & Lincoln, 1983, study) and ranged from a minimum of 54 to a maximum of 544 (mean = 154) in the three positive studies that reported the information (number of sessions is unknown in the Gloning et al., 1976, study). This difference in the number of therapy sessions can explain, or partially explain, the difference in results.

Table 1 summarises the results of studies that did not find a significant difference between treated and untreated subjects, and Table 2 reports the results of the studies that did find a significant difference between treated and untreated subjects.

The intensity and duration of treatment have been directly dealt with in a few studies all of which confirm the importance of these factors in recovery. Table 3 reports information from these studies (Basso, 1987; Brindley, Copeland, Demain, & Martyn, 1989; Denes, Perazzolo, Piani, & Piccione, 1996; Marshall, Tompkins, & Phillips, 1982).

TABLE 1

Group studies that did not find a significant difference in recovery between treated and untreated patients

Authors	Number of patients		Duration of therapy	Number of sessions
	Rehab. +	Rehab. –		
Vignolo (1964)	42	27	min 40 days	min 20
Levita (1978)	17	18	8 weeks	5 h/weeks
Pickersgill & Lincoln (1983)	36	20	8 weeks	n.r.
Lincoln et al. (1984)	104	87	max 24 weeks	2 h/weeks

Min = minimum, max = maximum, h = hour, n.r. = not reported.

The number of sessions, independently of whether delivered for equivalent periods of time or for longer periods of time, was always found to have a significant effect on recovery; subjects who received a higher number of therapy sessions improved more than subjects who received a lower number of therapy sessions.

A study by Bhogal et al. (2003) directly addressed in a rigorous fashion the question of whether the conflicting results found in aphasia therapy efficacy studies are related to differences in intensity and duration of treatment. By means of a MEDLINE literature search and a search through studies cited in review articles, studies investigating the effect of aphasia therapy were identified and the length of treatment, hours of therapy per week, and total number of aphasia therapy sessions were recorded for each study. Pearson bivariate correlation was used to determine the association between level/amount of recovery and length of treatment and hours of therapy. The outcome measures were the token test and the PICA scores, which were the tests most used in the selected articles. Eight studies provided the necessary data to tackle the question of the relationship between amount of recovery and length and intensity of treatment. Four studies (David et al., 1982; Hartman & Landau, 1987; Lincoln et al., 1984; Prins, Schoonen, & Vermuelen, 1989) were negative studies, i.e., no significant effect of therapy was found. Four studies (Brindley et al., 1989; Marshall et al., 1989; Poeck et al., 1989; Wertz et al., 1986) were positive studies that found a significant effect of therapy. In the negative studies, therapy was provided on average for 2.0 hours per week for an average of 22.9 weeks (range: 20

TABLE 2

Group studies that did find a significant difference in recovery between treated and untreated patients

Authors	Number of patients		Duration of therapy	Number of sessions
	Rehab. +	Rehab. –		
Hagen (1973)	10	10	12 months	12 h/week
Basso et al. (1975)	91	94	min 6 months	3 h/week
Gloning et al. (1976)	107		min 6 months	n.r.
Basso et al. (1979)	162	119	min 5 months	3 h/week
Shewan & Kertesz (1984)	52	23	up to 12 months	3 h/week
Poeck et al. (1989)	68	69	6–8 weeks	9 h/week
Mazzoni et al. (1995)	13	13	6 months	4–5 h/week
	(matched in pairs)			

Min = minimum, h = hour, n.r. = not reported.

TABLE 3
Studies on duration and frequency/intensity of therapy

Authors	Number of patients	Treatment/method	Results
Marshall et al. (1982)	110	Studied effect of 11 factors including number of sessions (range: 10–345)	Number of sessions is the most powerful predictor of improvement
Basso (1987)	95 untreated; 21 treated 3 months; 58 treated more than 6 months	Studied effect of therapy and duration of therapy for oral production and comprehension	Significantly more effective in patients treated more than 6 months
Brindley et al. (1989)	10 chronic Broca's aphasic subjects	12 weeks/2 sessions per week (1st period) 12 weeks/25 hours per week (2nd period)	No improvement in the first period, significant improvement in the second
Denes et al. (1996)	17 acute global aphasic subjects subdivided in two groups	Regular therapy: average 60 sessions Intensive therapy: average 130 sessions	Significant better results for writing in the intensive therapy group

to 34 weeks); in the positive studies, therapy was provided on average for 8.8 hours per week (8 to 25) for 11.2 weeks (range: 6 to 12 weeks). Differences in length and hours per week were significant: $t = 12.8$, $p < .001$ and $t = 8.72$, $p < .001$ respectively. The number of hours per week and the total number of therapy sessions were significantly higher in the positive studies; total length of therapy time was inversely correlated with the hours of therapy provided per week.

The mean improvements in the PICA and token test were significantly higher in the positive studies (15.1, $SD = 3.1$; 13.7, $SD = 6.7$ respectively) than in the negative studies (1.4, $SD = 1.4$; 0.6, $SD = 0.8$; $t = 8.79$, $p < .001$; $t = 2.56$, $p < .05$). Bhogal et al. (2003, p. 991) concluded, "Given the association between intensity of SLT and aphasia recovery, greater attention needs to be given to structuring the most appropriate treatment regimen."

The question of the intensity of treatment was also tackled in recent research (Pulvermueller et al., 2001). A total of 17 aphasic subjects were randomly allocated to two groups: a conventional therapy group and a constraint-induced therapy group. All subjects but one were chronic, with a mean length of illness of 98 months in the constraint-induced therapy and 24 months in the conventional therapy group. Treatment was delivered for 3 to 4 hours daily for 10 days (mean treatment hours: 31.5) in the constraint-induced group; and for 3 to 5 weeks resulting in a total of 20 to 54 hours (mean: 33.9) in the conventional therapy group. Conventional therapy was syndrome specific and was based on exercises such as naming, repetition, and sentence completion. Constraint-induced therapy was more pragmatic and communicatively based. Subjects were asked to participate in language games in which the material used, the rules of the game, and the reinforcements were adjusted to the needs of each subject. Before and after treatment subjects underwent a language examination including the Token Test, and naming, repetition, and comprehension tasks.

After treatment the group that received the constraint-induced therapy showed significant overall improvement, which was evident in three of the four tests used; no improvement in repetition was found. The conventional therapy group showed improvement in one task only and no significant overall improvement. Pulvermueller et al. (2001) concluded, "The present study demonstrates that improvement of language performance in chronic aphasia after stroke can be achieved by intensive CI aphasia therapy in only a few days" (p. 1624).

The important recovery in the constraint-induced group can be due to either type (conventional and constraint-induced) or intensity of treatment (3 to 4 hours daily for 2 weeks or the same number of hours distributed over 3 to 5 weeks). To clarify which of these two factors was responsible for the outcome, the study should be replicated, maintaining the same treatment but using different treatment regimens or vice versa, although it may well be the case that both factors affected recovery.

None of the studies reported above are free from methodological weaknesses and none, taken singly, provide sufficient evidence of the reliable importance of the amount of aphasia therapy. Results of primary studies can be mathematically pooled to yield a meaningful average effect size. A meta-analysis is a mathematical means for synthesising results scattered through the literature. The outcome of a meta-analysis is a means for determining the weight of the scientific evidence bearing on a given research hypothesis. The products of a meta-analysis are the average effect size, which measures the ampli-tude of the effect studied, and its confidence interval, which allows estimation of the degree to which a null hypothesis (e.g., that aphasia therapy is not efficacious) is false.

Four meta-analyses have been conducted on efficacy studies in aphasia therapy (Greener, Enderby, & Whurr, 1999 Robey, 1994, 1998; Whurr, Lorch, & Nye, 1992;) and three of these (Robey, 1994, 1998; Whurr et al., 1992) confirmed the efficacy of aphasia therapy. Of interest here is Robey's (1998) second meta-analysis, which also evaluated the effect of amount of treatment. Robey examined 55 reports on clinical outcome in aphasia. Studies were subdivided in three categories according to the amount of treatment delivered: low, moderate, and high. Amount of treatment was classified as low when it did not exceed 1.5 hours per week; it was classified as moderate when it lasted 2 to 3 hours per week; and high when it lasted at least 5 hours per week. Only 12 studies entered this analysis; many studies could not enter the analysis because they did not fit any of the above categories since the amount of treatment varied across subjects. The effect of amount of treatment was separately calculated for acute, post-acute, and chronic subjects. The effect size was greater in acute than in post-acute and chronic subjects but did not differ for these last two groups. More importantly, the more intensive the treatment, the greater was the change. Furthermore, the amount of change was positively correlated with the duration of treatment in weeks ($r = .76$, $p < .004$) and the total number of treatment hours ($r = .64$, $p < .026$). Robey (1998, p. 184) concluded that "Treatment length in excess of 2 hours per week brings about gains exceeding those that result from shorter duration: Two hours of treatment per week should constitute a minimum length for patients who can withstand the rigors of receiving treatment."

The outcome of a well-conducted meta-analysis is taken as well-grounded scientific evidence, as also shown by the "Level of Evidence" scales. It is now a general practice to evaluate results obtained in outcome research by "Level of Evidence" scales. The "Level of Evidence" scale developed by Birch and Davis (1997) employs three levels of evidence, level A being represented by a meta-analysis that includes at least two ran-domised controlled trials (RCT) and other studies with good internal and external validity. The Level of Evidence scale adopted by the European Federation of Neurolo-gical Societies (Hughes, Barnes, Baron, & Brainin, 2001) classifies a meta-analysis of RCTs as Ia level of evidence.

To conclude, the importance of the amount of therapy in affecting recovery is now well established. Whenever the effect of treatment intensity has been analysed in group studies it has been found to have a positive effect on recovery; Robey's meta-analysis supports this conclusion.

SINGLE-CASE STUDIES

The importance of treatment duration appears to be contradicted by results of single-case studies since there are many examples in the literature of short and successful treatments (e.g., Byng, 1988; Marshall, Pring, & Chiat, 1990; Penn, 1993). The explanation for this incongruity may be found in the characteristics of single-case studies. In many single-case therapy studies, the set of stimuli is experimentally controlled, the therapeutic techniques are model driven, detailed, and tailored to the subjects' functional damage. At the end of therapy it is possible to establish precisely the number of stimuli that subjects have learned. In group studies, as argued by Robey (1998), the question asked was whether "heterogeneous patients improve with the administration of heterogeneous treatments provided on heterogeneous schedules in heterogeneous contexts" (p. 183). Apparently, then, a detailed and model-driven treatment can be effective even if carried out for a short time, whereas a more general and nonspecific treatment necessitates longer periods of time. This is probably true, but the aims of the treatments may be different: learning to name 50 pictures or to read 20 irregular words in order to evaluate the efficacy of a therapeutic method for a specific type of cognitive damage on the one hand, and achieving generalised improvement of their language capacities on the other.

Many single-case studies are more akin to an efficacy study than to clinical intervention. They are an important step in the evaluation of a given treatment. If the treatment is shown to be effective in a subject with a given type of damage, it can then be applied to a large population having the same damage.

BUT HOW LONG AND INTENSIVE SHOULD TREATMENT BE?

All the studies reviewed so far pointed to the importance of the amount of therapy, but the amounts of treatment considered were always relatively limited, except in Hagen's (1973) study where subjects were treated for 12 hours per week for 12 months, receiving a maximum of 544 therapy sessions. Moreover, amount of recovery was only evaluated by standardised test scores; whether or not the improvement was also evident in the subjects' daily lives was generally not reported.

The amount of therapy provided to the aphasic subjects at the Aphasia Unit at Milan University has increased steadily during the years. In the last three to four years it has reached very high standards, requiring great efforts on the part of the aphasic subjects and their families. The regimen we now offer consists of 1-hour daily sessions, supported by intensive homework (2–3 hours per day) supervised by the speech therapist. Treatment is protracted for many months or years and is discontinued only when no recovery is observable between two control examinations.

Before starting treatment we ask the patients and their families to sign a symbolic contract. Signing a contract implies that therapy is a mutual endeavour which sees the aphasic subjects, their families, and the speech therapists as actors who must collaborate actively; therapy is not something delivered by speech therapists and passively received by aphasic individuals. Speech therapists are no longer the only persons to deliver therapy but they still have to locate the functional damage, decide what is the best treatment, establish which tasks aphasic subjects can carry out on their own and which with the help of the family, show them how to perform the required tasks, regularly check what is going on between the subject and the lay person delivering therapy, perform the control examinations, and adapt the intervention to the subject's recovery.

Having so profoundly changed our interaction with the aphasic individuals and their families, and asking them to sustain such a great effort, we were interested in knowing whether the results were worth the effort. We (Basso & Caporali, 2001) set out to compare three pairs of matched aphasic subjects—three control and three experimental—who all received long and intensive therapy that was, however, much more intensive with the three experimental subjects. Subjects were matched as far as possible for the variables known to influence recovery: age, sex, educational level, aetiology, site and size of lesion, time post-onset, type of aphasia, and severity of the disorder. Five subjects were between 6 and 22 months post-onset and were rehabilitated before entering the study; in two experimental subjects, therapy had been suspended because it was thought that further recovery was not possible. The reasons for suspending therapy for the other three subjects are unknown. The last subject, a control subject, was only 2 months post-onset, and was not rehabilitated before entering the study.

The first pair of subjects had mixed non-fluent aphasia, the second pair had global aphasia, and the third pair had agrammatism. Five of the six subjects were treated by the same speech therapist. The three control subjects received 1 hour of therapy daily for 20, 6, and 22 months respectively, when treatment was interrupted because they had reached a plateau. The three experimental subjects were treated 7 days per week, 3–4 hours per day, for 14, 40, and 14 months respectively. When the study ended, two were still improving.

At the last evaluation, all subjects showed some recovery in test results, which were better for the three experimental subjects. More importantly, the three control subjects did not show any improvement in their daily use of language, whereas the three experimental subjects all showed better spontaneous speech and conversational capacities. Recovery was exceptional in one of the experimental subjects, DT.

DT was a 35-year-old fashion designer with a degree in architecture who was 6 months post-onset when he was first seen at the aphasia unit. He had severe global aphasia; his spontaneous speech was scanty, totally incomprehensible, and apparently made up of short sequences of phonemes. He scored two on the token test and his comprehension was nil in a conversational setting. Reading and writing were totally lost. His recovery was very slow; 6 months after starting rehabilitation (i.e., 12 months after onset) he could name some pictures and scored 13 on the token test. Treatment was carried on for approximately 3 years with continuous improvement. When the study ended, DT's comprehension was quick and correct and he could sustain a normal conversation despite some anomias and some errors in grammatical construction. He scored 31/36 in a written version of the token test. Asked to describe a day at the seaside he said: "[...] Later I want to play with my child and we play we play. We eat and we play. In the evening we sleep and we dream [...]." He could read and write, although rather slowly and with some errors. DT had resumed work and led a normal life. He only reported a tendency to tire and a need to concentrate when he was spoken to.

To conclude, three pairs of very similar patients treated for very long periods of time with different intensity showed different outcomes. All subjects improved but the more intensively treated subjects improved more and, more importantly, used their partially recovered language in their daily living, which is the aim of any therapeutic intervention.

CONCLUSIONS

There is unanimous agreement in the literature concerning the importance of the amount of therapy for recovery: greater amounts of therapy have better chances to affect recovery positively than a smaller amount of therapy. Other questions, such as whether therapy should be delivered in a more or less distributed way, do not as yet have unambiguous answers. However, if Basso and Caporali's (2001) data are replicated, we should consider intensive and long-lasting treatments.

This paper has dealt with the duration and intensity of treatment in the hope of clarifying an important, though rather peripheral, issue about aphasia therapy. Moreover, it is argued, the question of aphasia therapy efficacy could be settled satisfactorily and would no longer need to be raised, if it were recognised that treatment regimen is an important determinant of recovery and that therapy was not sufficiently protracted in negative aphasia therapy efficacy studies.

Aphasia treatment outcome research has played an important role in compelling people to deal critically with the problem, but at the same time it has diverted too many resources from other, at least equally important questions. The content of therapy has not aroused as much interest as whether or not therapy is efficacious, but it goes without saying that efficacy mainly depends on what is done, and not for how long or with what frequency it is done. We now know a lot about aphasic disorders and we should concentrate our efforts on understanding what treatment is beneficial to such and such functional damage and why.

One final comment: if, as I argue, the therapist can no longer be the only person to deliver therapy, and aphasic individuals and their families must become directly involved in treatment, the role of the speech therapist must change. They should no longer be the first violinists, but should become conductors of a harmonious orchestra.

REFERENCES

Albert, M. (2003). Aphasia therapy works! Editorial. *Stroke, 34*, 992–993.

Basso, A. (1987). Approaches to neuropsychological rehabilitation: Language disorders. In M. J. Meier, A. L. Benton, & L. Diller (Eds.), *Neuropsychological rehabilitation* (pp. 294–314). London: Churchill Livingstone.

Basso, A., Capitani, E., & Vignolo, L. A. (1979). Influence of rehabilitation of language skills in aphasic patients: A controlled study. *Archives of Neurology, 36*, 190–196.

Basso, A., & Caporali, A. (2001). Aphasia therapy or the importance of being earnest. *Aphasiology, 15*, 307–332.

Basso, A., Faglioni, P., & Vignolo, L. A. (1975). Etude controlée de la rééducation du langage dans l'aphasie: comparaison entre aphasiques traités et non-traités. *Revue Neurologique, 131*, 607–614.

Bhogal, S. K., Teasell, R., & Speechley, M. (2003). Intensity of aphasia therapy, impact on recovery. *Stroke, 34*, 987–993.

Birch & Davis Associates, Inc. (1997). *The state-of-the-science medical rehabilitation, Volume 1*. Falls Church, VA: Birch and Davis Associates, Inc.

Brindley, P., Copeland, M., Demain, C., & Martyn, P. (1989). A comparison of the speech of ten Broca's aphasics following intensive and non-intensive periods of therapy. *Aphasiology, 3*, 695–707.

Byng, S. (1988). Sentence processing deficits: Theory and therapy. *Cognitive Neuropsychology, 5*, 629–676.

David, R. M., Enderby, P., & Bainton, D. (1982). Treatment of acquired aphasia: Speech therapists and volunteers compared. *Journal of Neurology, Neurosurgery and Psychiatry, 45*, 957–961.

Denes, G., Perazzolo, C., Piani, A., & Piccione, F. (1996). Intensive versus regular speech therapy in global aphasia: A controlled study. *Aphasiology, 10*, 385–394.

Gloning, K., Trappl, R., Heiss, W. D., & Quatember, R. (1976). Prognosis and speech therapy in aphasia. In Y. Lebrun & R. Hoops (Eds.), *Recovery in aphasics* (pp. 57–62). Atlantic Highlands, NJ: Humanities Press.

Greener, J., Enderby, P., & Whurr, R. (1999). Speech and language therapy for aphasia following stroke (Cochrane review). In: *The Cochrane Library, Issue 4*. Oxford: Update Software.

Hagen, C. (1973). Communication abilities in hemiplegia: Effect of speech therapy. *Archives of Physical Medicine and Rehabilitation, 54*, 454–463.

Hartman, J., & Landau, W. M. (1987). Comparison of formal language therapy with supportive counselling for aphasia due to acute vascular accident. *Archives of Neurology, 24*, 646–649.

Hughes, R. A., Barnes, M. P., Baron, J. C., & Brainin, M. (2001). European Federation of Neurological Societies Guidance for the preparation of neurological management guidelines by EFNS scientific task force. *European Journal of Neurology, 8*, 549–550.

Levita, E. (1978). Effects of speech therapy on aphasics' responses to the Functional Communication Profile. *Perceptual and Motor Skills, 47*, 151–154.

Lincoln, N. B., McGuirk, E., Mulley, G. P., Lendrem, W., Jones, A. C., & Mitchell, J. R. A. (1984). Effectiveness of speech therapy for aphasic stroke patients: A randomized controlled trial. *Lancet, 1*, 1197-1200.

Marshall, J., Pring, T., & Chiat, S. (1990). Sentence processing therapy: Working at the level of the event. *Aphasiology, 7*, 177–199.

Marshall, R. C., Tompkins, C., & Phillips, D. S. (1982). Improvement in treated aphasia: Examination of selected prognostic factors. *Folia Phoniatrica, 34*, 305–315.

Marshall, R. C., Wertz, R. T., Weiss, D. G., Aten, J. L., Brookshire, R. H., Garcia-Bunuel, L., et al. (1989). Home treatment for aphasic patients by trained nonprofessionals. *Journal of Speech and Hearing Disorders, 54*, 462–470.

Mazzoni, M., Vista, M., Geri, E., Avila, L., Bianchi, F., & Moretti, P. (1995). Comparison of language recovery in rehabilitated and matched, non-rehabilitated aphasic patients. *Aphasiology, 9*, 553–563.

Meikle, M., Wechsler, E., Tupper, A., Benenson, M., Butler, J., Mulhall, D. Et al. (1979). Comparative trial of volunteer and professional treatments of dysphasia after stroke. *British Medical Journal, 2*, 87–89.

Pedersen, P. M., Jorgensen, H. S., Nakayama, H., Raashou, H. O., & Olsen T. S. (1995). Aphasia in acute stroke: Incidence, determinants, and recovery. *Annals of Neurology, 38*, 659–666.

Pedersen, P. M., Jorgensen, H. S., Nakayama, H., Raaschou, H. O., & Olsen, T. S. (1996). Aphasia in acute stroke: Incidence, determinants, and recovery. Reply. *Annals of Neurology, 40*, 130.

Penn, C. (1993). Aphasia therapy in South Africa: Some pragmatic and personal perspectives. In A. L. Holland & M. M. Forbes (Eds.), *Aphasia treatment. World perspectives* (pp. 25–53). San Diego, CA: Singular Publishing Group.

Pickersgill, M. J., & Lincoln, N. B. (1983). Prognostic indicators and the pattern of recovery of communication in aphasic stroke patients. *Journal of Neurology, Neurosurgery and Psychiatry, 46*, 130–139.

Poeck, K., Huber, W., & Willmes, K. (1989). Outcome of intensive language treatment in aphasia. *Journal of Speech and Hearing Disorders, 54*, 471–479.

Prins, R. S., Schoonen, R., & Vermeulen, J. (1989). Efficacy of two different types of speech therapy for aphasic stroke patients. *Applied Psycholinguistics, 10*, 85–123.

Pulvermueller, F., Neininger, B., Elbert, T., Mohr, B., Rockstroh, B., Koebbel, P. et al. (2001). Constraint-induced therapy of chronic aphasia after stroke. *Stroke, 32*, 1621–1626.

Robey, R. R. (1994). The efficacy of treatment for aphasic persons: A meta-analysis. *Brain and Language, 47*, 582–608.

Robey, R. R. (1998). A meta-analysis of clinical outcomes in the treatment of aphasia. *Journal of Speech, Language, and Hearing Research, 41*, 172–187.

Shewan, C. M., & Kertesz, A. (1984). Effects of speech and language treatment in recovery from aphasia. *Brain and Language, 23*, 272–299.

Vignolo, L. A. (1964). Evolution of aphasia and language rehabilitation: A retrospective exploratory study. *Cortex, 1*, 344–367.

Wertz, R. T. (1996). Aphasia in acute stroke. Incidence, determinants, and recovery. Letter to the Editor. *Annals of Neurology, 40*, 129–130.

Wertz, R. T. (2003). Efficacy of aphasia therapy, Escher, and Sisyphus. In I. Papathanasiou & R. De Bleser (Eds.), *The sciences of aphasia: From therapy to theory* (pp. 259–271). Amsterdam: Pergamon.

Wertz, R. T., Collins, M. J., Weiss, D. G., Kurtzke, J. F., Friden, T., Brookshire, R. H., et al. (1981). Veterans Administration cooperative study on aphasia: A comparison of individual and group treatment. *Journal of Speech and Hearing Disorders, 24*, 580–594.

Wertz, R. T., Weiss, D. G., Aten, J. L., Brookshire, R. H., Garcia-Bunuel, L., Holland, A. L., et al. (1986). Comparison of clinic, home, and deferred language treatment for aphasia: A Veterans Administration cooperative study. *Archives of Neurology, 43*, 653–658.

Whurr, R., Lorch, M. P., & Nye, C. (1992). A meta-analysis of studies carried out between 1946 and 1988 concerned with the efficacy of speech and language therapy treatment for aphasic patients. *European Journal of Disorders of Communication, 27*, 1–17.

APHASIOLOGY, 2005, 19 (10/11), 985–993

Contributions and limitations of the cognitive neuropsychological approach to treatment: Illustrations from studies of reading and spelling therapy

Argye Elizabeth Hillis and Jennifer Heidler

Johns Hopkins University, Baltimore, MD, USA

Background: Cognitive neuropsychological research is focused on improving the under-standing of cognitive processes and representations underlying normal tasks such as reading and spelling, on the basis of impaired performance of these tasks after brain damage. Functional architectures of cognitive tasks developed through this approach have often assisted speech-language pathologists and other therapists in understanding the task to be treated, and in identifying the impaired and spared components of the task to be treated in each individual with brain damage.

Aims: To review the benefits and limitations of this approach, focusing on illustrations from treatment of reading and spelling, and to provide ideas about how the limitations might be addressed.

Contributions: We provide examples that demonstrate how disruption of particular cognitive functions in the process of reading or spelling might be identified and rationally treated. Additionally, we provide some illustrations of how limitations of this approach might be addressed by considering evidence from cognitive neuroscience regarding neural mechan-isms of recovery and learning.

Conclusions: Insights from cognitive neuropsychology should be integrated with insights from neuroscience in developing rehabilitation strategies.

Cognitive neuropsychology is the science devoted to characterising mental processes and representations underlying normal cognitive tasks—such as memory, reading, writing, comprehending or producing sentences, and calculation tasks—on the basis of patterns of impaired performance of these tasks after brain injury (see Rapp, 2001, for review). The primary goal is to specify the functional architecture of each normal cognitive task, and when possible to specify the internal structure of representations that are computed for the task. It is assumed that there is no major difference in how cognitive tasks are carried out across normal subjects, and that the pattern of impaired performance transparently reflects normal processing, minus the function(s) impaired in that individual.

This discipline has yielded models of the cognitive processes underlying various language tasks such as naming, reading, spelling, and sentence production (see Ellis & Young, 1988; Rapp, 2001; Shallice, 1988; for reviews). Speech-language pathologists have often used these models of normal language tasks to identify impaired and spared components of the cognitive tasks to be treated in each patient, based on detailed analysis of the performance across tasks by that individual, as described below. This method has

---

Address correspondence to: Argye Hillis MD, Department of Neurology, Phipps 126, Johns Hopkins Hospital, 600 North Wolfe Street, Baltimore, MD 21287, USA. Email: argye@JHMI.edu

© 2005 Psychology Press Ltd

http://www.tandf.co.uk/journals/pp/02687038.html   DOI:10.1080/02687030544000191

allowed the therapist to tailor rehabilitation with the goal of improving impaired com-
ponent(s), or to use spared components to compensate for the impaired one(s). A number
of illustrations of how cognitive neuropsychological models have been useful in focusing
treatment in various domains have been reviewed previously (Hillis, 1994, 2001, 2002a;
Mitchum & Berndt, 1988, 1994, 1995; Riddoch & Humphreys, 1994a, 1994b; Seron &
Deloche, 1989). In this paper, we will review some representative therapies that have
been used to treat reading and spelling of single words, since these domains have long
been the focus of research in cognitive neuropsychology. This review is not meant to be
exhaustive (see Beeson & Hillis, 2001, for a more comprehensive review), but illus-
trative. It will be used as a springboard for discussing how these cognitive neuropsychological models might be used in conjunction with advances in neuroscience to
develop a theory of rehabilitation that would be useful not only in focusing therapy, but
also in guiding specific procedures of rehabilitation.

TREATMENT OF ACQUIRED DYSLEXIA

Reading a single word is a more elaborate cognitive task than one might think. It entails,
at the least, early visual and spatial processing of the printed stimulus, recognising the
printed word as a known word (accessing the orthographic representation in the
"orthographic input lexicon"), accessing its meaning or semantic representation,
accessing its phonological representation in the "phonologic output lexicon" or
assembling its phonology via sub-lexical orthography-to-phonology conversion (OPC)
mechanisms, as schematically represented in Figure 1. Unfamiliar words are thought to
demand assembly through OPC mechanisms (see Ellis & Young, 1988; Shallice, 1988; or
Hillis, 2002b, for discussion). Alternative, "connectionist" models of reading do not
distinguish between mechanisms for reading familiar or unfamiliar words, and assume

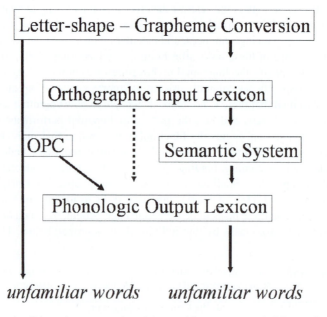

Figure 1.   Schematic representation of the cognitive processes underlying reading.

that processing in various components takes place in parallel rather than serially (for example, see Plaut & Shallice, 1993).

Each component of reading has been the focus of rehabilitation for individuals with damage to that component. For example, impaired access to orthographic representations in the orthographic input lexicon from vision ("pure alexia" or "letter-by-letter reading") is characterised by poor oral reading and reading comprehension of printed words, but better word recognition when words are spelled aloud. This deficit has been treated with methods, using Multiple Oral Re-reading of the same text (Beeson, 1998), brief exposure of words and/or pseudowords for rapid decisions about the stimuli (Friedman & Lott, 2000; Rothi & Moss, 1992), or multi-modality cueing (Maher, Clayton, Barrett, Schober-Peterson, & Rothi, 1998; Seki, Yajima, & Sugishita, 1995) to improve access (e.g., lower the "threshold of activation") to specific words. In contrast, impaired access to representations in the orthographic input lexicon from all modalities, characterised by poor recognition of written words or words spelled aloud, has often been treated by improving reading through sub-lexical OPC mechanisms (Berndt & Mitchum, 1994; Hillis, 1993; Nickels, 1992). This approach (or treatment of selectively impaired OPC mechanisms) often entails retraining single grapheme–phoneme correspondences, using "relay" words that the patient can spell (e.g., "b is for baby"), just as a child might learn phonics (dePartz, 1986). Some investigators have taught OPC procedures by training bigraphs, rather than individual letters, to improve blending (Friedman & Lott, 1996). However, when these OPC mechanisms are intact or fully retrained, patients still have trouble reading irregular words (e.g., yacht) and homographs (e.g., *lead* pencil versus *lead* the way) and understanding homophones (e.g., *write* versus *right*). These words often require item-specific training, using tasks such as matching printed words to definitions or pictures (e.g., Hillis, 1993) or training homophones in context-rich sentences (Scott & Byng, 1989). Patients who are impaired in accessing representations in the phonological output lexicon are able to understand written words, but often cannot read them aloud. If they are also impaired in using OPC mechanisms, focusing treatment on retraining these mechanisms can be helpful in reading aloud both familiar and unfamiliar words. Item-specific training of irregular words, using cued oral reading (with repetition if necessary) can also be successful (Hillis & Caramazza, 1994). Item-specific gains in oral reading in these cases are expected to show generalisation to oral naming of the same items.

TREATMENT OF ACQUIRED DYSGRAPHIA

Whether spelling can best be characterised as simply the "reverse" of the reading process, utilising the same orthographic and phonologic lexicons and sub-lexical orthography–phonology correspondences, or as sharing only a semantic system, has been a matter of prolonged debate in the literature, and is beyond the scope of this paper (see Hillis & Rapp, 2004, for review of the neuropsychological and neuroimaging evidence for each position). It is not likely that there are separate input and output lexicons for orthographic and phonologic representations. However, for heuristic purposes, the lexicons are depicted in Figure 2 as though they were specific to the spelling process.

Spelling a word to dictation is at least as complex as reading a word. It demands: recognising the spoken word as familiar by accessing the phonological representation in the lexicon; accessing its meaning (semantics); accessing the orthographic representation or assembling it from phonology-to-orthography conversion mechanisms; holding the orthographic string in the "graphemic buffer" (a short-term memory system) while

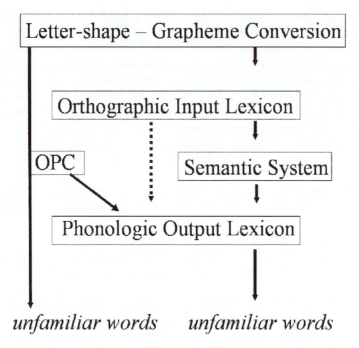

Figure 2.   Schematic representation of the cognitive processes underlying spelling.

individual letters are written or spelled aloud; and converting individual graphemes to specific letter shapes for writing. Each of these components of the spelling system has been addressed in individualised therapy. To illustrate, impaired access to orthographic representations for spelling is manifested by poor oral and written spelling of irregular words, although spelling of regular words and pseudowords though POC mechanisms may be spared. Thus, the patient may make phonologically plausible spelling errors (e.g., pizza spelled *peetsa*). Generally, high-frequency words are spelled more accurately than low-frequency words in such cases. Improving access to orthographic representations of irregular words has often entailed various methods of repetitive practice of copying or cued spelling with correction (Aliminosa, McCloskey, Goodman-Schulman, & Sokol, 1993; Carlomagno, Iavarone, & Colombo, 1994; Beeson, 1999; Weekes & Coltheart, 1996). Sometimes training with a mnemonic to help recall the spelling has been helpful (dePartz, Seron, & Van der Linden, 1992). As in reading, when patients are impaired in both accessing orthographic representations and in sub-lexical assembly mechanisms, training of the latter (POC mechanisms for spelling) may result in improvement of spelling both familiar and unfamiliar words, since the patient might use POC mechanisms to self-cue access to orthographic representations (Hillis & Caramazza, 1994). Thus, unlike repetition and cued spelling practice of specific words, this therapy can result in generalisation to untrained words (see Beeson & Rapscak, 2002, for further discussion of effectiveness and generalisation of treatment for impaired components of spelling).

Selective impairment at the level of the graphemic buffer affects all spelling tasks except direct copying, since all sorts of words and pseudowords must be held in the buffer while individual letters are written or spelled aloud. Thus, impairment results in the following profile of performance across tasks: impaired oral and written spelling within all input modalities (e.g., written naming and spelling to dictation); equally impaired spelling of high- and low-frequency words and pseudowords; comparable spelling to dictation and delayed copying (since both require the buffer); and a significant effect of word length on spelling accuracy (since longer words place greater demands on the buffer) (see Hillis & Caramazza, 1987, for further details). Spelling errors are generally not phonologically plausible, but involve insertion, deletion, transposition, and sub-stitution of letters (e.g, chair–*ckeaf*). Treatment at the level of the graphemic buffer has sometimes emphasised self-correction, using intact access to orthographic representations and intact OPC and POC mechanisms (e.g. Hillis & Caramazza, 1987; but see Rapp, 2005 this issue, for other approaches).

LIMITATIONS OF COGNITIVE MODELS FOR DESIGNING TREATMENT AND POTENTIAL CONTRIBUTIONS FROM NEUROSCIENCE

A number of authors have pointed out that cognitive neuropsychological models of normal language tasks do not entail or provide a theory of rehabilitation. They are more useful in focusing treatment on what to treat rather than how to treat it (Caramazza, 1989; Caramazza & Hillis, 1991; Wilson & Patterson, 1990; Wilson, 1997). Nevertheless, they do provide an essential first step—understanding what it is that needs to be treated. Furthermore, specific predictions about the results of particular treatments that follow from either ''box and arrow'' models or localist computational models of the cognitive processes and representations underlying the language task to be treated have been supported by empirical results (Martin, Fink, & Laine, 2004a). For example, such models allow predictions about the generalisation of treatment effects across modalities or across stimuli (Hillis, 1991), predictions about the sorts of patients (i.e., in terms of type of deficit) who are likely to respond to a particular treatment, or even predictions about the time course of treatment effects (e.g., Martin, Fink, Laine, & Ayala, 2004b). For example, Martin et al. (2004b) predicted from a localist computational model of naming that massive repetition of semantically related words (contextual priming) would result in initial interference with naming accuracy, followed by short-term facilitation, which was confirmed in a treatment study. Whether such predictions follow from characteristics specific to the model, or from general principles common to a number of alternative models, is less clear.

Some authors have suggested that connectionist models that entail simulations of learning provide a better basis for designing rehabilitation (Baddeley, 1993; Plaut, 1996). However, to date, the main contribution from these connectionist simulations to reha-bilitation has been to constrain what stimuli to treat, rather than methods of how best to treat them. That is, on the basis of a simulation of naming, Plaut (1996) predicted that patients should show better generalisation of improved naming to untrained items of atypical rather than typical exemplars of a category (e.g., pelican rather than robin as an exemplar of bird). Predictions from this model have been borne out in treatment studies that were designed specifically to improve accessibility of names of typical and atypical exemplars by treating one set or the other, in order to test these predictions (Kiran & Thompson, 2003). However, again, it is uncertain whether these predictions follow from specific characteristics of the model that distinguish it from other models or from more general principles that are not specific to the model (e.g., training a wider, more divergent range of exemplars allows generalisation to more items than training a narrow range of more similar exemplars).

Nevertheless, there are certain principles of learning captured by computational models of this sort that reflect neural processing, and thus may provide insight on how to treat language. First, connectionist models are based on Hebbian learning—the principle that "cells that fire together wire together". This principle reflects a well-described mechanism of synaptic plasticity in the brain—long-term potentiation. In long-term potentiation (LTP), rapid firing of neuron B by neuron A results in a change in the synapse between neurons A and B, such that neuron B will fire with less and less activation from neuron A over time. Since LTP requires rapid, intense repetitions of this pairing, rehabilitation may be most effective if it entails intense practice. Indeed, one treatment study documented that intense therapy using the same items (2 hours per day, 5 days per week) resulted in rapid item-specific improvement in naming that generalised to untrained settings, whereas the same therapy administered less intensely (1 hour per day, 2 days per week) resulted in no improvement of items matched in difficulty (Hillis, 1998).

An important aspect of LTP that is not captured in connectionist models is that LTP depends on the chemical milieu in the brain. That is, LTP (and a similar mechanism, long-term depression, or LTD) depends on the presence of adequate neurotransmitters. For example, LTD occurs only in the presence of norepinephrine and acetylcholine together (Kirkwood, Rozas, Kirkwood, Perez, & Bear, 1999). Norepinephrine and other neurotransmitters (such as serotonin and dopamine) may be depleted in conditions such as stroke and depression, either by the disease process or by medications used to treat concomitant conditions like hypertension. Therefore, medications that increase the availability of these neurotransmitters, such as antidepressants or acetylcholine esterase inhibitors (of the sort used to slow memory decline in Alzheimer's disease), may be useful adjuncts to rehabilitation. A number of studies have documented positive effects of amphetamines (which increase available norepinephrine) in conjunction with rehabilitation—in some cases through small randomised clinical trials (Clark & Mankikar, 1979; Walker-Batson, 2000; Walker-Batson et al., 2001; Walker-Batson, Devous, Curtis, Unwin, & Greenlee, 1991). Other studies have reported positive effects of bromocriptine (which stimulates dopamine receptors) along with rehabilitation, although contradictory results have also been reported (Albert, Bachman, Morgan, & Helm-Estabrooks, 1988; Gupta & Mlcoch, 1992; Sabe, Leigarda, & Starkstein, 1992). It is likely that pharmacological adjuncts to rehabilitation will be used with increasing success in the coming years. However, behavioural methods involved in increasing available neurotransmitters (like norepinephrine) during rehabilitation—such as inducing excitement through rewards or incentives—may be equally important (see Hillis, in press, for discussion).

In summary, cognitive neuropsychology has provided some invaluable insights towards understanding the cognitive processing underlying various language tasks such as reading and spelling. Although models of language tasks may help to focus treatment, they do not always predict which patients will respond to a specific treatment, or narrow down the possible effective treatment strategies. Rather, they may help to predict whether or not a specific treatment, or change at a specific level of processing, will result in generalisation across items or tasks (Hillis, 1989; Rapp, 2005 this issue). However, recent advances in neuroscience (including computational models) that provide insights into how learning takes place in the brain, how the brain is damaged by stroke, head injury, or disease, and how it recovers from damage, may be useful in designing treatment, as long as these insights are effectively integrated with models of the cognitive processes to be treated.

REFERENCES

Albert, M. L., Bachman, D. L., Morgan, A., & Helm-Estabrooks, N. (1988). Pharmacotherapy for aphasia. *Neurology, 38*, 877–879.

Aliminosa, D., McCloskey, M., Goodman-Schulman, R., & Sokol, S. (1993). Remediation of acquired dysgraphia as a technique for testing interpretations of deficits. *Aphasiology, 7*, 55–69.

Baddeley, A. (1993). A theory of rehabilitation without a model of learning is a vehicle without an engine: A comment on Caramazza and Hillis. *Neuropsychological Rehabilitation, 3*, 235–244.

Beeson, P. M. (1998). Treatment for letter-by-letter reading: A case study. In N. Helm-Estabrooks & A. L. Holland (Eds.), *Approaches to the treatment of aphasia* (pp.153–177). San Diego, CA: Singular Press.

Beeson, P. M. (1999). Treating acquired writing impairment. *Aphasiology, 13*, 367–386.

Beeson, P., & Hillis, A. E. (2001). Comprehension and production of written words. In R. Chapey (Ed.), *Language intervention strategies in aphasia and related neurogenic communication disorders* (pp. 572–604). Baltimore: Williams & Wilkens.

Beeson, P. M., & Rapcsak, S. Z. (2002). Clinical diagnosis and treatment of spelling disorders. In A. E. Hillis (Ed.), *The handbook of adult language disorders: Integrating cognitive neuropsychology, neurology and rehabilitation* (pp. 101–120). New York: Psychology Press.

Berndt, R. S., & Mitchum, C. C. (1994). Approaches to the rehabilitation of "phonological assembly". In M. J. Riddoch & G. Humphreys (Eds.), *Cognitive neuropsychology and cognitive rehabilitation* (pp. 503–526). Hove, UK: Lawrence Erlbaum Associates Ltd.

Caramazza, A. (1989). Cognitive neuropsychology and rehabilitation: An unfulfilled promise? In T. Seron & G. DeLoche (Eds.), *Cognitive approaches in rehabilitation* (pp. 383–398). Hillsdale, NJ: Lawrence Erlbaum Associates Inc.

Caramazza, A., & Hillis, A. E. (1991). For a theory of remediation of cognitive deficits. *Neuropsychological Rehabilitation, 3*, 217–234.

Carlomagno, S., Iavarone, A., & Colombo, A. (1994). Cognitive approaches to writing rehabilitation: From single case to group studies. In M. J. Riddoch & G. W. Humphries (Eds.), *Cognitive neuropsychology and cognitive rehabilitation* (pp. 485–502). Hove, UK: Lawrence Erlbaum Associates Ltd.

Clark, A. N. G., & Mankikar, G. D. (1979). D-amphetamine in elderly patients refractory to rehabilitation procedures. *Journal of the American Geriatrics Society, 27*(4), 174–177.

dePartz, M-P. (1986). Re-education of a deep dyslexic patient: Rationale of the method and results. *Cognitive Neuropsychology, 3*(2), 149–177.

dePartz, M-P., Seron, X., & Van der Linden, M. V. (1992). Re-education of surface dysgraphia with a visual imagery strategy. *Cognitive Neuropsychology, 9*, 369–401.

Ellis, A. W., & Young, A. (1988). *Human cognitive neuropsychology*. Hove, UK: Lawrence Erlbaum Associates Ltd.

Friedman, R. B., & Lott, S. N. (1996). Phonologic treatment for deep dyslexia using bigraphs instead of graphemes. *Brain and Language, 55*, 116–118.

Friedman, R. B., & Lott, S. N. (2000). Rapid word identification in pure alexia is lexical but not semantic. *Brain and Language, 72*(3), 219–237.

Gupta, S. R., & Mlcoch, A. G. (1992). Bromocriptine treatment of nonfluent aphasia. *Archives of Physical Medicine and Rehabilitation, 73*, 373–376.

Hillis, A. E. (1993). The role models of language processing in rehabilitation of language impairments. *Aphasiology, 7*, 5–26.

Hillis, A. E. (1994). Contributions from cognitive analysis. In R. Chapey (Ed.), *Language intervention strategies in adult aphasia* (pp. 207–219). Baltimore: Williams & Wilkens.

Hillis, A. E. (1989). Efficacy and generalization of treatment for aphasic naming errors. *Archives of Physical Medicine and Rehabilitation, 70*, 632–636.

Hillis, A. E. (1991). Effects of separate treatments for distinct impairments within the naming process. In T. Prescott (Ed.), *Clinical aphasiology, Vol. 19* (pp. 255–265). Austin, TX: Pro-Ed.

Hillis, A. E. (1998). Treatment of naming disorders: New issues regarding old therapies. *Journal of the International Neurological Society, 4*, 648–660.

Hillis, A. E. (2001). Cognitive neuropsychological approaches to rehabilitation of language disorders. In R. Chapey (Ed.), *Language intervention strategies in adult aphasia*. Baltimore: Williams & Wilkens.

Hillis, A. E. (2002a). *Handbook of adult language disorders: Integrating cognitive neuropsychology, neurology, and rehabilitation*. Philadelphia: Psychology Press.

Hillis, A. E. (2002b). The cognitive processes underlying reading. In A. E. Hillis (Ed.), *Handbook of adult language disorders: Integrating cognitive neuropsychology, neurology, and rehabilitation* (pp. 3–14). Philadelphia: Psychology Press.

Hillis, A. E. (in press). For a theory of rehabilitation: Progress in the decade of the brain. In P. Halligan & D. Wade (Eds.), *Effectiveness of rehabilitation of cognitive deficits.* Oxford: Oxford University Press.

Hillis, A. E., & Caramazza, A. (1987). Model-driven treatment of dysgraphia. In R. H. Brookshire (Ed.), *Clinical aphasiology* (pp. 84–105). Minneapolis, MN: BRK Publishers.

Hillis, A. E., & Caramazza, A. (1994). Theories of lexical processing and theories of rehabilitation. In M. J. Riddoch & G. Humphreys (Eds.), *Cognitive neuropsychology and cognitive rehabilitation* (pp. 449–484). Hove, UK: Lawrence Erlbaum Associates Ltd.

Hillis, A. E., & Rapp, B. S. (2004). Cognitive and neural substrates of written language comprehension and production. In M. Gazzaniga (Ed.), *The new cognitive neurosciences.* Cambridge, MA: MIT Press.

Kiran, S., & Thompson, C. (2003). The role of semantic complexity in treating of naming deficits: Training semantic categories in fluent aphasia by controlling exemplar typicality. *Journal of Speech-Language and Hearing Research, 46,* 773–787.

Kirkwood, A., Rozas, C., Kirkwood, J., Perez, F., & Bear, M. (1999). Modulation of long-term synaptic depression in visual cortex by acetylcholine and norepinephrine. *Journal of Neuroscience, 19,* 1599–1609.

Maher, L. M., Clayton, M. C., Barrett, A. M., Schober-Peterson, D., & Rothi, L. J. G. (1998). Rehabilitation of a case of pure alexia: Exploiting residual abilities. *Journal of the International Neuropsychological Society, 4,* 636–647.

Martin, N., Fink, R., & Laine, M. (2004a). Treatment of word retrieval with contextual priming. *Aphasiology, 18,* 457–471.

Martin, N., Fink, R., Laine, M., & Ayala, J. (2004b). Immediate and short-term effects of contextual priming on word retrieval. *Aphasiology, 18,* 867–898.

Mitchum, C., & Berndt, R. (1988). Aphasia rehabilitation: An approach to diagnosis and treatment of disorders of language production. In M. G. Eisenberg (Ed.), *Advances in clinical rehabilitation* (pp. 160–185). New York: Springer.

Mitchum, C., & Berndt, R. (1994). Verb retrieval and sentence construction: Effects of targeted intervention. In G. W. Humphreys & M. J. Riddoch (Eds.), *Cognitive neuropsychology and cognitive rehabilitation* (pp. 317–348). Hove, UK: Lawrence Erlbaum Associates Ltd.

Mitchum, C., & Berndt, R. (1995). The cognitive neuropsychological approach to treatment of language disorders. *Neuropsychological Rehabilitation, 5,* 1–16.

Nickels, L. (1992). The autocue? Self-generated phonemic cues in the treatment of a disorder of reading and naming. *Cognitive Neuropsychology, 9,* 155–182.

Plaut, D. (1996). Relearning after damage in connectionist networks: Toward a theory of rehabilitation. *Brain and Language, 52,* 25–82.

Plaut, D., & Shallice, T. (1993). Deep dyslexia: A case study of connectionist neuropsychology. *Cognitive Neuropsychology, 10,* 377–500.

Rapp, B. (2001). *The handbook of cognitive neuropsychology: What deficits reveal about the human mind.* Ann Arbor, MI: Taylor & Francis.

Riddoch, M. J., & Humphreys, G. (Eds.). (1994a). *Cognitive neuropsychology and cognitive rehabilitation.* Hove, UK: Lawrence Erlbaum Associates Ltd.

Riddoch, M. J., & Humphreys, G. (1994b). Cognitive neuropsychology and cognitive rehabilitation: A marriage of equal partners? In M. J. Riddoch & G. Humphreys (Eds.), *Cognitive neuropsychology and cognitive rehabilitation* (pp. 1–15). Hove, UK: Lawrence Erlbaum Associates Ltd.

Rothi, L. J. G., & Moss, S. (1992). Alexia without agraphia: Potential for model assisted therapy. *Clinical Communication Disorders, 2,* 11–18.

Sabe, L., Leigarda, R., & Starkstein, S. E. (1992). An open-label trial of bromocriptine in nonfluent aphasia. *Neurology, 42,* 1637–1638.

Scott, C., & Byng, S. (1989). Computer assisted remediation of a homophone comprehension disorder in surface dyslexia. *Aphasiology, 3*(3), 301–320.

Seki, K., Yajima, M., & Sugishita, M. (1995). The efficacy of kinesthetic reading treatment for pure alexia. *Neuropsychologia, 33,* 595–609.

Seron, T., & DeLoche, G. (1989). *Cognitive approaches in rehabilitation.* Hillsdale, NJ: Lawrence Erlbaum Associates Inc.

Shallice, T. (1988). *From neuropsychology to mental structure.* Cambridge: Cambridge University Press.

Walker-Batson, D. (2000). Use of pharmacotherapy in the treatment of aphasia. *Brain and Language, 71*(1), 252–254.

Walker-Batson, D., Curtis, S., Natarajan, R., Ford, J., Dronkers, N., Salmeron, E. et al. (2001). A double-blind placebo-controlled study of the use of amphetamine in the treatment of aphasia. *Stroke, 32,* 2093–2098.

Walker-Batson, D., Devous, M. D., Curtis, S., Unwin, D. H., & Greenlee, R. G. (1991). Response to amphetamine to facilitate recovery from aphasia subsequent to stroke. *Clinical Aphasiology, 21*, 137–143.

Weekes, B., & Coltheart, M. (1996). Surface dyslexia and surface dysgraphia: Treatment studies and their theoretical implications. *Cognitive Neuropsychology, 13*(2), 277–315.

Wilson, B. A. (1997). Cognitive rehabilitation: How it is and might be. *Journal of the International Neuropsychological Society, 3*, 487–496.

Wilson, B. A., & Patterson, K. E. (1990). Rehabilitation and cognitive neuropsychology. *Applied Cognitive Psychology, 4*, 247–260.

APHASIOLOGY, 2005, 19 (10/11), 994–1008

The relationship between treatment outcomes and the underlying cognitive deficit: Evidence from the remediation of acquired dysgraphia

Brenda Rapp

Johns Hopkins University, Baltimore, MD, USA

Background: It is unclear to what extent treatment outcomes are significantly influenced by the specific cognitive deficits that underlie an individual's language impairment. That is, it is not well understood if treatment benefits such as item-specific relearning, generalisation to untreated items, and long-term maintenance vary according to deficit type.

Aims: The aim of this investigation was to look at the relationship between deficit type and responsiveness to treatment by examining the results of applying the same remediation protocol to individuals suffering from deficits affecting different components of the spelling process.

Methods & Procedures: Three adults with acquired dysgraphia were identified as suffering from deficits to either the orthographic lexicon or the graphemic buffer. They were administered the same spell-study-spell treatment protocol during bi-weekly sessions for periods of 7–11 weeks with periodic follow-up evaluations that continued for 40–112 weeks after the end of treatment.

Outcomes & Results: All three individuals exhibited significant item-specific treatment benefits that were apparent even 40–112 weeks after the end of treatment. Furthermore, the individuals with the graphemic buffer deficits showed generalisation to untreated words, while the individual with the orthographic lexicon deficit showed an item-specific benefit merely from the repeated testing of words.

Conclusions: The presence or absence of generalisation effects appears to be related to the nature of the underlying deficit, while the long-term stability of treatment benefits does not.

Rehabilitation following neural injury is a complex process directed at facilitating different aspects of an individual's recovery. Acknowledgment of the many facets of rehabilitation—psychological, social, cognitive, occupational—represents recognition of the complex nature of human health and well-being. The research presented here is specifically concerned with the rehabilitation of particular cognitive functions deployed in written language production (i.e., spelling). This work recognises the extraordinary complexity of the cognitive machinery that gives rise to skilled human language use, and assumes that in order to maximise rehabilitation of a particular skill it will be necessary to understand the component cognitive operations that make up that skill as well as the treatment conditions that favour their remediation. More fundamentally, this work is based on the assumption that not only is it possible to objectively evaluate the

Address correspondence to: Brenda Rapp, Department of Cognitive Science, Johns Hopkins University, Baltimore, MD 21218, USA. Email: rapp@cogsci.jhu.edu

This work was made possible by the support of NIH grants MH55758 and DC006740. In addition, I would like to express my appreciation of Delia Kong's dedication and many contributions to this project.

    DOI:10.1080/02687030544000209

effectiveness of cognitive interventions, it is also essential to do so if we are to make progress towards the goal of maximising the brain's capacity to recover from neural injury.

Despite the critical role of written language production in employment and its importance in everyday life (grocery lists, telephone messages, agenda entries, email correspondence, greeting cards, etc.), there have only been a handful of studies concerned with the treatment of acquired spelling deficits (for a review see Beeson & Rapcsak, 2002). This paucity is especially troubling given the evidence that for individuals with severe impairment in both spoken and written language production, remediation of the written language deficits is sometimes more successful than remediation of the spoken language deficits (Beeson, 1999; Robson, Marshall, Chiat, & Pring, 2001). Written language rehabilitation may, therefore, provide a means of communication for individuals with very limited communication abilities.

Treatment studies are often designed to evaluate the effectiveness of particular treatments by comparing the outcomes of applying *different treatments* across individuals suffering from the *same deficits*. In contrast, the work described in this paper is directed at furthering our understanding of specific cognitive functions and the factors affecting their rehabilitation by comparing the *same treatment* in individuals that suffer from *different deficits*. It is assumed that by keeping the treatment protocol constant, the role that the deficit type plays in the treatment outcomes will be more evident.

In this investigation we studied three individuals with acquired dysgraphia,[1] and we: (1) used a theory of the spelling process to identify which of the component operations involved in spelling were affected in these individuals, (2) applied the same treatment protocol to the two different deficits types that we identified and, finally, (3) evaluated the relationship between the treatment outcomes and the deficit types. The treatment protocol was designed to address the following questions: Is there a benefit achieved from simply evaluating a set of words repeatedly? Is the treatment that was applied beneficial beyond any effects of repeated testing? Do treatment benefits generalise to untreated words? What is the stability of the treatment benefits over time? Our results indicate that the answers to these questions vary in systematic ways that may be related to the particular cognitive function that has been affected by neural injury.

THE SPELLING PROCESS AND DAMAGE TO INDIVIDUAL COMPONENTS

According to the theory schematised in Figure 1 (Caramazza, 1988; Ellis, 1989), spelling to dictation can be achieved by two sets of processes or "routes"—lexical and sublexical. The lexical route uses information about words that has been stored in long-term memory, while the sublexical route uses learned information regarding the regular relationships between sounds and letters. With regard to the lexical route, when an individual hears a word (e.g., in the spelling to dictation task, listening to a lecture or telephone conversation, etc.) a phonological representation of the word is activated in the long-term memory store of the phonological forms of words referred to as the phonological input lexicon. Activation of this representation allows the listener to gain access to the word's meaning in the semantic system and, at this point, the representation of the word's spelling can be accessed in the orthographic output lexicon (OOL)—the long-term

---

[1] A significant portion of the results obtained for two of the three participants (RSB and MMD) was previously reported in Rapp and Kane, 2002.

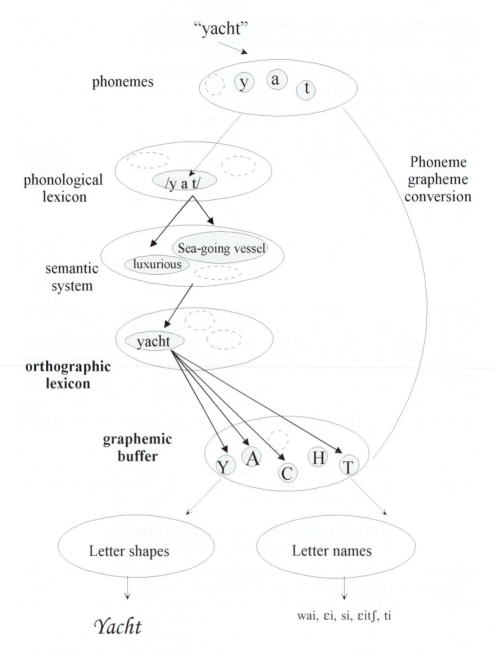

Figure 1. A schematic depiction of the cognitive components involved in spelling.

memory repository of the spellings of familiar words. The OOL can also be accessed in response to semantic activation prompted by a visual object or a thought. In contrast, the sublexical process responds to any phonological string, whether or not it is a word that is familiar to the listener. That is, unfamiliar words or pseudowords (e.g., "flope") are processed in the same manner as words. The sublexical process applies stored knowledge of sound-to-spelling correspondences to the phonological stimulus and yields a phonologically plausible spelling (e.g., "once" → WUNS). The spellings generated by either the lexical or sublexical processes are then held in a short-term working memory component called the graphemic buffer (GB) that maintains these representations active while each letter is assigned either a shape (upper/lower case, cursive) for written spelling, or a letter name for oral spelling. Finally letter shapes or letter names are produced by engaging the appropriate motor systems.

Numerous studies have shown that individual components of the spelling system can be selectively affected by neurological injury (for a review see Rapp & Gotsch, 2001). Impairment to each component has a characteristic manifestation, which assists in identifying the locus of the deficit/s. Given that the cases described in this paper have deficits affecting either the OOL or the GB, the subsequent discussion is restricted to these two components.

Damage restricted to the OOL gives rise to the following: (1) because the OOL is a post-semantic component we expect to see *intact single word comprehension*; (2) given that the OOL is sensitive to the frequency with which a word has been encountered, damage to the OOL results in a *lexical frequency effect* (high-frequency words spelled better than low-frequency words); (3) the OOL is assumed to be insensitive to the length of a word (Caramazza, Miceli, Villa, & Romani, 1987), thus deficits to the OOL affect long and short words comparably, yielding an *absence of a length effect*; (4) damage to the OOL will increase reliance on the sublexical process (if it is relatively intact), yielding phonologically plausible spelling responses (PPEs; such as "yacht" spelled as YOT). Damage to the GB yields a performance pattern that largely, although not entirely, contrasts with this; specifically: (1) given that damage to the GB is also post-semantic, we should observe *intact single word comprehension*; (2) because the GB is thought to be entirely (or largely) insensitive to lexical frequency, an *absence of a frequency effect* is expected; (3) the GB is essentially a working memory process that it is sensitive to the length of the word whose activation must be maintained and, therefore, a *length effect* is expected; and (4) GB damage does not prompt reliance on the sublexical system, as a result instead of PPEs the errors that are expected to arise following GB damage are *letter substitutions, deletions, additions, and transpositions* (e.g., "yacht" → YECT).

TREATMENTS TARGETING THE ORTHOGRAPHIC LEXICON AND THE GRAPHEMIC BUFFER

The majority of treatment studies that have targeted specific components of the spelling architecture have been directed at strengthening the representations of word spellings in the OOL. These studies have generally employed techniques in which the correct spellings of words are repeatedly presented for study and spelling and/or delayed copy (Aliminosa, McCloskey, Goodman-Schulman, & Sokol, 1993; Beeson, 1999; Beeson & Hirsch, 1998; Behrman, 1987; Behrmann & Byng, 1992; Carlomagno, Iavarone, & Colombo, 1994; Clausen & Beeson, 2003; DePartz, Seron, & Van der Linden, 1992; Hatfield & Weddel, 1976; Hillis & Caramazza, 1987; Rapp & Kane, 2002; Raymer, Cudworth, & Haley, 2003; Seron, Deloche, Moulard, & Russelle, 1980; Weekes & Coltheart, 1996). This general method is based on the assumption that neural injury has weakened/damaged the representations of words in long-term memory and that the repeated presentation of words will strengthen or build up these representations. On this basis, and given the assumption that the OOL stores the spellings of the specific words with which an individual is familiar, the expectation for successful treatment of an OOL deficit is that there should be: (a) word-specific improvement for trained words that have been "strengthened" and (b) an absence of generalisation to untreated words since these have not been specifically targeted.

There have been very few treatment studies specifically directed at remediating GB deficits and, unlike in the case of OOL deficits, there has been no consensus regarding a rationale for a treatment method. Hillis and Caramazza (1987) taught error detection and correction strategies; Hillis (1989) used a cueing hierarchy; and Rapp and Kane (2002) applied the same repeated study and spelling technique used for OOL deficits. Given the characterisation of the GB as a working memory component that is used in the spelling of all words and pseudowords, the expectations for successful treatment of a GB deficit are: (a) no special benefit for treated words, but rather (b) generalisation of treatment benefits to untrained words.

A review of the treatment outcomes in these studies reveals a mixed picture that does not clearly conform to the expectations for either OOL or GB deficits, particularly with regard to generalisation effects. Thus, studies directed at strengthening spelling representations in the OOL uniformly report success with the words targeted in treatment but vary with regard to finding generalisation to untrained words. With GB deficits, some researchers have reported generalisation effects (Hillis & Caramazza, 1987; Rapp & Kane, 2002) while others have not (Hillis, 1989).

Understanding the reasons for variable outcomes such as these is critical for developing a real understanding of the mechanisms that underlie and support successful recovery and rehabilitation of cognitive functions. A number of possible accounts of this variability can be briefly considered. One possibility is that the deficits of the individuals participating in these studies have not been characterised with sufficient precision and that, in fact, individuals who were classified as having the same deficit actually had different deficits. If that were the case, variable outcomes would be expected. Another possibility is that the differences in outcomes stem from differences across studies with regard to treatment protocols. That is, although treatments for the OOL deficits were generally similar, there were a number of differences across studies that may have influenced the outcomes. Finally, it is possible that treatment outcomes are entirely unrelated to the nature of the functional deficit suffered by an individual. It may be that, instead, outcomes are entirely determined by other factors, ranging from the cognitive to the motivational to the metabolic. For example, it could be that treatment outcomes are determined not by the cognitive component that has been affected by neurological injury but by the integrity of fundamental cognitive functions such as memory or spoken language abilities. The research reported here attempts to address some of these possibilities in order to further our understanding of the factors that are relevant to facilitating recovery and rehabilitation of acquired deficits of written language.

EXPERIMENTAL STUDY

Three individuals with acquired dysgraphia subsequent to embolic stroke participated in this study. Prior to the initiation of this investigation, all three individuals had participated for fairly extensive time periods (18 months to 4 years) in spelling research studies that did not involve any rehabilitation.

MMD was a 67-year-old right-handed woman with a high-school diploma who worked in a clerical position until retirement. Premorbid writing samples revealed fewer than .2% spelling errors. She suffered a stroke 2 years prior to the onset of this investigation and CT scans indicated damage to the left posterior parietal and temporal areas.

The stroke produced mild spoken language difficulties and a significant spelling impairment but no evidence of neglect or field loss. MMD was able to live completely independently.

RSB was a 58-year-old right-handed man who held a PhD and worked as a toxicology researcher until suffering a stroke 4 years prior to this investigation. He reported no premorbid spelling difficulties and was a bilingual speaker of English and Spanish (Spanish was spoken infrequently after the age of 15). MRI scans revealed a lesion in the left anterior parietal region which produced moderate difficulties in spoken language production, significant difficulties in number processing and spelling, as well as some mild somatosensory abnormalities (Rapp, Hendel, & Medina, 2002). RSB showed no signs of visual or tactile neglect and did not suffer any visual field loss. Subsequent to the stroke, RSB retired from his employment but was able to read for pleasure, drive, and manage most of his family's affairs.

JRE was a 62-year-old right-handed woman who worked as a rehabilitation nurse until the time of her stroke, 4 years prior to the onset of this investigation. MRI scanning revealed left posterior frontal as well as posterior parietal and temporal damage. Prior to the stroke JRE was an excellent speller, avid reader, and crossword puzzle aficionada. The stroke produced moderate/severe spoken language production difficulties, moderate spelling difficulties, and paralysis of the left arm, which left her unable to drive. JRE managed most of her affairs with some assistance and was able to enjoy international travel.

In addition to a comprehensive spelling assessment, pre-treatment assessments include the Wechsler Memory Scale–Revised (Wechsler, 1987), and spoken word comprehension and production evaluations using the Snodgrass & Vanderwart picture set (Snodgrass & Vanderwart, 1980). As indicated in Table 1, all three individuals were within normal limits on the WMS–R, they all demonstrated excellent auditory single word comprehension, and suffered mild-moderate difficulties in picture naming.

TABLE 1
Comparison of language, cognitive skills, and other factors for RSB, JFE, and MMD

	RSB	JRE	MMD
Age/hand	58/Rt-handed	62/Rt-handed	67/Rt-handed
Ed/work	PhD/researcher	Rehab nurse	High school/clerical
Aetiology	CVA: left anterior parietal (4 years post)	CVA: left frontal, temporo-parietal (4 years post)	CVA: left posterior parietal/temporal (2.5 years post)
Premorbid spelling	excellent	excellent	excellent
WMS-R	101	95	88
Confrontation naming	75%	90%	92%
Auditory word comp	100%	100%	95%
Quasi-weekly spelling research prior to treatment	18 months	4 years	2 years

Characterising the spelling deficits

All three participants were administered the JHU Dysgraphia Battery (Goodman & Caramazza, 1985) in order to evaluate the integrity of the components of the spelling process depicted in Figure 1 (see for a review of the diagnostic process, see Rapp & Gotsch, 2001).

As discussed in the Introduction, damage to the orthographic lexicon and the graphemic buffer yields characteristic performance and error profiles. As indicated in Table 2, the evaluation revealed that MMD suffered from a deficit to the orthographic lexicon (see also Folk, Rapp, & Goldrick, 2002), while RSB and JRE had primary deficits to the graphemic buffer.

Consistent with damage to the orthographic lexicon, MMD (1) was more accurate with high- vs low-frequency words (71%, 25/35 vs 41%, 14.35) ($\chi^2 = 5.8$, $p < .02$); (2) exhibited no difference in spelling four-letter vs seven-letter words (four-letter words = 57% correct, 8/14, vs seven-letter words = 57%, 8/14); and (3) produced a number of phonologically plausible errors such as "copy" spelled as COPPIE. In addition to this primary orthographic lexicon deficit, MMD also had a deficit affecting sublexical phonology-to-orthography conversion, as indicated by her difficulties in nonword spelling, 24% (32/132) accuracy.

As expected from damage to the graphemic buffer, both RSB and JRE (1) exhibited no or weak effects of frequency; RSB: high- (46%, 16/35) vs low- (37%, 13/35) frequency words ($\chi^2 = 0.24$, ns); JRE: high- (59%, 17/29) vs low- (66%, 19/29) frequency words ($\chi^2 = .07$, ns); (2) were significantly more accurate in spelling short vs long words; RSB: four-letter words (79%, 11/14 correct) vs eight-letter words (21%, 3/14 correct) ($\chi^2 = 7.0$, $p < .01$); JRE: four-letter words (64%, 9/14 correct) vs eight-letter words (0%, 0/14 correct) ($\chi^2 = 10.5$, $p < .01$); and (3) only very rarely produced PPEs, with their primary error types being letter substitutions (RSB: "edit" → IDIT; JRE: "taxi" → TIXI) and deletions (RSB: "recital" → RE_AL; JRE: symbol" → SYOL). JRE showed no evidence of an additional sublexical deficit, exhibiting very similar error types and accuracy with words and nonwords. RSB produced the same error types with words and nonwords but was less accurate with nonwords, an indication of an additional deficit affecting sublexical processing.

TABLE 2
Key features for identification of an orthographic lexicon or graphemic buffer deficit

| | Orthographic lexicon deficit | Graphemic buffer deficit | |
	MMD	RSB	JRE
Length effect	−	+	+
Frequency effect	+	−	−
Phon plausible, similar words, semantic	"urban" → ERBAN "tease" → TEZE "trout" → TROOP	−	−
Letter errors: subs, deletions, movement, insertions	−	"recital" → RE_AL "scalp" → SCAPL "crawl" → CRAWAL	"symbol" → SYOL "thief" → THEIEF "taxi" → TIXI

Summary.   It is important to note that while the three participants clearly differ with regard to their spelling deficits, they are quite similar in their memory and spoken language skills. This will allow us to address one of the concerns raised in the Introduction: the possibility that variable results across studies applying apparently similar treatments to apparently similar deficits could be due to variability across participants with regard to other basic (non-spelling) cognitive skills. The similarity of the three participants in this study with regard to their general cognitive profiles diminishes the likelihood that differences in these areas would be the source of any differences in treatment outcomes we might observe. Nonetheless, it is possible that the assessment of these skills that has been carried out is not sufficiently sensitive to detect differences that may be relevant for determining efficacy and treatment outcomes. It is also possible that what we have considered to be relatively minor differences (e.g., differences in naming abilities or IQ) may actually be significant with regard to their impact on treatment outcomes. These issues will be taken up in the General Discussion.

Remediation of the spelling deficits

The treatment protocol was designed to evaluate the following: (1) word-specific treatment effects, (2) generalisation of treatment to untreated words, (3) word-specific effects of repeated testing, (4) long-term maintenance of any of the observed treatment gains. In order to do so, three matched word sets consisting of 20–30 items were developed for each of the participants: Treated, Repeated, and Control words. Word sets were matched for lexical frequency and letter length and consisted of uninflected, non-homophones. Performance was evaluated during three phases: *pre-treatment baseline, treatment, and follow-up.* Spelling accuracy was evaluated in terms of the number of target letters spelled correctly. Each target letter was assigned a score of 0, 0.5, or 1. A score of 1 was assigned if the target letter was present and in the correct position, 0.5 if it was present but in the incorrect position, and 0 if it was absent. Accuracy was also evaluated according to whether or not the word was correct. Both scoring methods yielded essentially the same patterns but we report letter accuracy as it is the more sensitive measure. Throughout the study, RSB and MMD produced written responses, while JRE (based on her preference) orally spelled her responses.

Pre-treatment baseline phase.   During this phase, spelling performance on all three word sets was evaluated twice (except that Control words were evaluated only once during pre-treatment baseline for RSB and MMD). Each word was read aloud by the experimenter, the participant repeated the word, and then attempted to spell it.

Treatment phase.   The Treated and Repeated words were administered in a blocked manner at each session, with the order of blocks alternating from session to session. Typically there were two treatment sessions per week and these continued until letter error rate was maintained below 5% for at least two consecutive sessions. When this criterion was reached, two *post-treatment evaluations* were administered. Control words as well as Treated and Repeated words were re-administered during these sessions.

Repeated words were administered at every session simply in a spelling to dictation task. Treated words were presented in the following three steps: (1) The participant heard a word, repeated it, and attempted to spell it. (2) After this initial response, and regardless of its accuracy, the participant was shown the correct spelling of the word on a note card while the experimenter said aloud each of the letters of the word. The participant was instructed to study the word, without any time restriction. (3) If the word had been spelled correctly at Step 1, then Step 3 was omitted and the experimenter went on to the next item; otherwise, after the note card was removed from view, the participant was given another opportunity to spell the word. Steps 2 and 3 were repeated until the word was correctly spelled.

   Follow-up phase.   Follow-up evaluations involved administering items from all three lists for spelling to dictation. MMD was evaluated at 12, 20, and 40 weeks following the end of the treatment phase; RSB at 8, 12, 20, 40, and 112 weeks; and JRE at 12, 20, 40, and 90 weeks.

Results

This study allows us to examine the extent to which the patterns of recovery are similar/ different depending on the locus of the primary spelling deficit. The four effects of interest, listed earlier, would be established as follows: (1) *Word-specific treatment effects*: greater accuracy on Treated words at the post-treatment evaluation than at baseline, as well as greater accuracy on Treated vs Repeated words at the end of treat- ment. The latter is necessary in order to distinguish a true treatment effect from an effect of repeated testing or generalised learning. (2) *Generalised learning effects*: greater accuracy on the Control words at the end of treatment than at the beginning. (3) *Word- specific repetition effects:* greater accuracy on the Repeated words at the end of treatment than at the beginning and either (a) no generalised learning effect or (b) an effect of repetition beyond that of generalised learning. The latter is necessary to distinguish a true repetition effect from a generalised learning effect. (4) *Long-term maintenance of treatment benefits:* greater accuracy on Treated, Repeated, or Control words at the time of the follow-up evaluations than at pre-treatment baseline.

   The results of pre-treatment and treatment phases and the post-treatment evaluation are presented in Figure 2; follow-up results are in Figure 3. For the purpose of increasing the stability of the data, the results from pairs of sessions were combined into single accuracy scores or "evaluations".

   Pre-treatment baseline results.   Pre-treatment baseline testing revealed no differ- ences in error rates among the three list types (MMD: $\chi^2 = 1.5$, *ns*; RSB: $\chi^2 = 0.33$, *ns*; JRE: $\chi^2 = 0.13$, *ns*); nor were there differences across the two pre-treatment testing sessions for any lists (MMD: treated $\chi^2 = 0.85$, *ns*, repeated $\chi^2 = 0.85$, *ns*; RSB: treated $\chi^2 = 0.32$, *ns*, repeated $\chi^2 = 0$, *ns*; JRE: treated $\chi^2 = 0$, *ns*, repeated $\chi^2 = 1.4$, *ns*, control $\chi^2 = 0.02$, *ns*). Thus, although the baseline testing period was short, there is no evidence of general amelioration of spelling abilities. This is not surprising given that all three individuals were at least $2\frac{1}{2}$ years post-stroke and had been participating in spelling research (not treatment related) for a considerable period of time (see Table 1).

   ### Treatment results

   Word-specific treatment effects.   All three participants showed significant treatment- related improvement for the words that were trained. As stated earlier, this is indicated by two things: a significant difference in the error rates between the pre-treatment baseline scores versus final evaluation at the end of treatment for the treated words (MMD: $\chi^2 = 61.5$, $p < .0001$; RSB: $\chi^2 = 52.3$, $p < .001$; JRE: $\chi^2 = 46.9$, $p < .001$) as well as a

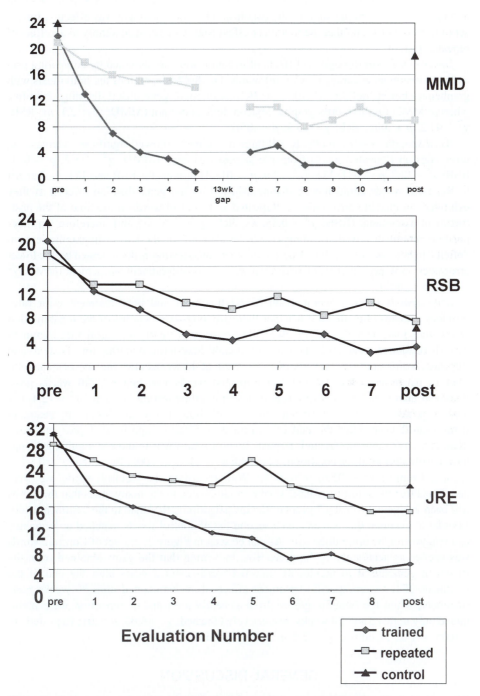

Figure 2. Percent letter errors in each evaluation, from pre-treatment baseline through treatment to post-treatment evaluation. Each evaluation score corresponds to the mean of two sessions.

significant difference between Treated and Repeated words at the end of treatment (MMD: $\chi^2 = 14.8$, $p < .001$; RSB: $\chi^2 = 6.8$, $p < .01$; JRE: $\chi^2 = 28.3$, $p < .001$). In combination these finding support the conclusion that the treatment was effective for the set of treated words and that the treatment effect cannot be reduced simply to an effect of repeated testing.

Generalised learning effects. Effects of generalisation are assessed by comparing pre- and post-treatment accuracy on Control words. On this basis, both of the individuals with graphemic buffer deficits (RSB and JRE) exhibited generalised learning benefits, whereas MMD (with an orthographic lexicon deficit) did not (MMD: $\chi^2 = 2.1$, *ns*; RSB: $\chi^2 = 41.2$, $p < .001$; JRE: $\chi^2 = 5.3$, $p < .05$).

Word-specific repetition effects. All three participants showed significant decreases in error rates on Repeated words from pre to post treatment (MMD: $\chi^2 = 18.2$, $p < .001$; RSB: $\chi^2 = 22.2$, $p < .001$; JRE: $\chi^2 = 9.9$, $p < .01$). However, for RSB and JRE the benefit to Repeated words could not be distinguished from the generalisation effects, as they exhibited comparable error rates on Repeated and Control words at the time of the post-treatment assessment (RSB: $\chi^2 = 0.35$, *ns*; JRE: $\chi^2 = 1.6$, *ns*) and, therefore, an independent benefit of repeated testing cannot be claimed for the two orthographic lexicon deficits. In contrast, for MMD a true effect of repeated testing is documented by the lower error rates on Repeated versus Control words at the post-treatment assessment (MMD: $\chi^2 = 12.0$, $p < .001$).

Long-term benefits. A comparison of pre-treatment and post-treatment error rates provides a means of evaluating whether there are long-term benefits of the rehabilitation (see Figure 3 and Table 3). Although MMD's error rates clearly increased once treatment was discontinued, she still showed significant long-term benefits for Treated and Repeated words until her final follow-up session at 40 weeks after the end of treatment. That is, performance on Treated and Repeated words was better at 40 weeks post-treatment than it had been during pre-treatment baseline testing (Treated: $\chi^2 = 12.4$, $p < .001$; Repeated: $\chi^2 = 3.1$, $p < .05$ one-tailed). RSB showed very little loss of his treatment gains even 2 years after the end of treatment, and the comparison of pre- and post-treatment error rates for Treated, Repeated, and Control words showed significant long-term benefits for all three conditions (Treated: $\chi^2 = 23.3$, $p < .001$; Repeated: $\chi^2 = 15.2$, $p < .001$; Control: $\chi^2 = 35.6$, $p < .001$). With regard to the Control words, we were concerned that the stability of RSB's gains could be due to the many times that the words had been evaluated over the 2 years of the investigation rather than to the treatment itself. In order to examine this, we created a second list of control words matched in frequency and length with the other three lists. As can be seen in Figure 3, this set of Control2 words was spelled as accurately as the other lists, indicating that the gains obtained from the treatment generalised to previously untested words even 2 years after the end of the treatment. JRE's word-specific treatment effects were maintained until 90 weeks post-treatment, while the benefits gained from generalisation and/or repetition were maintained only until 12 and 20 weeks, respectively (Treated: $\chi^2 = 6.63$, $p < .01$; Repeated: $\chi^2 = 0.05$, $p < .05$; Control: $\chi^2 = 3.5$, $p < .05$ one-tailed).

GENERAL DISCUSSION

We applied the same spell-study-spell remediation protocol to three dysgraphic individuals with deficits affecting different components of the spelling process. The results indicate that all three participants, whether they suffered from an orthographic output lexicon deficit or a graphemic buffer deficit, benefited from the remediation protocol. In

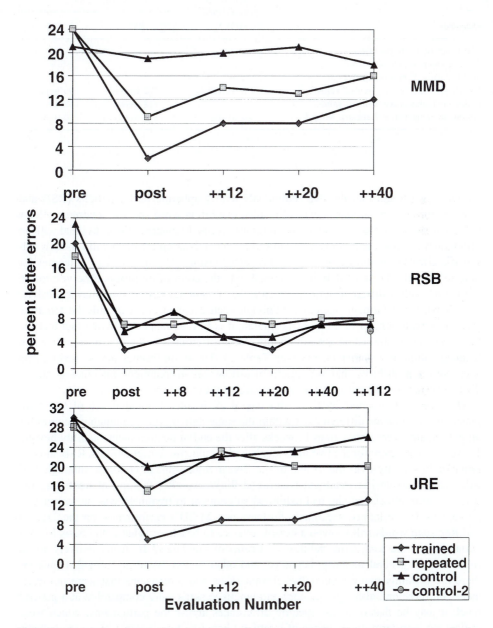

Figure 3. Percent letters correct in each evaluation, from pre-treatment baseline, to post-treatment evaluation and through post-treatment follow-ups. ++ = weeks post-treatment. Each evaluation score corresponds to the mean of two sessions.

TABLE 3
A summary of the major empirical findings reported for MMD, RSB, and JRE

Outcomes	Orthographic lexicon deficit MMD	Graphemic buffer deficit	
		RSB	JRE
Word-specific treatment effects?	+	+	+
Generalisation to untreated words?	−	+	+
Word-specific repetition effects?	+	−	−
Follow-up maintenance: Treated words?	40 weeks	112 weeks	90 weeks
Follow-up maintenance: Control words?	−	112 weeks	12 weeks
Follow-up maintenance: Repeated words?	40 weeks	112 weeks	20 weeks

particular we found that the two individuals with graphemic buffer deficits (RSB and JRE) showed a very similar pattern of results, exhibiting word-specific treatment effects as well as significant generalisation to untrained words. In contrast, the individual with an orthographic lexicon deficit (MMD) showed no generalisation effects but did show word-specific effects of treatment as well as of repeated testing. The similarity of outcomes for individuals with the same deficit, combined with the contrasting results observed for an individual with a different deficit, indicate that functional deficit type may contribute significantly to treatment outcome. Although such a conclusion can only be tentative given the small number of individuals studied, it is further supported by the fact that the three individuals studied do not exhibit any major differences in their basic cognitive and language abilities or other factors (see Table 1). These similarities across participants decrease the probability that the pattern of differences in treatment outcomes is due to differences across the participants with regard to these factors.

However, it is noteworthy that, with regard to long-term maintenance of treatment gains, the participants differed even within the same deficit type. Although outcomes for all participants were stable up to 12 weeks after the end of the treatment, stability beyond 12 weeks varied even for the two individuals with graphemic buffer deficits. RSB showed remarkable stability over the course of the 2-year follow-up. In contrast, although JRE exhibited word-specific treatment benefits at 90 weeks after the end of treatment, the generalisation effect that she had exhibited subsequent to treatment was no longer significant by 12 weeks post-treatment. Furthermore, MMD's performance on the Treated and Repeated words still showed a benefit relative to baseline. What is the basis for this variability in the long-term stability of treatment outcomes? It seems unlikely to be related to the general memory, language, and other factors listed in Table 2. However, there are certainly many potentially relevant skills and dimensions that were not evaluated. Furthermore, although memory and language skills were comparable at a general level, it may be that there are specific differences across the participants, which were critical for long-term maintenance of treatment benefits. For example, there is evidence that phonological and semantic components of verbal short-term memory abilities may be differentially affected in aphasia (Martin, Shelton, & Yaffee, 1994) with possible consequences for long-term learning (Martin, Fink, & Laine, 2004; Martin & Saffran, 1999). Despite the considerable complexity of this topic, it is essential that future research should be directed at developing a better understanding of the factors that contribute to the longevity of treatment gains.

It is also worth considering whether the outcomes conform to predictions derived from our current understanding of the orthographic lexicon and graphemic buffer. As indicated in the Introduction, successful treatment of the orthographic lexicon would be expected to strengthen the specific words treated, without generalising to untreated words. This is indeed what was observed in MMD's case. It is of further interest that for MMD there was a clear benefit from repeatedly attempting to spell (without feedback regarding the accuracy of her responses). It may be important for future studies to control for this possibility, particularly in studies specifically directed at determining the effectiveness of a particular remedial technique. Additionally, with regard to theory-based predictions, we indicated in the Introduction that given the assumption that the buffering function applies to all words, generalisation effects are predicted for the effective treatment of graphemic buffer deficits. Thus, Treated, Repeated, and Control words would be expected to benefit from successful intervention in graphemic buffer cases. This is indeed what was observed for RSB and JRE. However, this view of the graphemic buffer would not have predicted a difference between Treated and Control words. However, both JRE and RSB showed greater benefits for Treated vs Control words. What is the basis of this word-specific treatment effect in graphemic buffer cases? It could be that our understanding of the graphemic buffer is incomplete and for this reason the predictions are incorrect; alternatively it could be that the word-specific treatment effects that go above and beyond the generalisation effects originate outside the target system. For example, it could be that word-specific learning involves the creation of episodic memory traces rather than changes to the spelling architecture itself.

In summary, this study reveals that behavioural intervention in acquired spelling deficits may be quite successful, with certain benefits maintained over the long term. The results further indicate that specific aspects of the response to treatment are determined by the nature of the underlying cognitive deficit itself. There are, however, also indications that other factors may be relevant, particularly in determining the longevity of the benefits. Clearly, to make progress towards the goal of maximising the brain's capacity to recover from neural injury, we will need to develop a detailed and comprehensive understanding of rehabilitation and the many factors—cognitive, biological, motivational—that contribute to its success.

REFERENCES

Aliminosa, D., McCloskey, M., Goodman-Schulman, R., & Sokol, S. (1993). Remediation of acquired dysgraphia as a technique for testing interpretations of deficits. *Aphasiology, 7*, 55–69.

Beeson, P. M. (1999). Treating acquired writing impairment: Strengthening graphemic representations. *Aphasiology, 13*, 367–386.

Beeson, P. M., & Hirsch, F. M. (1998, November). *Writing treatment of severe aphasia.* Paper presented at the Annual Convention of the American Speech-Language-Hearing Association, San Antonio, TX.

Beeson, P. M., & Rapcsak, S. Z. (2002). Clinical diagnosis and treatment of spelling disorders. In A. E. Hillis (Ed.), *Handbook on adult language disorders: Integrating cognitive neuropsychology, neurology, and rehabilitation.* Philadelphia: Psychology Press.

Behrmann, M. (1987). The rites of righting writing: Homophone remediation in acquired dysgraphia. *Cognitive Neuropsychology, 4*, 365–384.

Behrmann, M., & Byng, S. (1992). A cognitive approach to the neurorehabilitation of acquired language disorders. In D. I. Margolin (Ed.), *Cognitive neuropsychology in clinical practice* (pp. 327–350). New York: Oxford University Press.

Caramazza, A. (1988). Some aspects of language processing revealed through the analysis of acquired dysgraphia: The lexical system. *Annual Review of Neuroscience, 11*, 395–421.

Caramazza, A., Miceli, G., Villa, G., & Romani, C. (1987). The role of the graphemic buffer in spelling: Evidence from a case of acquired dysgraphia. *Cognition, 26*, 59–85.

Carlomagno, S., Iavarone, A., & Colombo, A. (1994). Cognitive approaches to writing rehabilitation: From single case to group studies. In M. J. Riddoch & G. W. Humphreys (Eds.), *Cognitive neuropsychology and cognitive rehabilitation* (pp. 485–502). Hove, UK: Lawrence Erlbaum Associates Ltd.

Clausen, N. S. & Beeson, P. M. (2003). Conversational use of writing in severe aphasia: A group treatment approach. *Aphasiology, 17*(6/7) 625–646.

DePartz, M-P., Seron, X., & Van der Linden, M. V. (1992). Re-education of surface dysgraphia with a visual imagery strategy. *Cognitive Neuropsychology, 9,* 369–401.

Ellis, A. (1989). *Reading, writing and dyslexia.* Hove, UK: Lawrence Erlbaum Associates Ltd.

Folk, J. R., Rapp, B., & Goldrick, M. (2002). The interaction of lexical and sublexical information in spelling: What's the point? *Cognitive Neuropsychology, 19,* 653–671.

Francis, W., & Kucera, H. (1982). *Frequency analysis of English usage.* Boston: Houghton Mifflin Co.

Goodman, R. A., & Caramazza, A. (1985). *The Johns Hopkins Dysgraphia Battery.* Baltimore: Johns Hopkins University.

Hatfield, M. F., & Weddel, R. (1976). Re-training in writing in severe aphasia. In Y. Lebrun & R. Hoops (Eds.), *Recovery in aphasics* (pp. 65–78). Amsterdam: Swets & Zeitlinger.

Hillis, A. E. (1989). Efficacy and generalisation for aphasic naming errors. *Archives of Physical Medicine and Rehabilitation, 70,* 632–636.

Hillis, A. E., & Caramazza, A. (1987). Model-driven treatment of dysgraphia. In R. H. Brookshire (Ed.), *Clinical aphasiology* (pp. 84–105). Minneapolis, MN: BRK Publishers.

Martin, N., Fink, R., & Laine, M. (2004). Treatment of word retrieval deficits with contextual priming. *Aphasiology, 18,* 457–471.

Martin, N., & Saffran, E. M. (1999). Effects of word processing and short-term memory deficits on verbal learning: Evidence from aphasia. *International Journal of Psychology, 34,* 339–346.

Martin, R. C., Shelton, J. R., & Yaffee, L. S. (1994). Language processing and working memory: Neuro-psychological evidence for separate phonological and semantic capacities. *Journal of Memory and Language, 33,* 83–111.

Rapp, B., & Gotsch, D. (2001). Cognitive theory in clinical practice. In R. Berndt (Ed.), *Handbook of neuropsychology* (2nd ed., Vol. 2, pp. 221–235). Amsterdam: Elsevier Science Publishers.

Rapp, B., Hendel, S., & Medina, J. (2002). Remodeling of somatosensory hand representations following cerebral lesions in humans. *NeuroReport, 13*(2), 207–211.

Rapp, B., & Kane, A. (2002). Remediation of deficits affecting different components of the spelling process. *Aphasiology, 16*(45/6), 439–454.

Raymer, A. M., Cudworth, C., & Haley, M. A. (2003). Spelling treatment for an individual with dysgraphia: Analysis of generalisation to untrained words. *Aphasiology, 17*(6/7), 607–624.

Robson, J., Marshall, J., Chiat, S., & Pring, T. (2001). Enhancing communication in jargon aphasia: A small group study of writing therapy. *International Journal of Language and Communication Disorders, 36,* 471–488.

Seron, X., Deloche, G., Moulard, G., & Russelle, M. (1980). A computer-based therapy for the treatment of aphasic subjects with writing disorders. *Journal of Speech and Hearing Disorders, 45,* 45–58.

Snodgrass, J. G., & Vanderwart, M. (1980). A standardized set of 260 pictures: Norms for name agreement, image agreement, familiarity, and visual complexity. *Journal of Experimental Psychology: Human Learning and Memory, 6,* 174–215.

Wechsler, D. (1987). *Wechsler Memory Scale–Revised.* San Diego, CA: The Psychological Corporation.

Weekes, B., & Coltheart, M. (1996). Surface dyslexia and surface dysgraphia: Treatment studies and their theoretical implications. *Cognitive Neuropsychology, 13,* 277–315.

APHASIOLOGY, 2005, 19 (10/11), 1009–1020

Therapy for sentence processing problems in aphasia: Working on thinking for speaking

Jane Marshall and Deborah Cairns

City University, London, UK

Background: There is evidence that language production requires specialised conceptual processes, or "thinking for speaking" (Slobin, 1996). These processes generate the pre-verbal message, which according to Levelt (1989, 1999) has propositional structure and perspective and is specifically adapted for the target language.
Aims/Main Contribution: This paper presents evidence that thinking for speaking may be impaired in aphasia. Even when not impaired, its complexities may prevent people with aphasia from revealing grammatical competencies. This may explain why therapy often fails to bring about improvements in open speaking conditions, such as narrative, which impose heavy message-level demands.
Conclusions: It is argued that, with some individuals, therapy should target thinking for speaking skills. Two therapy studies are reviewed that support this conclusion.

THINKING FOR SPEAKING

Different models of language production agree that the first level of processing involves the generation of a pre-verbal message (e.g., Garrett, 1988; Levelt, 1989, 1999; Thompson & Faroqi-Shah, 2002). Here, decisions about content will determine what is and is not mentioned, as well as more subtle modifications, such as quantification, mood, and aspect.

The idea that production begins with a message is not controversial. More contentious is how that message is translated into language. Many commentators point out that our concepts do not readily map onto language (e.g., Black & Chiat, 2000; Pinker, 1989). Rather, we express a selective or "pared down" version of our concepts, a version that is adapted to the language being used: "Any utterance is a selective schematization of a concept – a schematization that is in some way dependent on the grammaticized meanings of the speaker's particular language, recruited for the purposes of verbal expression" (Slobin, 1996, pp. 75–76).

Slobin suggests that, during utterance formulation, speakers direct their attention to the properties of events and situations that are most readily expressed in their language. Such selective attention can be observed through cross-linguistic differences. Take the following examples of children describing a picture from the Frog Story (Slobin, 1996). The picture illustrates two events. One has just occurred and is now complete (a boy falling

Address correspondence to: Jane Marshall, Department of Language and Communication Science, City University, London EC1V OHB, UK. Email: J.Marshall@city.ac.uk

The work reported in this paper was supported by a scholarship from the Stroke Association to Jane Marshall and by a bursary from Connect – The Communication Disability Network to Deborah Cairns.

http://www.tandf.co.uk/journals/pp/02687038.html   DOI:10.1080/02687030544000218

out of a tree); the other is ongoing (bees chasing a dog). This temporal difference was typically marked by speakers of English (a language with grammatical aspect):

"the boy fell out and the dog was being chased by the bees" (English)

In contrast, it was typically omitted by speakers of Hebrew (a language without grammatical aspect):

"the boy fell and the dog ran away" (Hebrew)

The pattern was not absolute, since just under a third of Hebrew speakers used other devices to mark the fact that one event was complete and the other ongoing. Clearly Hebrew speakers can detect the temporal properties of events. However, because aspect is not marked in their language, it is typically not attended to. English speakers, in contrast, are much more likely to attend to this feature, as it can be expressed in the verb form.

Other examples are less subtle. If an English speaker describes a picture of a man throwing either a big or a small ball, they might mention the size of the ball, but equally might not. A user of British Sign Language (BSL), however, is duty bound to attend to this feature of the event. This is because the BSL verb THROW must be modified according to the nature of the direct object.

Similarly, an English speaker could describe the activity depicted in Figure 1 as "The woman attacks the man", leaving the nature of the attack unspecified. This option is less available to the user of BSL, where no exact equivalent verb exists. Here the likely verb is STAB, which will be modified to express the manner and direction of the action in the picture. Again, the BSL user has to attend to features of the event that can be disregarded by the user of English (for further examples see Sutton-Spence & Woll, 1999)

These cross-linguistic differences highlight the need for language to act as a filter on one's thoughts, a process that has been described as "thinking for speaking" (Slobin, 1996). Sensitivity to the target language is not the only requirement proposed in message generation. Levelt (1989, 1999), for example, argues that messages must additionally have propositional structure. This specifies the main protagonists and their roles in the

Figure 1.   The woman attacks the man.

event, and will eventually map onto the verb argument structure composed by the language formulator. The message must also be marked for perspective. This is particularly evident in language about spatial relationships, for example where a ball can be described as "to the left" or "to the right" of a chair, depending on the perspective adopted by the speaker (Brown & Levinson, 1993; Levelt, 1996). However, it is also a general feature of all speech, as illustrated in the following pairs of utterances:

I'll bring it round after lunch.
I'll take it round after lunch.

I lent him a fiver.
He borrowed a fiver from me.

She's my mother.
I'm her daughter.

IMPLICATIONS FOR APHASIA

If production entails thinking for speaking, this could be a locus of impairment in aphasia. In other words, some people with aphasia may be unable to build grammatically principled, constrained schematisations of events that can be mapped onto their language. Is there any evidence that this is the case?

Some evidence comes from aphasic people's performance on nonverbal tasks exploring event knowledge. One task (Dipper, 1999) explored the very preliminary level of analysis that distinguishes events from static situations. This task was adapted from the photograph-sorting task devised by Nickels, Byng, and Black (1991), and was based upon Langacker's (1987, 1991, 1997) notion that we conceptualise the temporal profile of an event by "scanning" its component movements. Participants watched video clips, half of which showed events (e.g., a person washing up) and half static scenes (e.g., crockery drying on a rack). They had to indicate whether anything was happening. Cunningly, Dipper ensured that the judgement could not be made simply by detecting movement, as the states were filmed with a moving camera. Controls performed at ceiling on this task, as did some of the people with aphasia. However, one person did not, suggesting that even this very early level of analysis was impaired (see also Byng, Nickels, & Black, 1994).

Nonverbal event judgement tasks are difficult to develop, and almost all can be criticised. For example, some individuals may fail these tasks for "trivial" reasons that have nothing to do with thinking for speaking. In themselves, therefore, they may provide only partial evidence. Further evidence comes from the output produced by some aphasic people when trying to describe events.

One study (Cairns, Marshall, Cairns, & Dipper, 2005) used naming to investigate people's focus of attention when talking about action pictures. Participants were shown pictures of events and asked not to describe them, but simply to name the entities taking part in the action. All the pictures showed a person using an instrument to act upon either another person or an object. In order to ensure that the three main nouns were matched in frequency and familiarity, the people had identifiable roles (such as "cowboy" or "fireman"). This resulted in some rather bizarre events, as illustrated in Figure 2. The pictures were also drawn with no left/right bias, so that in half the items the agent was shown on the left and in half on the right.

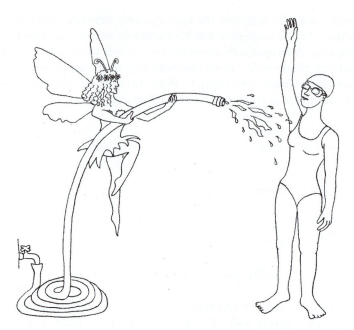

Figure 2. An example of the stimuli used by Cairns et al.

This task was given to 20 controls with unimpaired language, and to two individuals with nonfluent aphasia. The first, "Ron", had good noun production, but very reduced verb and sentence output. For example, he scored 116/162 when naming object pictures, but just 17/100 when naming action pictures (Druks & Masterson, 2000), and his output contained virtually no verb argument structure. Ron had also previously demonstrated difficulties with a number of nonverbal event judgement tasks. The second participant with aphasia, "Helen", also had impaired verb and sentence production, but did not demonstrate the same difficulty on event-processing tasks.

How did Ron, Helen, and the controls differ? One point of contrast was in the number of items named. The mean number named by controls was 3.01 (SD 0.03), indicating that they pretty much only named the main protagonists (agent, theme, and instrument). Helen showed a similar pattern, naming a mean of 3.07 items per picture. Ron, on the other hand, was less focused in his naming (mean number of items = 4.93), as this example illustrates:

"tap, hose, and pixies, elf, woman, long hair – no, short – no, bob, and pixie and then swimming woman, and cap, obviously, and [gestures goggles]"

The order of naming was also different. On a later occasion, the controls were asked to describe the pictures, and from their descriptions a modal sentence order could be determined for each item. This was significantly related to their original naming order. In other words, even when just naming the objects and people in the picture, non-brain-damaged controls typically started with the agent, then named the theme, and finally the instrument. Their attention over the items in the picture, as reflected in their naming, seemed to be driven by the thematic structure of the event. Helen demonstrated a similar focus. Indeed she achieved higher scores than the controls for the relationship between her order of naming and sentence order. Ron was very different. His naming order showed no relationship either with his own attempts at sentence description or with the controls' modal sentence order.

Ron's performance on this task invites a number of interpretations. For example he may have listed all the nouns that he could access in order to demonstrate his competence with this aspect of language. An alternative view is that Ron's attention over these events was qualitatively different from the non-aphasic controls', and was not driven by thematic prominence. As a result he names peripheral as well as key entities and displays a more random order of naming. It is interesting that Helen performs normally on this task, despite her verb and sentence impairments. Her constrained and ordered naming may point to retained event analysis skills, which are less available to Ron.

IMPLICATIONS FOR THERAPY: STUDY 1

If aphasia can affect thinking for speaking, this could become a target for intervention. This possibility was pursued in one therapy study (Marshall, 1994; Marshall, Pring, & Chiat, 1993). MM, the person studied, had severe nonfluent aphasia, with reduced verb production and virtually no sentence output.

A number of factors suggested that thinking for speaking might be impaired. First, MM had difficulty with nonverbal tasks requiring event judgements. One was the Role Video. Here MM watched 32 events (twice) on video, 16 of which were reversible and 16 nonreversible. After the first presentation she was given three photos, and after the second she was asked to select the photo showing the outcome of the event. Examples are given below:

woman burns paper   burnt paper (target)
                                burnt box (role distractor – the box was present in the video
                                but uninvolved in the event)
                                torn paper (event distractor)

woman shoots man   man dead (target)
                                woman dead (role distractor)
                                man now wearing coat (event distractor)

Controls, and many aphasic people, make virtually no errors on this task. MM was different. Her picture selections were perfect for the nonreversible events, showing that she understood the task and had no visual difficulties with the video or pictures. However, she made five errors with the reversible items, suggesting some difficulty schematising the role structure of these events.

As with Ron, further evidence came from MM's naming. We noticed that when MM attempted to describe event pictures she often named items that were peripheral to the main event:

"my car ... Ford Escort ... blue [writes mirror] .. and er Ford"
(target: woman driving a car)

In describing 50 event pictures, MM named a total of 34 optional items; that is, nouns and adjectives that would appear within modifying phrases in normal production. This contrasted with five non-aphasic controls, who on average named just 20.6 optional items (range 8–28). As with Ron, MM's naming seemed to be less focused on key arguments than that of the controls.

The evidence suggested that MM's thinking about events was out of kilter. She was not focusing on the main protagonists, or laying down explicit representations of their role in the event. We hypothesised that if therapy could help her to think about events in a more organised and language-compatible way, production might improve.

The main therapy task involved making decisions about the roles of people and objects in events. MM watched an event on video, such as a man ironing a shirt. First she was asked to identify the agent, e.g., by selecting a photograph of the man (rather than a picture of a woman, the shirt, or the iron). Then she was asked to identify the object that was changed in the event, again through photo selection. The third stage required her to think about the action. She was given pictures showing contrastive outcomes (e.g., an ironed shirt vs a torn shirt) and asked to pick the correct one for the event. She was also asked to gesture the action and attempt to name the verb.

Therapy was evaluated by comparing pre- and post-therapy descriptions of 50 event pictures, of which 20 illustrated verbs that had featured in therapy, while 30 illustrated untreated verbs. The latter included 10 items illustrating three argument events (such as a woman selling a car to a man), which were an untreated event type. Encouragingly, MM's picture descriptions improved, both in terms of the number of verbs named and word order structure, and these gains generalised to the untreated two argument verbs. There was also evidence that the gains were communicatively valuable. MM's attempts to describe the pictures were shown to four observers, who were asked to judge their content. These observers understood significantly more post- than pre-therapy descriptions. Less encouragingly, MM's descriptions of three argument events did not improve, and nor did her narrative production.

One way of interpreting these outcomes is to suggest that therapy gave MM the skill to analyse the role structure of already constrained event representations (that is, pictures of two-argument events). When the pictures were less constrained (three-argument events) she was still out of her depth. The unconstrained origins of narrative production were even more problematic.

Some support for this view came from a video-description task administered post-therapy (Byng & Black, unpublished; results reported in Marshall, 1994). A total of 50 events were presented on video for description. These fell into three categories:

single events (20 items):
  a man playing a piano
  a woman tickling a child
multiple events (20 items):
  a woman climbing a ladder while a child builds a tower
  a woman kisses a man while he eats a biscuit
single events with multiple perspectives (10 items):
  a woman feeding a child/a child eating
  a man talking to a woman/a woman listening to a man

MM's output was scored for verb production and structure. The latter scoring awarded one point if a single noun was correctly positioned in relation to the verb, and two points for a complete verb argument structure (thus the maximum possible structural score for the single events was 40, and 80 for the multiple events). If the degree of constraint present in the stimulus influences production, MM should cope better at describing single rather than multiple events. We would also predict difficulties with the multiple-perspective items, where MM would be required to constrain her own thinking for speaking by adopting an appropriate perspective over the events. This prediction was

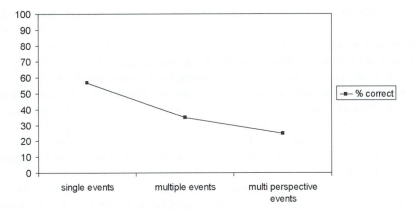

Figure 3.   MM's structure scores on the multiple event description task.

borne out, although only in terms of the structure score (see Figure 3). MM's difficulties with the multiple events and multiple perspective events are illustrated by the following samples:

bye bye boy paints colours woman
(a boy paints a woman, the woman waves)

ball ... man girls ... er boy no no catch boy
(a man catches a ball thrown by a woman)

It seems that the degree to which MM can employ her new-found structural skills depends on the nature of the stimulus. She achieves some success with highly focused representations of single events, including reversible ones, but starts to fail when multiple events, or multiple perspectives, have to be processed. Of course, this condition applies whenever MM attempts spontaneous speech or narrative, which may explain why therapy effects did not generalise to these contexts.

A second therapy case pursues the issue of generalisation, and describes another therapy approach that may assist thinking for speaking in more open conditions.

IMPLICATIONS FOR THERAPY: STUDY 2

Like MM, EM (Marshall, 1999; Marshall, Pring, & Chiat, 1998) had nonfluent, agrammatic speech, with most of her output consisting of isolated noun phrases. Initial testing pointed to severe problems in verb production. There were virtually no verbs in her spontaneous speech and, in matched spoken picture naming tasks, she named nouns much more successfully than verbs. Despite this, EM could write verbs and comprehend them. It seemed, therefore, that her difficulties lay in linking verb semantics to phonology. There was evidence that this difficulty underpinned her sentence-production problems, since simply providing her with a verb dramatically improved sentence generation.

The first therapy programme was developed in the light of these findings. Therapy aimed to improve access to a vocabulary of 35 treated verbs (using semantic naming tasks). We hypothesised that therapy should improve verb naming, and that there would be a corresponding increase in sentence production. To some extent, these predictions were upheld, in that picture descriptions involving the 35 treated verbs improved, both with respect to verb production and argument structure. However, there were some important limitations. Untreated verbs were unchanged, which mirrors the results obtained from many studies of naming therapy with nouns (see Nickels, 2002). More disappointingly, there were no gains in spontaneous speech or narrative. In one evaluation task, EM was required to retell two short stories, one of which was constructed using the treated verbs. Given that EM's naming of these verbs had improved, we might anticipate improvements in her narrative. Yet this was not the case. After therapy, most of her narrative comprised single noun phrases, and the number of utterances containing a verb had not increased.

In summary, it seemed that therapy had restored access to a corpus of verbs and that once the verb was accessed, EM could use it to build argument structure. However, this access depended on condition. When the task was constrained (describing pictures with a single sentence) the verb was available; when it was unconstrained (narrative) it was not.

This observation stimulated the second therapy programme. One element of this programme aimed to "train" a small group of general verbs (go, come, leave, give, get, put, take, bring, make, and change), with the rationale that access to these verbs would enable EM to describe a very wide range of events and situations. The second element aimed to manipulate the way EM thought about events, so that she would become more able to describe them. In essence, this component aimed to help her reduce complex, multiple situations to highly focused unitary concepts.

Overall, EM was given 20 hours of therapy. A major component involved retelling clips of commercial video films. Before watching the clips EM was reminded of her general verbs. She and the therapist also discussed strategies for recounting the story, such as thinking about one event at a time, focusing on the main action of each segmented event, gesturing that action, attempting to name her gesture, and referring to the list of general verbs. EM then watched the clips and attempted to retell what had happened, with cues from the therapist.

After this therapy there were some further gains in verb picture naming, at least when the general verbs could be employed. More importantly, there were also gains in the open narrative task, particularly in terms of the number of utterances containing verb argument structure. Furthermore, these changes seemed to have communicative value. EM's pre- and post-therapy narratives were played to four observers, who were asked to judge their content. These observers understood significantly more of EM's output after therapy than before (see narrative samples in Figure 4).

What was the active component of therapy? One element aimed to train a group of general verbs. If mastered, these could be used to express a wide range of propositions and might, therefore, account for the narrative gains. However, there was little evidence that this was the case, since across both EM's post-therapy narratives there were only seven uses of these verbs. The alternative possibility is that EM benefited from the thinking strategies taught in therapy. This view receives more support, in that 17 of EM's verbs and verb phrases (65%) were accompanied by a gesture post-therapy, and on a number of occasions she repeated or refined her gestures until a verb was achieved. This was an overt sign that she was employing at least one of the taught strategies—a strategy that encouraged EM to break down complex situations into more focused concepts that can be expressed in a single gesture.

Pre Therapy
the pack ... a car ... roof rack ... going to ... drive ... the policeman ... followed the motorway ... the car ...cut ... back in the garage ... the car is damaged ... is going to the station ... the man ... friend ... thirty pounds ... home

Post Therapy
today ... home to holiday ... pack the bags ... roof rack ... cover ... canvas ... open the car ... get in the car ... drive ... the motorway ... drive the car for twelve miles ... the police chased the car ... speeding no way ... drive to the garage ... Peter was map ... the man is showing the way ... drive the motorway ... skidded to stop ... cutting the hand ... back to the garage ... bandaged the hand ... build the car ... the man is driving to the station ... burglar ... wallet ... the ticket and money all gone ... old friend on the platform ... thirty pounds for the ticket ... three o'clock in the morning go home

Target story:
Peter decided to drive home for Christmas. He packed his case, put it on the roof rack and covered it in canvas. Finally he set off. On the motorway a police car followed him for ten miles. Luckly he was not speeding. After he left the motorway he had to stop at a garage to ask the way. The attendant showed him directions on the map. He set off again. At the next bend his car spun off the road. Peter cut his hand in the crash. He went back to the garage. They cleaned his hand and agreed to mend the car. They also took him to the nearest station. In the ticket hall a thief stole Peter's wallet. He had no money or credit cards. Then he noticed an old friend on the opposite platform. The friend lent him £30. Now Peter could buy his ticket. He finally got home at three in the morning.

Figure 4.   Narrative samples produced by EM.

DISCUSSION AND CONCLUSIONS

This paper has argued that describing events and situations requires processes of thinking for speaking, which translate our general ideas about the world into selective, language-compatible representations. According to Levelt (1989, 1999) such representations have propositional structure, encode perspective, and are tuned to the target language of the speaker.

If thinking for speaking is a stage of language production, it may be impaired in aphasia. In line with this view, some people with aphasia perform poorly on tasks in which they are required to make judgements about events. We also presented evidence from "Ron" whose naming from event pictures suggests that he perceives these differently from controls, at least when he is required to talk about them.

Thinking for speaking may also be a focus for therapy, particularly if there is evidence that it is impaired. This hypothesis was pursued with MM (Marshall et al., 1993). Therapy aimed to help MM compose more structured event representations that delineate who or what was performing which role. Despite the fact that tasks were largely non-verbal, there were post-therapy gains in MM's production.

Although encouraging, there was an important limitation in the results achieved with MM, in that picture description improved, but narrative did not. This pattern has been reported in a number of previous therapy studies (e.g., Berndt & Mitchum, 1995; Weinrich, Shelton, McCall, & Cox, 1997) and suggests that generalising the effects of therapy to open speech is very difficult. One reason for this may be that different speaking conditions impose different message-level demands. Pictures, by their very nature, do some of the work involved in thinking for speaking. For example, they tend to focus on the main event and the key protagonists, while omitting extraneous detail. Spontaneous speech and narrative, where the starting point typically involves complex and multiple events, do not provide the same facilitation. These conditions also require what Levelt terms "macroplanning", that is, an ability to sequence a series of propositions and so direct the focus of the listener over the developing discourse (Levelt, 1999).

The complex message-level demands imposed by spontaneous speech or narrative may disadvantage people with aphasia, even when there is no impairment in thinking for speaking. This seemed to be the case for EM (Marshall, 1999). She performed well on nonverbal event-judgement tasks, like the Role Video. This, together with her good comprehension and writing of verbs, would argue against an event-level impairment. Yet, after the first therapy programme EM's production, like MM's, was sensitive to the nature of the task. She could produce learnt verbs in response to pictures, but not when she had to use them in narratives. This observation drove the second therapy programme, which provided EM with strategies for thinking about complex and multiple events. Encouragingly, this extended her gains to more open speaking situations.

A number of researchers suggest that agrammatic speakers retain considerable grammatical competence. Evidence includes their ability to judge the grammaticality of sentences (Linebarger, Schwartz, & Saffran, 1983) and their ability to improve the syntactic quality of their output, e.g., when supported by priming (Hartsuiker & Kolk, 1998) or a computer-based communication system (Linebarger, McCall, & Berndt, 2004; Linebarger, Schwartz, Romania, Kohn, & Stephens, 2000). It is argued therefore, that agrammatism reflects a problem of *performance*, in which retained skills can no longer be employed because of limitations in processing resources. For example, if lexical retrieval is costly, or slow, this will mop up resources that might otherwise be available for computing grammatical structure. One drain on resources may be the demands of thinking for speaking. If this can be facilitated, it may permit expression of otherwise submerged grammatical competence.

One source of facilitation may come from conversation partners. Many of the questions and prompts used in supported conversation techniques (Kagan, 1995, 1998; Pound, Parr, Lindsay, & Woolf, 2000) serve at least in part to "pare down" the thinking of the person with aphasia, focusing them on the key concept or component of their message. As a result, supported conversation may enable people with aphasia to express complex ideas that could not otherwise be communicated.

Another source of facilitation may derive from stimulus materials that, in themselves, support thinking for speaking. Similar arguments have recently been put forward by Dean and Black (2005), who compared descriptions of simple line drawings with those of more complex photographs. We have developed a new task in which people are asked to describe filmed events that pose a perspective dilemma. For example, one shows a man pushing a box while a woman pulls it. The format of the stimulus, and the type of additional cue provided, are manipulated in order to investigate the effects on output. Data collection is ongoing. However, we have found that some individuals with aphasia produce more verbs when the event is filmed in such a way as to help them focus on one, rather than both, of the individuals involved.

A third way of facilitating thinking for speaking is through direct therapy. At a basic level such therapy may focus on single events, and aim to clarify the roles of the people and objects involved. More "advanced" therapy requires tasks that impose heavy thinking for speaking demands, such as narrative, and entails the teaching of cognitive strategies, such as segmentation and selectivity.

Therapies working on sentence production should aim to improve spontaneous, everyday speech. If we are to achieve this, our therapy needs to help people with aphasia accomplish the conceptual preparations necessary for such speech. Preliminary studies with MM and EM show that this is a realistic target for intervention with some promising outcomes. The approach now needs to be tested with more individuals, to find out whether better thinking really does lead to better speaking.

REFERENCES

Berndt, R., & Mitchum, C. (1995). Cognitive neuropsychological approaches to the treatment of language disorders. *Neuropsychological Rehabilitation, 5*, 1–6.

Black, M., & Chiat, S. (2000). Putting thoughts into verbs: Developmental and acquired impairments. In W. Best, K. Bryan, & J. Maxim (Eds.), *Semantic processing theory and practice*. London: Whurr.

Brown, P., & Levinson, S. C. (1993). "Uphill" and "downhill" in Tzeltal. *Journal of Linguistic Anthropology, 3*(1), 46–74.

Byng, S., Nickels, L., & Black, M. (1994). Replicating therapy for mapping deficits in agrammatism: Remapping the deficit? *Aphasiology, 8*, 315–341.

Byng, S., & Black, M. (unpublished). *The Multiple Event Test*.

Cairns, D., Marshall, J., Cairns, P., & Dipper, L. (2005). *Event processing through naming: investigating event focus in a person with aphasia*. Manuscript submitted for publication.

Dean, M.P. & Black, M. (2005). Event processing and description in people with aphasia. *Aphasiology, 19*, 521–544.

Dipper, L. (1999). *Event processing for language: An investigation of the relationship between events, sentences and verbs, using data from 6 people with non-fluent aphasia*. Unpublished PhD thesis, University College London, UK.

Druks, J., & Masterson, J. (2000). *An Object and Action Naming Battery*. Hove, UK: Psychology Press.

Garrett, M. (1988). Processes in language production. In N. Frederick (Ed.), *Linguistics: The Cambridge Survey, Volume 3*. Cambridge: Cambridge University Press.

Hartsuiker, R., & Kolk, H. (1998). Syntactic facilitation in agrammatic sentence production. *Brain and Language, 62*, 221–254.

Kagan, A. (1995). Revealing the competence of aphasic adults through conversation: A challenge to health professionals. *Topics in Stroke Rehabilitation, 2*(1), 5–28.

Kagan, A. (1998). Supported conversation for adults with aphasia: Methods and resources for training conversation partners. *Aphasiology, 12*, 816–830.

Langacker, R. W. (1987). *Foundation of cognitive grammar: Volume 1*. Stanford, CA: Stanford University Press.

Langacker, R. W. (1991). *Foundation of cognitive grammar: Volume 2*. Stanford, CA: Stanford University Press.

Langacker, R. W. (1997). The contextual basis of cognitive semantics. In J. Nuyts & E. Pederson (Eds.), *Language and conceptualization*. Cambridge: Cambridge University Press.

Levelt, W. (1989). *Speaking: From intention to articulation*. Cambridge, MA: MIT Press.

Levelt, W. (1996). Perspective taking and ellipsis in spatial descriptions. In P. Bloom, M. Peterson, L. Nadel, & M. Garrett (Eds.), *Language and space*. Cambridge, MA: MIT Press.

Levelt, W. (1999). Producing spoken language: A blueprint of the speaker. In C. Brown & P. Hagoort (Eds.), *The neurocognition of language*. Oxford: Oxford University Press.

Linebarger, M., McCall, D., & Berndt, R. (2004). The role of processing support in the remediation of aphasic language production disorders. *Cognitive Neuropsychology, 21*, 267–282.

Linebarger, M., Schwartz, M., Romania, J., Kohn, S., & Stephens, D. (2000). Grammatical encoding in aphasia: Evidence from a "processing prosthesis". *Brain and Language, 75*, 416–427.

Linebarger, M., Schwartz, M., & Saffran, E. (1983). Sensitivity to grammatical structure in so called agrammatic aphasics. *Cognition, 13*, 361–392.

Marshall, J. (1994). *Sentence processing in aphasia: Single case treatment studies*. Unpublished PhD thesis, City University, London, UK.

Marshall, J. (1999). Doing something about a verb impairment: Two therapy approaches. In S. Byng, K. Swinburn, & C. Pound (Eds.), *The aphasia therapy file*. Hove, UK: Psychology Press.

Marshall, J., Pring, T., & Chiat, S. (1993). Sentence processing therapy: Working at the level of the event. *Aphasiology, 7*, 177–199.

Marshall, J., Pring, T., & Chiat, S. (1998). Verb retrieval and sentence production in aphasia. *Brain and Language, 63*, 159–183.

Nickels, L. (2002). Therapy for naming disorders: Revisiting, revising and reviewing. *Aphasiology, 16*, 935–980.

Nickels, L., Black, M., & Byng, S. (1991). Sentence processing deficits: A replication of therapy. *British Journal of Disorders of Communication, 26*, 175–201.

Pinker, S. (1989). *Learnability and cognition: The acquisition of argument structure*. Cambridge, MA: MIT Press.

Pound, C., Parr, S., Lindsay, J., & Woolf, C. (2000). *Beyond aphasia: Therapies for living with communication disability*. Bicester, UK: Winslow Press.

Slobin, D. (1996). From ''thought and language'' to ''thinking for speaking''. In J. Gumperz & S. Levinson (Eds.), *Rethinking linguistic relativity*. Cambridge: Cambridge University Press.

Sutton-Spence, R., & Woll, B. (1999). *The linguistics of British Sign Language: An introduction*. Cambridge: Cambridge University Press.

Thompson, C., & Faroqi-Shah, Y. (2002). Models of sentence production. In A. Hillis (Ed.), *The handbook of adult language disorders*. New York: Psychology Press.

Weinrich, M., Shelton, J., McCall, D., & Cox, D. (1997). Generalisation from single sentence to multisentence production in severely aphasic patients. *Brain and Language, 58*, 327–352.

APHASIOLOGY, 2005, 19 (10/11), 1021–1036  Psychology Press
Taylor & Francis Group

Treating agrammatic aphasia within a linguistic framework: Treatment of Underlying Forms

Cynthia K. Thompson

Northwestern University, Evanston, IL, USA

Lewis P. Shapiro

San Diego State University, CA, USA

Background: Formal linguistic properties of sentences—both lexical, i.e., *argument structure*, and syntactic, i.e., *movement*—as well as what is known about normal and disordered sentence processing and production, were considered in the development of Treatment of Underlying Forms (TUF), a linguistic approach to treatment of sentence deficits in patients with agrammatic aphasia. TUF is focused on complex, non-canonical sentence structures and operates on the premise that training underlying, abstract, properties of language will allow for effective generalisation to untrained structures that share similar linguistic properties, particularly those of lesser complexity.

Aims: In this paper we summarise a series of studies focused on examining the effects of TUF.

Methods & Procedures: In each study, sentences selected for treatment and for generalisation analysis were controlled for their lexical and syntactic properties, with some structures related and others unrelated along theoretical lines. We use single-subject experimental designs—i.e., multiple baseline designs across participants and behaviours—to chart improvement in comprehension and production of both trained and untrained structures. One structure was trained at a time, while untrained sentences were tested for generalisation. Participants included individuals with mild to moderately severe agrammatic, Broca's aphasia with characteristic deficits patterns.

Outcomes & Results: Results of this work have shown that treatment improves the sentence types entered into treatment, that generalisation occurs to sentences which are linguistically related to those trained, and that treatment results in changes in spontaneous discourse in most patients. Further, we have found that generalisation is enhanced when the direction of treatment is from more to less complex structures, a finding that led to the Complexity Account of Treatment Efficacy (CATE, Thompson, Shapiro, Kiran, & Sobecks, 2003). Finally, results of recent work showing that treatment appears to affect processing of trained sentences in real time and that treatment gains can be mapped onto the brain using functional magnetic resonance imaging (fMRI) are discussed.

Conclusions: These findings indicate that TUF is effective for treating sentence comprehension and production in patients who present with language deficit patterns like those seen in our patients. Patients receiving this treatment show strong generalisation effects to untrained language material. Given the current healthcare climate, which limits the amount of treatment that aphasic patients receive following stroke, it is important that clinicians deliver treatment that results in optimal generalisation in the least amount of time possible.

Address correspondence to: Cynthia K. Thompson, Department of Communication Sciences and Disorders, Northwestern University, 2240 Campus Drive, Evanston, Illinois 60208-3540, USA.
Email: ckthom@northwestern.edu

http://www.tandf.co.uk/journals/pp/02687038.html   DOI:10.1080/02687030544000227

This paper summarises a linguistic approach to treatment of sentence production and comprehension deficits found in individuals who have agrammatic Broca's aphasia. The programme, "Treatment of Underlying Forms", is labelled as such for good reason: the underlying, abstract, properties of language are seriously considered, with the assumption that training such properties will allow for effective generalisation to untrained structures that share similar linguistic properties.

The effects of this treatment approach have been studied extensively in a series of studies by Thompson, Shapiro, and colleagues (Ballard & Thompson, 1999; Jacobs & Thompson, 2000; Thompson, Ballard, & Shapiro, 1998; Thompson & Shapiro, 1994; Thompson, Shapiro & Roberts, 1993; Thompson, Shapiro, Ballard, Jacobs, Schneider, & Tait, 1997b; Thompson, Shapiro, Kiran, & Sobecks, 2003; Thompson, Shapiro, Tait, Jacobs, & Schneider, 1996). Our treatment investigations use a single subject experimental design in order to allow us to directly examine generalisation as it emerges during treatment, while experimental control is maintained. From this work we have learned the following: (a) treatment improves production (and comprehension) of the sentence types entered into treatment, (b) generalisation to untrained sentences occurs to those that are linguistically similar to those trained, (c) generalisation is enhanced when the direction of treatment is from more to less complex structures, (d) treatment results in substantial changes in spontaneous discourse in most patients,[1] (e) treatment appears to affect processing of trained sentences in real time, and (f) treatment gains can be mapped onto the brain using functional magnetic resonance imaging (fMRI).

THEORETICAL FRAMEWORK

Treatment of Underlying Forms considers both lexical, i.e., *argument structure*, and syntactic, i.e., *movement*, aspects of sentences that become the focus of treatment. In most theories of grammar there is an intimate relationship between these properties. In addition, they have been the focus of much work in psycholinguistics and neurolinguistics. Here we briefly review these properties (see Shapiro & Thompson, in press; Thompson, 2001, for a more complete discussion).

Argument structure is a lexical property of verbs that characterises the number and types of participants in an event described by the verb. This property interacts with the syntax and thus places constraints on the well-formedness of sentences. There are several different types of verbs determined (a) by the number of participants (i.e., arguments) that go into the action described by the verb, (b) by the number of different argument structure arrangements that are possible given a certain verb, and (c) by the semantic (*thematic*) roles that the arguments play. Verbs such as *sleep*, *snore*, and *laugh* are one-place (intransitive, unergative) verbs, requiring only a single external argument assigned the thematic role of "Agent of the action". Verbs such as *chase*, *cut*, and *tickle* are two-place verbs, which assign the Agent role to the external argument and the Theme role to the internal argument. Verbs such as *give*, *put*, and *send* have three arguments, Agent, Theme, and Goal.

Sentences are derived from the output of two operations: *Merge*, which combines syntactic objects selected from the lexicon to form higher-order categories, e.g., a selected verb combines with its arguments to form a verb phrase (VP), and *Move*, which displaces a category to another position in the syntactic tree. It has long been recognised

---

[1] We note that this treatment has been shown to result in different generalisation patterns in patients with fluent aphasia (Murray, Ballard, & Karcher, 2004).

that there are several types of movement (Chomsky 1991, 1993). The most relevant to our work are wh-movement (or A′ movement) and NP-movement (A movement). These operations are crucial for deriving non-canonical sentence forms.

In English, object-extracted wh-questions, clefts, and object relatives are formed via wh-movement. Consider the following, an object-extracted wh-question:

1. Who did the thief chase?

Formation of sentences of this type involves movement of a direct object argument from its base position, occurring after the verb, to a position higher in the syntactic tree as shown in Figure 1.

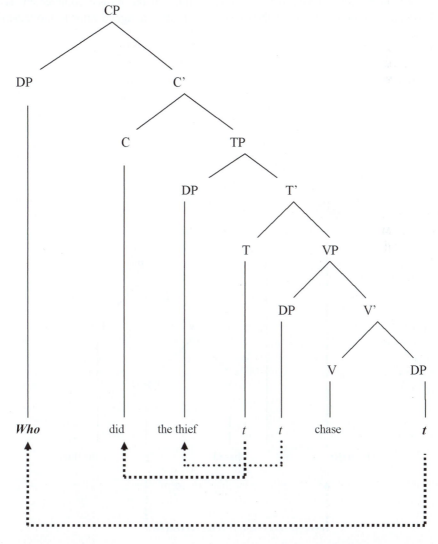

Figure 1.   Tree structure denoting Wh-movement (A′ movement) in an object extracted wh-question construction. Movement occurs from the direct object position to the specifier position of the complementiser phrase (CP), a non-argument occupied position. A copy or trace is left behind in its original position.

The complement of *chase* moves from the direct object position after the verb to the specifier position of CP, a non-argument (A′) position. This operation leaves behind a copy or trace of the moved complement. Once moved, the displaced constituent is linked (co-indexed) with the position from which it was derived and the thematic role, originally assigned to the complement, is inherited by the moved constituent.

NP-movement is involved in formation of English passives and subject raising constructions. Consider the following passive sentence:

2. The artist was chased by the thief.

In formation of the passive, the complement of the verb, i.e., *the artist*, is moved from its canonical, post-verbal position to the specifier position of TP, an argument (A) position, as shown in Figure 2. Once again, a copy or trace of the moved complement is left behind, and the thematic role of the moved constituent, assigned prior to movement, is retained.

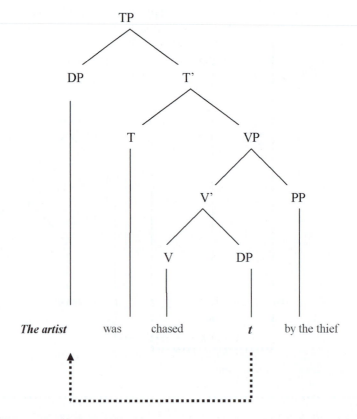

Figure 2.   Tree structure depicting NP-movement (A movement). Here, the complement of the verb *chase* is moved to the subject position—the specifier position of the Tense Phrase (Spec-TP)—leaving a copy or trace. Thus, an argument is moved to another argument position.

Processing and production implications

Verb argument structure.   The sentence-processing literature indicates that the lexical entries for verbs are available for some, if not all, Broca's aphasic subjects. In a series of on-line experiments it has been shown that individuals with Broca's aphasia and anterior brain damage activate the argument-taking properties of verbs when they are encountered in sentences, as do normal listeners (e.g., Shapiro, Gordon, Hack, & Killackey, 1993; Shapiro, Nagel, & Levine, 1993; Shapiro, Zurif, & Grimshaw, 1987, 1989; Tanenhaus, Carlson, & Trueswell, 1989; Trueswell & Kim, 1998). Once active, these properties are used by the processing system, perhaps during a secondary routine, to establish thematic relations among the arguments in the sentence, allowing for final interpretation. Interestingly, however, individuals with Wernicke's aphasia, resulting from damage to posterior perisylvian regions, do not show normal on-line sensitivity to these argument structure properties, suggesting that the conceptual-semantic aspects of these lexical properties influence the types of "semantic-like" deficits observed in these individuals.

The results of recent neuroimaging studies coincide with these patterns, i.e., verb argument structure processing relies heavily on posterior regions of the brain (Ben-Shachar, Hendler, Kahn, Ben-Bashat, & Grodzinsky, 2003; Thompson, Bonakdarpour, Fix, Parrish, Gitelman, & Mesulam, 2004). Thompson et al., for example, in a study comparing activation patterns for verbs controlled for their argument structure found that verbs with a greater number of arguments, e.g., three-argument versus two- or one-argument verbs, yield bilateral posterior, superior temporal gyri/sulci activation.

Verb argument structure also influences production. Several studies with Broca's aphasic patients have shown that verb production becomes more difficult as the number of argument structures entailed within the verb's representation increases. This has been shown in English and also across languages, including Dutch, German, Italian, and Hungarian (DeBleser & Kauschke, 2003; Jonkers & Bastiaanse, 1996, 1998; Kegl, 1995; Kemmerer & Tranel, 2000; Kim & Thompson, 2000, 2004; Kiss, 2000; Luzzatti, Raggi, Zonca, Pistarini, Contardi, & Pinna, 2002; Thompson, Lange, Schneider, & Shapiro, 1997), i.e., three-argument verbs are more difficult to produce than two- or one-argument verbs. Further, verbs with even greater argument structure complexity, i.e., complement verbs such as *know*, which entail a clausal argument or proposition within their representation, present difficulty for Broca's aphasic patients (Thompson et al., 1997a), and intransitive unaccusative verbs such as *melt*, and *amuse*-type psychological (psych) verbs, which involve syntactic movement, are more difficult to produce than intransitive unergatives such as *run*, and *admire*-type psych verbs which do not (Lee & Thompson, 2004; Thompson, 2003).

Complex sentences.   There is a large body of evidence suggesting that normal listeners show sensitivity to the movement operations involved in non-canonical sentences (see Swinney & Osterhaut, 1990, for an example). This shows up in sentences like "The policemen saw the boy *who* the crowd at the party accused _[trace/copy]_ of the crime". When processing such sentences, the complement of *accused* (the moved element) is "reactivated" at the trace/copy site for processing, perhaps to satisfy the thematic requirements of the verbs. Importantly, agrammatic Broca's aphasic patients do not show this normal processing pattern. That is, they have difficulty in properly assigning thematic roles to arguments that have been moved out of their canonical position (Grodzinsky, 1995; Schwartz, Linebarger, Saffran, & Pate, 1987; Zurif, Swinney, Prather,

Solomon, & Bushell, 1993). On the production side, these patients use primarily simple sentence structures, avoiding complex sentences in which binding relations are essential.

Treatment of Underlying Forms exploits these patient strengths and weaknesses. The facts that Broca's aphasic individuals retain access to verb argument structure during on-line processing, yet show deficits in verb and verb argument structure production, are central to the approach. In addition, the rules that govern non-canonical sentence for-mation are exploited to help patients overcome their difficulty with both comprehension and production of these structures. That is, the representational similarities and differ-ences underlying the surface realisations of sentences that are the focus of our work are considered.

TREATMENT OF UNDERLYING FORMS

Treatment of Underlying Forms (TUF) considers both the lexical and syntactic properties of (a) the sentences entered into treatment and (b) the sentences selected for general-isation analysis. Treatment begins with tasks concerned with establishing and improving knowledge of and access to the thematic role information around verbs,[2] using the active, declarative form of non-canonical sentences. Then instructions concerning the movement of various sentence constituents are provided and subjects are taken through the proper movement to derive the surface form of target sentences. In essence, the procedures involve ''meta-linguistic'' knowledge of verb properties and movement. Additional morphemes required in the surface form of various sentences are provided and inserted into sentence frames.[3] Throughout treatment, we examine generalisation to sentences that are similar to those trained in terms of their semantic and syntactic properties.

Participant characteristics

Patients who have participated in experiments examining the effects of TUF show pro-files on the *Western Aphasia Battery* (WAB, Kertesz, 1982) consistent with a diagnosis of mild to moderately severe agrammatic, Broca's aphasia with Aphasia Quotients (AQs) ranging from around 65 to 85.[4] Our agrammatic subjects demonstrate a characteristic pattern of comprehension: (a) lexical comprehension of both nouns and verbs is superior to overall sentence comprehension, (b) semantically reversible sentences are more dif-ficult to understand than non-reversible sentences, and (c) comprehension of canonical sentences (i.e., actives and subject relatives) is superior to non-canonical sentences (i.e., passives and object relatives).

In production, greater difficulty in producing verbs as compared to nouns is the typical pattern, and a verb argument structure production hierarchy is common, with verbs with a greater number of arguments more difficult to produce than those with fewer. Greater impairments in producing complex sentences (i.e., passives, object relatives, object clefts,

---

[2] We note that other available treatments are similar to Treatment of Underlying Forms in this regard, i.e., ''verb as core'' (Loverso, Prescott, & Selinger, 1986) and ''mapping therapy'' (see Schwartz, Saffron, Fink, Myers, & Martin, 1994) focus on the thematic roles of sentence NPs. Our approach, however, departs from these in that we focus on both comprehension and production of the verb and its arguments as well as adjuncts contained in target sentences. Additionally, we exploit the movement operations involved in creating gram-matically correct non-canonical sentences and emphasise how thematic roles are retained in the surface string of complex sentences in which NPs have been moved out of their canonical positions.

[3] See Thompson (2001) for detailed treatment protocols.

[4] We note that patients with lower AQs, i.e., below 50, have not responded successfully to treatment (see Ballard & Thompson, 1999).

object-extracted wh-questions) as compared to simple, active sentences, is also characteristic of our patients. These production patterns show up in both constrained sentence production tasks[5] and in narrative discourse samples.[6]

Training and generalisation of wh-movement structures

Training and generalisation of wh-questions.   Our treatment approach evolved from early work concerned with training agrammatic patients to produce wh-questions (e.g., Wambaugh & Thompson, 1989) in which we found no generalisation from *what* to *where* questions. In keeping with our theoretical framework, we surmised that this lack of generalisation across wh-questions that are roughly analogous in their surface form could have resulted because of differences in the lexical properties of the verbs utilised by the two question types as well as differences in movement operations required. The *what*-questions trained included two-place verbs such as *cook*, and therefore deriving the surface question form involved argument movement. Conversely, the *where*-questions trained included one-place verbs such as *sleep*. To derive a question form, *adjunct* movement was required. Adjuncts, unlike arguments, are phrases contained within sentences that are not a part of the verb's lexical representation; thus they are not assigned a thematic role by the verb and they are not obligatorily present in sentences.

We therefore theorised that the lack of generalisation from *what*- to *where*-questions was related to the distinction between argument and adjunct movement. We further conjectured that, if this postulate were correct, wh-questions that are alike not only in surface form, but also in their underlying linguistic representation, would be better candidates for generalisation. For example, we predicted generalisation from *what*- to *who*-questions that are identical in both phrase structure and in argument structure, i.e., both constructions involve verbs that select a direct object. Both questions also rely on argument movement.

Training and generalisation of argument movement.   In a follow-up study, we (Thompson et al., 1993) investigated generalisation across wh-questions that involve argument movement, i.e., *what* and *who*-questions—as in *What is the boy fixing?* and *Who is the boy helping?* Note that the verbs *help* and *fix* are both two-place verbs, which assign the thematic role of Theme to the direct object argument. To derive both question types, the direct object DP is replaced by a wh-morpheme, and moved to the sentence initial position. Wh-questions were trained using NP^V^NP^PP sentences in which the PP was either an argument or an adjunct.

Results were encouraging. Training *who*-questions resulted in generalisation to untrained *who*- and untrained *what*-questions (and vice versa), and in addition, training wh-questions in the more complex phrasal configuration resulted in generalised wh-question production in less complex ones. We attributed this successful generalisation to our controlling the lexical properties of verbs as well as the movement operations required for *what* and *who* questions.

---

[5] We use the *Northwestern Assessment of Verbs and Sentences* (NAVS) (Thompson, 2005) to detail both comprehension and production patterns.

[6] Narrative samples are collected by asking subjects to tell the story of Cinderella and describe a Charlie Chaplin silent film. Samples are analysed using a coding system developed by Thompson, Shapiro, Tait, Jacobs, Schneider, & Ballard (1995).

Training and generalisation of argument vs adjunct movement

To further establish the distinction between training wh-questions that utilise argument movement versus those that utilise adjunct movement we (Thompson et al., 1996) trained an additional seven agrammatic aphasic individuals to produce *who*, *what*, *where*, and *when* questions. As previously noted, *who* and *what* questions require similar movement of the direct object argument, whereas *when* and *where* questions require adjunct movement. As in our other treatment work, the primary outcome of interest was generalisation across wh-question types. We predicted that training sentences derived from movement of an argument (e.g., *who*-questions) would only generalise to untrained wh-questions that also rely on movement of an argument (e.g., *what*-questions), but not to sentences derived from movement of an adjunct phrase (e.g., *when*- and *where*-questions). Similarly, we predicted that training sentences derived from movement of an adjunct would not generalise to those derived from movement of an argument. Using a set of 20 two-place verbs, 80 active sentence stimuli (NP^V^NP^PP) were developed to depict the underlying form of the four question constructions trained as in (3) – (6).

3. The soldier is pushing the woman into the street. Who is the soldier pushing into the street?
4. The boy is kicking the cow in the barn. What is the boy kicking in the barn?
5. The student is helping the doctor during the evening. When is the student helping the doctor?
6. The guard is protecting the clerk at the store. Where is the guard protecting the clerk?

Results supported our previous work. When treatment was applied to wh-questions requiring movement of the direct object argument (e.g., *what*-questions), generalised production of untrained wh-questions was restricted to those also involving direct object argument movement (e.g., *who*-questions). Similarly, when treatment was applied to wh-questions requiring adjunct movement (e.g., *where*-questions), generalisation occurred to untrained wh-questions relying on adjunct movement (e.g., *when*-questions). Importantly, argument movement did not generalise to adjunct movement constructions, and vice versa.

Training and generalisation of wh-movement vs NP-movement structures

As described previously, a distinction can be made between two types of movement. One type is Wh-movement, which displaces a complement from its underlying position after the verb (in English) to Spec-CP, a non-argument (A′) position. The other is NP-movement, which moves elements into the subject argument (A) position (Spec-TP). Given this theoretical distinction—and our premise and earlier findings that generalisation should occur only among constructions that have like-structural properties—we addressed the following question: Will training sentences that rely on one type of movement generalise only to those constructions also relying on that type of movement, or, alternatively, will any type of movement generalise to any other type of movement? This is a much stronger test of our underlying forms premise than the argument/adjunct distinction, since the spell-out forms of sentences generated from Wh-movement (e.g., wh-questions, object clefts, and object relatives) cannot be said to be similar in any analogical way to each other, or to sentences generated by NP-movement (e.g., passives, subject raising).

In Thompson et al. (1997b), we trained agrammatic aphasic subjects to produce sentences derived from Wh-movement—i.e., either wh-questions (7) or object clefts (8)—and tested generalisation to NP-movement structures—i.e., passive (9) and subject raising structures (10)), and vice versa.

7. Who did the girl hit? (wh-question)
8. It was the boy who the girl hit. (object cleft)
9. The boy was hit by the girl. (passive)
10. The girl seems to have hit the boy. (subject raising)

The data revealed the following patterns: the sentences entered into treatment were acquired very quickly once treatment began, and remained significantly above baseline performance levels throughout the study. Observed generalisation patterns aligned with our predictions: Participant 1 who was trained on wh-movement structures showed increased performance on both trained and untrained wh-movement sentences. Training object clefts resulted in generalisation to *who*-questions. Yet this training did not influence production of passives or subject-raising constructions. For Participant 2, training on passives yielded improved performance on subject-raising constructions, but no generalisation to untrained object clefts or wh-questions was noted. These patterns corroborated and extended the results from our studies examining argument and adjunct distinctions in wh-movement; that is, generalisation occurred only to constructions that have similar underlying properties as those trained. In follow-up studies, we have found similar constraints on generalisation across sentence types (Ballard & Thompson, 1999; Jacobs & Thompson, 2000).

Complexity effects

One other pattern noted in our work is that training more complex but related structures yields more wide-ranging treatment effects than using simpler structures as a starting point for treatment. As noted above, in Thompson et al. (1993) we found that training wh-questions that relied on "denser" underlying phrase structure configurations generalised to wh-questions based on less dense structures. In addition, in a closer analysis of response patterns from our previous studies that examined wh-questions and object clefts (Thompson & Shapiro, 1994; Thompson et al., 1997b) we found that several of our participants evinced better generalisation when first trained on object clefts relative to when first trained on wh-questions. Considering the differences between these two structures, the syntax of object cleft constructions involves movement within an embedded relative clause; the maximal projection (CP) of this clause is dominated by another TP in the matrix clause. In simple object extracted wh-questions, movement to Spec-CP is also involved, but movement is within the matrix clause. The CP dominates all other nodes in the construction. Thus, the syntax of a simple wh-question forms a *subset* of the entire phrasal configuration of an object-cleft construction. Therefore, object clefts can be considered to be more complex than wh-questions.

Given this complexity metric, and assuming that such a notion can be transferred to the processing routines underlying sentence production and comprehension, we conducted some formal tests of this complexity hypothesis. In one of our efforts (Thompson et al., 1998) we tested three agrammatic Broca's aphasic individuals who were trained on object clefts (e.g., *It was the artist who the thief chased*) and wh-questions (e.g., *Who did the thief chase?*). Using, again, a single-subject experimental design, participants were trained to produce either object clefts or simple object extracted wh-questions in counterbalanced order, while generalisation to untrained structures was assessed.

Results showed that when treatment was first applied to object clefts, object cleft production increased significantly above baseline levels, and so too did wh-question production, with similar learning curves noted for both constructions. Conversely, the two participants who received initial treatment focused on wh-questions, showed no generalised effect to object clefts. Both showed improved wh-question production (and comprehension), which did not influence object clefts. Rather these structures required direct treatment. For all three participants, the production of passives, generated from NP-movement, did not increase above initial baseline levels during treatment of wh-movement structures, replicating our earlier work.

These patterns aligned with our complexity predictions: treatment effects are more pronounced when treatment is initiated on complex structures; in such a case simpler structures emerge without direct treatment. The reverse approach, while espoused in traditional language intervention approaches, i.e., beginning treatment with simpler structures and progressively increasing the complexity of material entered into treatment, appears to be less efficacious, and indeed, other similar treatment experiments have indicated this as well.

In our most recent effort (Thompson et al., 2003) we replicated and extended this work by adding an additional structure, i.e., object relative constructions as in (11) below.

11. The man saw the artist that the thief chased. (object relative)
12. It was the artist who the thief chased. (object cleft)
13. Who did the thief chase? (wh-question)

Note that object relatives and object clefts are similar to one another, yet there are crucial differences between the two (see Figure 3). In the matrix clause of object relatives (e.g., *The man saw the artist* ...), the subject is base-generated in the verb phrase, as per the VP internal subjects hypothesis (Koopman & Sportiche, 1991) and moves to Spec-TP (the subject position). Furthermore, the subject (*the man*) acquires the Agent role from the verb (*saw*). In the matrix clause of object cleft constructions (e.g., *It was the artist* ...), however, the subject is represented by a pronoun (*It*) that lacks semantic content, as no thematic role is assigned. Further it is base generated in its subject position, thus subject movement is not required. These differences indicate that object relatives are more complex than object clefts, i.e., the material in the matrix clause of object clefts is more complex than that in object relatives. Matrix wh-questions as in (13) are less complex than both object relatives and object clefts, as discussed above.

Given these complexity differences, we predicted that training patients to produce complex object relatives would result in generalisation to both object clefts, and object-extracted wh-questions, but that training simpler forms would not result in improved production or comprehension of the more complex ones. Results showed that this is the case: training object relatives resulted in generalisation to untrained object clefts and wh-questions, while training wh-questions did not show generalisation to untrained object relatives or clefts. Furthermore, when object clefts were entered into treatment,

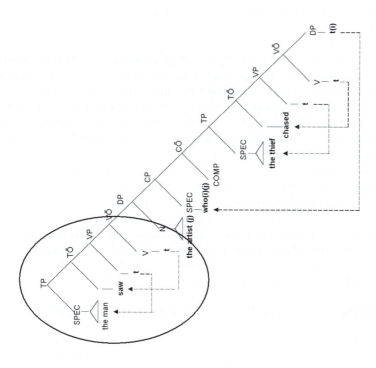

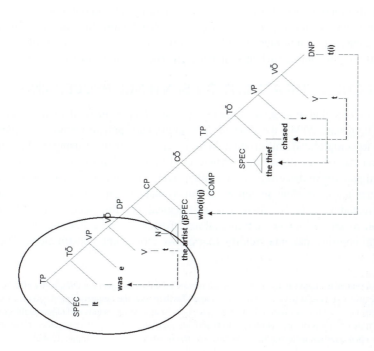

Figure 3. Tree diagram showing object cleft (left) and object relative (right) constructions. Note that the material in the matrix clause (circled) in the two structures is different, i.e., subject movement from Spec of VP to Spec of IP is shown for object relatives. Such movement is not seen in object cleft constructions. However, both structures involve identical wh-movement in the embedded clause.

generalisation was not observed to object relatives.[7] Consideration of these findings as well as our earlier observations led us to coin the Complexity Account of Treatment Efficacy (CATE) (Thompson et al., 2003).

The complexity account is buttressed by mounting evidence from multiple sources. For example, Eckman and colleagues showed that teaching relative clauses to L2 learners of English generalises to untrained canonical structures (actives and subject relatives) (Eckman, Bell, & Nelson, 1988), much like what we have found with our Broca's aphasic participants. Gierut and colleagues, in numerous studies, have shown that unmarked phonological structures replace marked structures in the error patterns observed in children with phonological disorders. Furthermore, training marked structures (e.g., defined in terms of sonority or cluster formation) results in greater system-wide changes than training unmarked structures (see, for example, Gierut, 1998; Gierut & Champion, 2001; see also Archibald, 1998; Barlow, 2001, for evidence from L2 phonological acquisition). We have also observed such complexity training effects with adult individuals with apraxia of speech (Maas, Barlow, Robin, & Shapiro, 2002) and those with fluent aphasia and naming deficits (Kiran & Thompson, 2003). Finally, evidence for the complexity hypothesis also comes from domains outside language (e.g., in maths learning, Yao, 1989; and in motor learning, Schmidt & Lee, 1999).

EFFECTS OF TREATMENT ON DISCOURSE PATTERNS

Changes in discourse characteristics have been noted in several of the aforementioned treatment studies. The most important changes noted across participants include (a) increases in mean length of utterance (MLU), (b) increases in the proportion of grammatical sentences, and (c) increases in the proportionate number of verbs as compared to nouns produced. Notably, subjects have also shown improvements in verb argument structure production with increases in correct usage of Agents, Themes, Goals, and even sentential complements seen following treatment. The proportion of adjuncts produced correctly has also increased with treatment. These findings are encouraging and suggest that treatment gains are not restricted to improvement on targeted sentence structures. Rather, they suggest that treatment results in improved access to a variety of language structures that are encountered when sentences become the focus of treatment.

EFFECTS OF TREATMENT ON SENTENCE PROCESSING

Importantly, we note that in a recent study using an auditory anomaly detection paradigm (Dickey & Thompson, 2004), we showed that agrammatic patients, who were successfully trained to comprehend and produce Wh-movement structures using TUF, evinced normal-like on-line processing of these structures. Treated patients were more successful than untreated patients in detecting the anomalies, rejecting anomalous sentences reliably more often than non-anomalous sentences, as did normal participants. This effect was not noted for untreated patients, i.e., there was no statistically significant difference between their rejection of anomalous or non-anomalous structures. These findings suggest that treatment can improve patients' ability to process movement constructions. We are

---

[7] We note that sentence length cannot be a serious contender for contributing to our complexity effects, given that our object relatives and clefts were controlled for length. Furthermore, the number of propositions expressed in the sentences cannot explain the observed patterns, since both matrix wh-questions and object clefts could be argued to entail only one proposition, yet object clefts and wh-questions did not pattern together. Nevertheless, we take it as an open question as to the set of factors that might contribute to a complexity metric.

currently following up on these findings by examining the eye-tracking patterns of patients as they listen to such sentences. These data will help us to understand whether or not patients begin to engage "normal" processing routines when off-line abilities improve, or whether they use abnormal processing strategies to solve the sentences that they encounter.

THE NEURAL CORRELATES OF TREATMENT EFFECTS

Finally, we note that treatment gains can be mapped onto the brain using fMRI. In a recent study (Thompson, Fix, Gitelman, Parrish, & Mesulam, 2000) we examined the neural correlates of treatment-induced (TUF) improvements in patients with agramma-tism. Six agrammatic patients participated in the study. Three patients were provided with treatment and underwent pre–post treatment behavioural testing and fMRI scans. Under scanning conditions, patients performed a sentence verification task for both syntactically complex object clefts and simpler subject cleft constructions. One of these subjects (OJ) also served as a control subject, receiving repeat behavioural testing and fMRI scans at 5-month intervals prior to undergoing treatment and post-treatment scanning. The remaining three subjects served as control subjects for the behavioural tasks only. Results showed significant changes in behavioural tests administered pre- and post-treatment for the treated subjects only. Concomitant changes were noted in activation patterns in the right hemisphere homologue of Wernicke's and surrounding areas for all treated subjects (BA 22, 21, and 37) and the right hemisphere homologue of Broca's area for two patients (HR and MK) for sentences as compared to words. Two patients (MK and OJ) also showed post-treatment recruitment of spared left hemisphere areas (see Figure 4). These findings show that the neural networks underlying language processing can be modified even in patients who are several years post-stroke. Indeed, our patients ranged from 1 (MK) to 10 years post-stroke (HR). However, further work is needed comparing the effects of various treatments on the ways in which the language network can be modified.

CONCLUSIONS

The findings from our research indicate that treatment for sentence production deficits in patients with agrammatic aphasia appears to be efficacious when the lexical and syntactic properties of (a) the language deficit exhibited by the aphasic individuals, (b) the sen-tences selected for treatment and generalisation analysis, and (c) the treatment strategy utilised, are considered and controlled. This approach results not only in improvement on trained structures, but also on linguistically related untrained structures. In addition, treatment influences spontaneous language usage; in particular improvements are seen in access to language structures involved in sentence production in general. Conversely, when linguistic underpinnings are not considered, generalisation effects are considerably diminished, or are absent, resulting in little or no discernible improvement in sentence production beyond the kind of constructions trained.

We also find that consideration of the complexity of material entered into treatment is important, i.e., generalisation is enhanced when the direction of treatment is from more to less complex structures. Once again, however, the linguistic relationship between trained and untrained items is important to consider, i.e., the relation must be grounded in what is known about language representation and processing.

Finally, we find that Treatment of Underlying Forms appears to affect on-line sentence processing, i.e., trained patients show more "normal" patterns of sentence processing than untrained patients, and the improvements resulting from treatment affect the neural

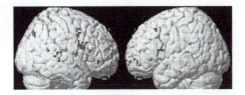

Patient 1 (HR)

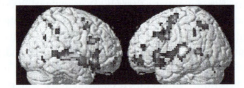

Patient 2 (MK)

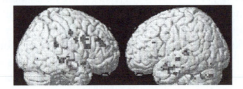

Patient 3 (OJ)

Figure 4. Areas of significant activation in three agrammatic aphasic patients' post-treatment scans as compared to pre-treatment scans.

network recruited to support language. While we have only begun our work in these areas, the results to date are encouraging.

In conclusion, our linguistic approach to treatment of sentence deficits as seen in agrammatic aphasia has been shown to be effective, perhaps more so than any other treatment designed for this purpose. While we are far from fully understanding the effects of brain damage on the language processing/production system or the full effects of treatment, we strongly suggest that this approach is the right one at least for some patients. Indeed, the more we learn about the linguistic and psycholinguistic under-pinnings of sentence production and comprehension in normals and how these processes are affected by brain damage, the more detailed we can be about the design of treatment.

REFERENCES

Archibald, J. (1998). Second language phonology, phonetics, and typology. *Studies in Second Language Acquisition*, *20*, 189–212.

Ballard, K. J., & Thompson, C. K. (1999). Treatment and generalisation of complex sentence structures in agrammatism. *Journal of Speech, Language, and Hearing Sciences*, *42*, 690–707.

Barlow, J. A. (2001). Individual differences in the production of initial consonant sequences in Pig Latin. *Lingua*, *111*, 667–696.

Ben-Shachar, M., Hendler, T., Kahn, I., Ben-Bashat, D., & Grodzinsky, Y. (2003). The neural reality of syntactic transformations: Evidence from fMRI. *Psychological Science*, *14*, 433–440.

Chomsky, N. (1991). Some notes on the economy of derivation and representation. In R. Friedin (Ed.), *Principles and parameters in comparative grammar.* Cambridge, MA: MIT Press.

Chomsky, N. (1993). A minimalist program for linguistic theory. In K. Hale, & S. Keyser (Eds.), *The view from building 20.* Cambridge, MA: MIT Press.

DeBleser, R., & Kauschke, C. (2003). Acquisition and loss of nouns and verbs: Parallel or divergent patterns? *Journal of Neurolinguistics, 16,* 213–229.

Dickey, M. W., Thompson, C. K. (2004). The resolution and recovery of filler-gap dependencies in aphasia: Evidence from on-line anomaly detection. *Brain and Language, 88*(1), 108–127.

Eckman, F. R., Bell, L., & Nelson, D. (1988). On the generalisation of relative clause instruction in the acquisition of English as a second language. *Applied Linguistics, 9,* 1–20.

Gierut, J. A. (1998). Treatment efficacy: Functional phonological disorders in children. *Journal of Speech, Language, and Hearing Research, 41,* S85–S100.

Gierut, J. A., & Champion, A. H., (2001). Syllable onsets II: Three-element clusters in phonological treatment. *Journal of Speech, Language, and Hearing Research, 44,* 886–904.

Grodzinsky, Y. (1995). Trace deletion, theta-roles and cognitive strategies. *Brain & Language, 51,* 467–497.

Jacobs, B., & Thompson, C. K. (2000). Cross-modal generalisation effects of training non-canonical sentence comprehension and production in agrammatic aphasia. *Journal of Speech, Language, and Hearing Sciences, 43,* 5–20.

Jonkers, R., & Bastiaanse, R. (1996). The influence of instrumentality and transitivity on action naming in Broca's and anomic aphasia. *Brain and Language, 55,* 37–39.

Jonkers, R., & Bastiaanse, R. (1998). How selective are selective word class deficits? Two case studies of action and object naming. *Aphasiology, 12,* 245–256.

Kegl, J. (1995). Levels of representation and units of access relevant to agrammatism. *Brain and Language, 50,* 151–200.

Kertesz, A. (1982). *Western Aphasia Battery.* New York: Grune & Stratton.

Kemmerer, D., & Tranel, D. (2000). Verb retrieval in brain-damaged subjects: I. Analysis of stimulus, lexical, and conceptual factors. *Brain and Language, 73,* 347–392.

Kim, M., & Thompson, C. K. (2000). Patterns of comprehension and production of nouns and verbs in agrammatism: Implications for lexical organization. *Brain and Language, 74,* 1–25.

Kim, M., Thompson, C. K. (2004). Verb deficits in Alzheimer's disease and agrammatism: Implications for lexical organization. *Brain and Language, 88*(1), 1–20.

Kiran, S., & Thompson, C. K. (2003). The role of semantic complexity in treatment of naming deficits: Training semantic categories in fluent aphasia by controlling exemplar typicality. *Journal of Speech Language, and Hearing Research, 46,* 773–787.

Kiss, K. (2000). Effects of verb complexity on agrammatic aphasics' sentence production. In R. Bastiaanse & Y. Grodzinsky (Eds.), *Grammatical disorders in aphasia* (pp. 123–151). London: Whurr Publishers.

Koopman, H., & Sportiche, D. (1991). The position of subjects. *Lingua, 85,* 211–258.

Lee, M., & Thompson, C. K. (2004). Agrammatic aphasic production and comprehension of unaccusative verbs in sentence contexts. *Journal of Neurolinguistics, 17,* 315–330.

Loverso, F. L., Prescott, T. E., & Selinger, M. (1986). Cueing verbs: A treatment strategy for aphasic adults. *Journal of Rehabilitation Research, 25,* 47–60.

Luzzatti, C., Raggi, R., Zonca, G., Pistarini, C., Contardi, A., & Pinna, G. D. (2002). Verb-noun double dissociation in aphasic lexical impairments: The role of word frequency and imageability. *Brain and Language, 81,* 432–444.

Maas, E., Barlow, J., Robin, D., & Shapiro, L. P. (2002). Treatment of phonological errors in aphasia and apraxia of speech: Effects of phonological complexity. *Aphasiology, 16,* 609–622.

Murray, L. L., Ballard, K., & Karcher, L. (2004). Linguistic specific treatment: Just for Broca's aphasia? *Aphasiology, 18,* 785–809.

Schmidt, R. A., & Lee, T. D. (1999). *Motor control and learning: A behavioural emphasis.* Champaign, IL: Human Kinetics.

Schwartz, M. F., Linebarger, M., Saffron, E. M., & Pate, D. (1987). Syntactic transparency and sentence interpretation in aphasia. *Language and Cognitive Processes, 2,* 85–113.

Schwartz, M. F., Saffron, E. M., Fink, R. B., Myers, J. L., & Martin, N. (1994). Mapping therapy: A treatment programme for agrammatism. *Aphasiology, 8,* 19–54.

Shapiro, L. P., Gordon, B., Hack, N., & Killackey, J. (1993). Verb-argument structure processing in complex sentences in Broca's and Wernicke's aphasia. *Brain and Language, 45,* 423–447.

Shapiro, L. P., Nagel, N., & Levine, B. A. (1993). Preferences for a verb's complements and their use in sentence processing. *Journal of Memory and Language, 32,* 96–114.

Shapiro, L. P., & Thompson, C. K. (in press). Treating language deficits in Broca's aphasia. In Y. Grodzinsky, & K. Amunts (Eds.), *Broca's region*. New York: Oxford University Press.

Shapiro, L. P., Zurif, E., & Grimshaw, J. (1987). Sentence processing and the mental representation of verbs. *Cognition, 27*, 219–246.

Shapiro, L. P., Zurif, E., & Grimshaw, J. (1989). Verb representation and sentence processing: Contextual impenetrability. *Journal of Psycholinguistic Research, 18*, 223–243.

Swinney, D., & Osterhaut, L. (1990). Inference generation during auditory language comprehension. In A. Graesser & G. Bower (Eds.), *Inferences and text comprehension*. San Diego, CA: Academic Press.

Tannenhaus, M. K., Carlson, G. N., & Trueswell, J. C. (1989). The role of thematic structures in interpretation and parsing. *Language and Cognitive Processes, 4*, 211–234.

Thompson, C. K. (2001). Treatment of underlying forms: A linguistic specific approach for sentence production deficits in agrammatic aphasia. In R. Chapey (Ed.), *Language intervention strategies in adult aphasia* (4th Ed., pp. 605–628). Baltimore: Williams & Wilkins.

Thompson, C. K. (2003). Unaccusative verb production in agrammatic aphasia: the argument structure complexity hypothesis. *Journal of Neurolinguistics, 16*, 151–167.

Thompson, C. K. (2005). *The Northwestern Assessment of Verbs and Sentences*. Manuscript in preparation.

Thompson, C. K., Ballard, K. J., & Shapiro, L. P. (1998). The role of complexity in training Wh-movement structures in agrammatic aphasia: Optimal order for promoting generalisation. *Journal of the International Neuropsychological Society, 4*, 661–674.

Thompson, C. K., Bonakdarpour, B., Fix, S., Parrish, T., Gitelman, D., & Mesulam, M-M. (2004). Neural correlates of word class processing. *Brain and Language, 91*, 15–16.

Thompson, C. K., Fix, S., Gitelman, D. R., Parish, T. B., & Mesulam, M. (2000). FMRI studies of agrammatic sentence comprehension before and after treatment. *Brain and Language, 74*, 387–391.

Thompson, C. K., Lange, K. L., Schneider, S. L., & Shapiro, L. P. (1997a). Agrammatic and non-brain damaged subjects' verb and verb argument structure production. *Aphasiology, 11*, 473–490.

Thompson, C. K., & Shapiro, L. P. (1994). A linguistic-specific approach to treatment of sentence production deficits in aphasia. In P. Lemme (Ed.), *Clinical aphasiology, Vol. 22* (pp. 307–323). Austin, TX: Pro-Ed.

Thompson, C. K., Shapiro, L. P., Ballard, K. J., Jacobs, B. J., Schneider, S. L., & Tait, M. (1997b). Training and generalised production of wh- and NP-movement structures in agrammatic aphasia. *Journal of Speech, Language, and Hearing Research, 40*, 228–244.

Thompson, C. K., Shapiro, L. P., Kiran, S., & Sobecks, J. (2003). The role of syntactic complexity in treatment of sentence deficits in agrammatic aphasia: The complexity account of treatment efficacy (CATE). *Journal of Speech, Language, and Hearing Research, 46*, 591–607.

Thompson, C. K., Shapiro, L. P., & Roberts, M. (1993). Treatment of sentence production deficits in aphasia: A linguistic-specific approach to wh-interrogative training and generalisation. *Aphasiology, 7*, 111–133.

Thompson, C. K., Shapiro, L. P., Tait, M., Jacobs, B. J., & Schneider, S. L. (1996). Training Wh-question productions in agrammatic aphasia: Analysis of argument and adjunct movement. *Brain and Language, 52*, 175–228.

Thompson, C. K., Shapiro, L. P., Tait, M. E., Jacobs, B., Schneider, S., & Ballard, K. (1995). A system for the linguistic analysis of agrammatic language production. *Brain and Language, 51*, 124–129.

Trueswell, J., & Kim, A. (1998). How to prune a garden-path by nipping it in the bud: Fast priming of verb argument structure. *Journal of Memory and Language, 39*, 102–123.

Wambaugh, J. L., & Thompson, C. K., (1989). Training and generalisation of agrammatic aphasic adults' wh-interrogative productions. *Journal of Speech and Hearing Disorders, 54*, 509–525.

Yao, K. (1989). *Acquisition of mathematical skills in a learning hierarchy by high and low ability students when instruction is omitted on coordinate and subordinate skills*. Unpublished doctoral dissertation, Indiana University, USA.

Zurif, E., Swinney, D., Prather, P., Solomon, J., & Bushell, C. (1993). On-line analysis of syntactic processing in Broca's and Wernicke's aphasia. *Brain and Language, 45*, 448–464.

APHASIOLOGY, 2005, 19 (10/11), 1037–1051

Degrees of severity and recovery in agrammatism: Climbing up the syntactic tree

Na'ama Friedmann

Tel Aviv University, Israel

Background: Agrammatic aphasia impairs syntactic abilities in production and comprehension. The Tree Pruning Hypothesis (TPH) suggests that the syntactic deficit in production can be described in terms of inability to access the high nodes of the syntactic tree.

Aims: The current study explored patterns of individual differences between individuals with agrammatic aphasia, and suggested a characterisation for different degrees of agrammatic severity using the syntactic tree. A second aim was to test the path of spontaneous recovery in agrammatic aphasia.

Methods & Procedures: The first experiment tested 18 individuals with agrammatism: 16 were Hebrew speakers, and 2 were speakers of Palestinian Arabic. The syntactic ability of the participants was assessed with respect to three levels of the syntactic tree. To test the ability at the Agreement Phrase (AgrP) level, a task of agreement completion was used. To test the ability at the Tense Phrase (TP) level, a task of tense inflection completion was used. The ability at the highest level of the tree, the Complementiser Phrase (CP), was tested using elicitation tasks for two structures: Wh-questions and relative clauses. The second experiment tested the recovery of these four abilities over time in SB, an individual with agrammatism, starting 4.5 months post her brain injury until 18 months post-onset.

Outcomes & Results: The main findings were that the variation between the performance of different individuals with agrammatism and degrees of agrammatic severity could be accounted for by different sites of pruning on the syntactic tree. Severe agrammatism results from inability to access TP and the nodes above it, which impairs both tense inflection and CP-related abilities like the production of embedded sentences and Wh-questions. Milder agrammatism results from the inaccessibility of a higher node, CP, which causes a deficit to embedded sentences and Wh-questions, but leaves tense unimpaired. For both degrees of severity, agreement inflection was unimpaired. The second experiment showed that the spontaneous recovery of SB proceeded on the syntactic tree: the starting point was impairment in AgrP, TP, and CP, at the next stage AgrP recovered, and at the following stage TP recovered too.

Conclusions: The results show that the syntactic tree is not only a useful tool for the characterisation of agrammatic aphasia at one point in time; it can also account for individual differences as well as for degrees of agrammatic severity, and can describe stages of spontaneous recovery. A milder impairment, or improvement in agrammatism, manifests itself in the ability to access higher nodes of the syntactic tree.

Address correspondence to: Dr Naama Friedmann, School of Education, Tel Aviv University, Tel Aviv 69978, Israel. Email: naamafr@post.tau.ac.il

Many thanks to Michal Biran for her help in repeatedly testing SB. The research was supported by the Joint German-Israeli Research Program grant GR01791 (Friedmann).

   DOI:10.1080/02687030544000236

INTRODUCTION

Agrammatic aphasia is an intriguing syntactic impairment that has yielded various descriptions over the years. This paper tries to account for some of the variability among individuals with agrammatism using a syntactic generalisation: the hierarchical order of various syntactic components on the syntactic tree.

Early accounts of speech production in agrammatism suggested that the syntactic ability is completely lost, and that agrammatic aphasics only lean on non-linguistic strategies to concatenate words into a sentence (Berndt & Caramazza, 1980; Caplan, 1985; Goodglass, 1976; Goodglass & Berko, 1960). A move towards a more selective account of the impairment resulted in the suggestion that only functional elements are impaired in agrammatic speech production (Grodzinsky, 1990). However, in recent years empirical evidence has accumulated, suggesting that the deficit is actually finer-grained, and that not all functional elements are equally impaired in agrammatism.

The current picture of speech production in agrammatism, based on the increasing number of detailed studies of various syntactic abilities conducted in recent years, is that of an intricate and highly selective pattern of deficit.

Inflections.   Inflections were found to be impaired in a selective way. In Hebrew and in Palestinian Arabic, tense inflection was found to be severely impaired, whereas agreement inflection was almost intact in a set of constrained tasks such as sentence completion, elicitation, and repetition (Friedmann, 1994, 2000, 2001; Friedmann & Grodzinsky, 1997). Subsequent studies in other languages have reported a similar dissociation between tense and agreement. Benedet, Christiansen, and Goodglass (1998), using a sentence completion procedure, reported that verb agreement was much better preserved than tense inflection in both Spanish and English. Ferreiro (2003) tested agrammatic aphasic patients in Catalan and Spanish, with the same completion and repetition tasks that were used in Friedmann (1994, 2001), and reported a similar pattern of dissociations: tense was more impaired than agreement in Catalan and Spanish. In Dutch, Kolk (2000) reported substantially higher error rate for tense than for agreement. Wenzlaff and Clahsen (2004) tested agrammatism in German using forced-choice completion of inflection and also showed a dissociation between completion of agreement, which was similar to that of the control subjects, and completion of tense, which was at chance level. Past participle agreement in Italian was also found to be relatively preserved (De Bleser & Luzzatti, 1994). In De Bleser and Luzzatti's study, most of the tasks in non-embedded sentences were performed at around 90% correct.

Embedding and questions.   Another domain of deficit in agrammatic production is embedding. Individuals with agrammatism either avoid embedded sentences altogether or produce an incomplete or ungrammatical sentence when they try to produce them. This has been shown in spontaneous speech in various languages: in English (Bates, Friederici, Wulfeck, & Juarez, 1988; Thompson, Shapiro, Ballard, Jacobs, Schneider, & Tait, 1997; Thompson, Shapiro, Tait, Jacobs, & Schneider, 1996), in Italian and German (Bates et al., 1988), in Japanese (Hagiwara, 1995), in Hebrew and Palestinian Arabic (Friedmann, 1998a, 2001), and in Dutch, Finnish, French, Hindi, Polish, and Swedish in the Menn and Obler (1990) corpora. Interestingly, individuals with agrammatism correctly produce embedded sentences that do not require the CP, such as reduced relatives ("I saw the boy crying") (Friedmann, 1998a, 2001).

The production of questions is another syntactic domain that has shown a selective pattern of impairment in agrammatism. Seminal treatment studies by Shapiro, Thompson, and their group (Thompson & Shapiro, 1994, 1995) showed that individuals with agrammatism cannot produce well-formed Wh-questions. Other studies that compared yes/no- to Wh-questions showed that in languages that require movement of the auxiliary, yes/no questions are impaired too. Studies in English (Friedmann, 2002) and in Dutch (Ruigendijk, Kouwenberg, & Friedmann, 2004) showed that both Wh- and yes/no questions are impaired, while in languages such as Hebrew and Arabic, in which Wh-questions require movement of the Wh element to the beginning of the question but yes/no questions do not require movement, Wh-questions are impaired, but yes/no questions are intact (Friedmann, 2002).

The *Tree Pruning Hypothesis* (TPH, Friedmann, 1994, 2001; Friedmann & Grodzinsky, 1997) was suggested to account for these seemingly unrelated deficits and for the dissociations between spared and impaired abilities within and across languages in agrammatic production. The TPH is a linguistic generalisation, formulated within the generative grammar framework. According to the TPH, individuals with agrammatic aphasia are unable to project the syntactic tree up to its highest nodes, and their syntactic tree is "pruned". As a result, syntactic structures and elements that require the high nodes of the tree are impaired, but structures and elements that involve only low nodes are preserved.

According to syntactic theories within the generative tradition (e.g., Chomsky, 1995), sentences are represented as phrase markers or syntactic trees. In these syntactic trees, content and function words are represented in different nodes (head nodes and phrasal nodes) (Figure 1). Functional nodes include, among others, inflectional nodes: an agreement phrase (AgrsP), the lowest functional node, which represents agreement between the subject and the verb in person, gender, and number, and a tense phrase (TP) above it, representing tense inflection of the verb. Finite verbs move from V, their base-generated position within the VP, to Agr and then to T in order to check (or collect) their inflection. Thus, the ability to correctly inflect verbs for agreement and tense crucially depends on the AgrP and TP nodes and the ability to move the verb to these nodes. The highest phrasal node in the tree is the complementiser phrase, CP, which hosts complementisers such as "that", Wh morphemes like "who" and "what" that moved from the base-generated position within the VP, and the auxiliary or the verb in yes/no questions in languages like English, German, and Dutch, which require movement of the

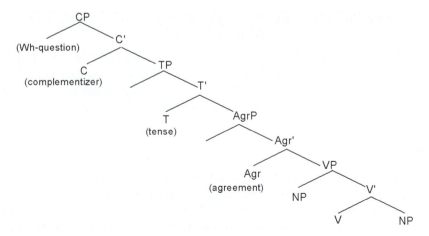

Figure 1.   Syntactic tree based on Pollock (1989).

auxiliary or the verb to the beginning. Thus, the construction of embedded sentences and Wh-questions depends on the CP node being intact and accessible. Crucially, the nodes in the syntactic tree are hierarchically ordered—the lowest node is the Verb Phrase, the nodes above it are the Agreement Phrase and the Tense Phrase (in this order according to Pollock, 1989), and the Complementiser Phrase is placed at the highest point of the syntactic tree.

The Tree Pruning Hypothesis uses this hierarchical order to account for the selective pattern of impairment in agrammatic production both within and between languages. If individuals with agrammatism cannot access a certain syntactic node, they will not be able to produce the syntactic structures that require this node, and they will also not be able to access higher nodes, and therefore will not be able to produce structures that relate to these higher nodes. Importantly, nodes below the pruning site are intact, and therefore structures that require only low nodes such as AgrP and VP are well formed in agrammatic production. This accounts for the dissociation between tense and agreement inflection: If tense and agreement reside on different nodes in the syntactic tree, with TP higher than AgrP, then it is possible for TP to be inaccessible, and therefore for tense inflection to be impaired, while the AgrP node, which is below the pruning site, remains intact, and consequently agreement inflection is intact.

The selective deficit with respect to embedded sentences and questions is accounted for by the inaccessibility of CP. Full relative clauses ("This is the man that the woman kissed") and sentential embeddings ("The man said that the woman kissed him") require the C node; Wh-questions ("Who did the woman kiss?") require the specifier of CP, and yes/no questions in Dutch and English ("Did the woman kiss the man?") require the C node. When CP is unavailable, these structures are impaired. This also accounts for the spared structures: embedded sentences that do not require the CP, such as reduced relatives ("I saw the boy crying"), were produced correctly by individuals with agrammatism. So were yes/no questions in Hebrew and Arabic, which also do not require any overt element in CP ("You like hummus?").

The following experiments focused on the performance pattern of each individual with agrammatism with respect to various syntactic abilities. They explored the validity of the TPH to further account for different patterns of agrammatism that relate to different degrees of severity of the agrammatic impairment.

EXPERIMENT 1: DEGREES OF AGRAMMATIC SEVERITY AND THE TREE

In order to test individual differences in the three layers of the syntactic tree, CP, TP, and AgrP, we assessed each individual's abilities using four tasks: an agreement completion task to assess abilities that relate to AgrP level, a tense completion task to assess TP level, and subject relative clause elicitation, as well as elicitation of Wh-questions, to assess CP level abilities.

Method

Participants.   The study included 18 individuals with agrammatic aphasia: 16 were native speakers of Hebrew, and 2 were native speakers of Palestinian Arabic. They were 9 women and 9 men, with a mean age of 42 (SD = 16), and a mean of 12 years of education (SD = 1.6). All participants had characteristic agrammatic speech: nonfluent and short with incomplete and ungrammatical utterances and reduction of sentence structure. They all failed in comprehension tests of reversible object relative clauses, tested using the syntactic test battery BAFLA (Friedmann, 1998b; for the comprehension performance of seven of the participants see Friedmann & Shapiro, 2003). Only parti- cipants who had at least two-word utterances were included in the study. All of them had brain lesion in the left cerebral hemisphere, and right hemiplegia or hemiparesis. The aetiology of the lesion of 14 of the participants was stroke, 3 had traumatic brain injury, and 1 had left fronto-parietal craniotomy following astrocytoma. They were patients in Israeli hospitals and rehabilitation centres, and were in a stable condition at the time of testing, at least 7 months post-onset (with a mean of 22 months post-onset).

In addition, a control group of 10 NORMALs (individuals with No Reported MAl- functioning Language) was tested using the same tasks, in order to evaluate the tasks as well as to get a notion of the way these tasks are performed without a language deficit. Because the agrammatic participants were either in their thirties or around age 65, the control group included five individuals of each of these age groups (this group's results were taken from Friedmann, 1998a).

General procedure.   Since the main interest was in errors that stemmed from the underlying grammatical deficit, no time limit was imposed during testing, and partici- pants were encouraged to take as much time as they needed for each item, to correct themselves until they reached the best response they could (without feedback from the experimenter), and to ask for as many repeats as they needed. They were also instructed to ask for a break, or to terminate the session altogether whenever they felt tired. Between tests, breaks of 5 to 10 minutes were given. The order of tests was randomly varied among participants. The structures that were tested in Hebrew and Palestinian Arabic were similar, and the results were similar for both languages, so the data for the speakers of Hebrew and Palestinian Arabic will be presented together.

Agreement inflection completion.   In the agreement completion task, the participant first heard a sentence containing an inflected verb, and then a second sentence without a verb, with a change in the subject. The participant was asked to produce the missing verb with the proper inflection (see example 1). In doing so the participant had to change the inflection of the given verb in one agreement feature—either person, gender, or num- ber—in order for it to agree with the subject of the second sentence. The test consisted of simple sentences of three to five words.

(1) Berega ze ha-yeled kotev. Berega ze gam ha-yeladim _____ (kotvim).
     Right now the-boy writes. Right now the-boys also _____ (write-pl,3rd,masc,present).

Each of the 24 inflection forms was tested twice (3 persons, 2 genders, 2 numbers, 3 tenses, which make 10 different forms in the past and future, and 4 forms in the present), with a total of 48 items per test.

Tense inflection completion.   In the tense completion task, the participant first heard a sentence containing an inflected verb and then a second sentence without a verb, this time with a change in the temporal adverb. The participant was asked to produce the missing verb with the proper inflection (see example 2).

(2) Berega ze ha-yeled kotev. Gam etmol ha-yeled _____ (katav)
     Right now the-boy writes. Also yesterday the-boy_____ (write-3rd,sg,masc,past)

Seven of the participants (HY, RN, RS, RA, TA, KA, AL) participated in an additional test, which tested tense and agreement together, without a temporal adverb. The test, as exemplified in 3, included the verb in the infinitival form, and the participant was asked to use the same verb in the missing place, in the correct inflection. In this task they had to inflect the verb for both tense and agreement, as the verb had to agree in person, gender, and number with the subject, and in tense with the sentential tense, which was presented in the inflected verb in the beginning of the sentence. This test also included 48 sentences.

(3) Ha-yeladim racu lehikanes, az hem patxu et ha-delet ve … (nixnesu)
     The-kids wanted to-enter, so they opened the-door and … (entered-past, 3rd, masc, pl)

Embedded sentence elicitation.   The production of embedded sentences was examined using a subject relative clause elicitation task. The task included 18 target sentences, elicited by nine pairs of drawings, each pair including a figure involved in two different actions. The participants were given the description of the two pictures together, and were asked to depict each figure separately, using a single sentence starting with the words "This is the …". So for Figure 2, for instance, (4) was used as the experimenter presentation of the question (translated), and sentence 5 is the target relative clause response. Prior to the task, a practice picture pair was given. The task was repeated twice (with at least 2 weeks between sessions), with a total of 36 target relative clauses per participant.

(4) Here are two men. One man is rowing a boat, another man is playing matkot [a favourite Israeli ball game]. Which man is this? Start with "This is the man . . ."
(5) ze ha-'ish **she**-xoter besira.
     This the-man that-rows in-boat
     "*This is the man that rows a boat*"

Wh-question elicitation.   In order to elicit Wh-questions, sentences were presented to the participants in which one of the details (phrases) was replaced by a non-specific term (such as someone, something, some place). The task was introduced using a context for asking questions: "Imagine that your son comes home from school and tells you about his day. The problem is that he omits important details and you ask questions to find out about the missing details. For example, he tells you someone pushed him in school and you want to know about this kid, so you ask: Who pushed you?". The patient

Figure 2.   An example of the drawings used in the relative clause elicitation task.

was instructed to ask the experimenter about the missing detail (see example 6 for the elicitation of an object question).

(6) Experimenter: Miri cyira **mashehu**. At roca lish'ol legabei ha-mashehu ha-ze, az at sho'elet ...
Miri drew something. You want to-ask about the-something the-this, so you ask ...
*"Miri drew **something**. You want to ask about this thing, so you ask ..."*
Target question: ma miri cyira?
what Miri drew
"What did Miri draw?"

The sentences were read aloud by the experimenter, and concurrently presented in large print (18 point font). The non-specific phrase was boldfaced. At least two practice items preceded each session, and training proceeded until we were sure that the participant understood the task. The task included 24 items. Target Wh-questions included 12 argument questions (subject and direct object) and 12 adjunct questions, randomly ordered. Argument questions included four subject, four animate object ("who"), and four inanimate object ("what") questions. Adjunct questions were four "where", four "when", and four "why" questions, see target questions of each type in example 7.[1] The test was repeated after 2 months for four of the participants.

(7) a. Subject question: mi sirek et dani? *who combed Danny?*
b. Object who question: et mi danny nishek? *Whom Danny kissed?*
c. Object what question: ma safta bishla? *What grandma cooked?*
d. Adjunct where question: eifo dani nirdam? *Where Danny fell-asleep?*
e. Adjunct when question: matai ha-shemesh zarxa? *When the-sun rose?*
f. Adjunct why question: lama hayeled baxa? *Why the-boy cried?*

The production of the various Wh-questions by the participants was analysed and compared to the production of the control group.

Results and discussion

Figure 3 presents the individual results in each of the syntactic levels AgrP, TP, and CP. For each participant, the left-hand column presents percent correct in agreement completion, the middle column presents percent correct in tense completion, and the rightmost column presents the performance that is related to the CP layer—the average performance on the relative clause elicitation and the Wh-question elicitation. Although each individual has different percentages in each of the tasks, the most important finding here is that the participants' performance was remarkably similar, creating two patterns: The performance of all participants was poor in structures that require CP, good in structures that require AgrP, and they differed with respect to their performance in structures that require TP—some were impaired in TP and some were unimpaired.

All the 18 individuals with agrammatism who participated in our study had severe difficulties in the production of structures that are related to CP: Wh-questions and subject relative clauses. Their average performance on the production of

---

[1] The test also included 24 yes/no questions, which do not require the use of high syntactic nodes in Hebrew and in Palestinian Arabic; these items were used as controls and to assure that the participants understood the task, which they did, and they will not be reported in the current paper (for details see Friedmann, 2002).

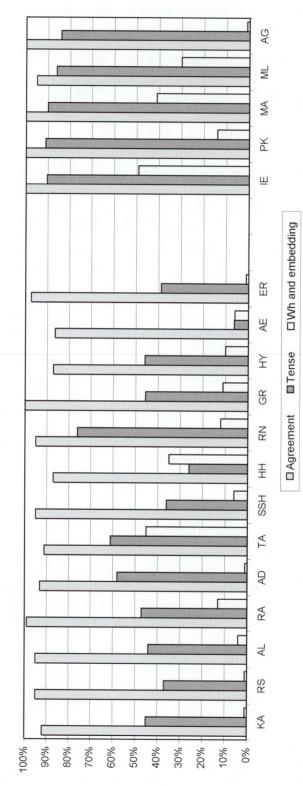

Figure 3. Individual performance of the 18 participants in agreement completion, tense completion, Wh-questions, and embedding elicitation.

subject relative clauses was 15% correct (SD = 14%), and on the Wh-question production it was 18% (SD = 22%). The performance of each of the participants in both
Wh-question elicitation and relative clause elicitation was significantly poorer than
that of the control group, $p < .0001$ (using Crawford & Howell's, 1998, significance test on the difference between individual's score and control sample). Difficulties in Wh-questions and relative clause production have already been reported in
the literature (Friedmann, 2002; Thompson & Shapiro 1994, 1995: Thompson et al.,
1996 for Wh-questions; Friedmann, 2001 for relative clauses). Other studies showed
difficulties in other types of CP-related structures as well, such as deficits in sentential complements (Friedmann, 1998a, 2001); impaired production of yes/no questions
in languages that require CP for these questions (Friedmann, 2002; Ruigendijk et
al., 2004); and impaired production of verb movement to C in Hebrew (Friedmann,
2005; Friedmann & Gil, 2001).

On the other hand, all participants had good performance (arbitrarily defined as performance above 85% correct) in agreement completion. The average performance was
95% correct, with SD of 5%. Twelve of the individuals did not differ significantly from
the control group in their performance in the agreement completion test (Crawford &
Howell's t-test, $p > .09$), and six participants performed significantly poorer than the
control group, but still above 85% correct.

The average performance on the tense completion task was 56% (SD = 25%).
As we found in previous studies (Friedmann, 1994, 1998a, 2000, 2001; Friedmann
& Grodzinsky, 1997), the comparison between tense and agreement at the group
level (using Wilcoxon Signed-Rank Test) showed that agreement completion was significantly better than tense completion, $z = 3.71$, $p = .0002$. However, on the individual level, Fisher's exact test yielded a significant difference between tense and
agreement for only 13 of the participants. Participants IE, PK, MA, ML, and AG
(in the right-hand columns on Figure 3) did well on both tense and agreement, and
showed no significant difference between tense and agreement ($p > .12$). Thus, the
participants differed with respect to their performance in tense inflection completion. Five of them performed well, and showed good tense inflection, while others
were also impaired in tense inflection. For the tense completion test, three of the individuals did not differ significantly from the control group (Crawford & Howell's t-
test, $p > .09$), two performed significantly less well than the healthy control group,
but still above 85% correct, and the other thirteen participants performed significantly less well than the control group and below 85%.

So all the participants have impaired CP and relatively unimpaired AgrP, and
some have TP impairment. This yields two very clear patterns of agrammatic
impairment: one pattern, manifested by the more severe agrammatic individuals, is
that of intact agreement, impaired tense, and impaired Wh-questions and CP
embeddings. The more mildly impaired individuals show a different pattern. In
their production, both tense and agreement are relatively intact (with agreement at
100% and tense at around 90% correct), but Wh-questions and embedding are
impaired.

Crucially, their pattern of performance showed that the syntactic tree defines a perfect
Guttman Scale (Guttman, 1944) for agrammatic production: if a node is accessible, all
nodes below it are also accessible, and if a node is inaccessible for a certain individual,
nodes above it are inaccessible as well. Indeed, none of the aphasic individuals showed a
deficit in a low node without a deficit in the nodes above it. In no case was there impaired
TP without a deficit in CP, and in no case was there a deficit in AgrP without a deficit in

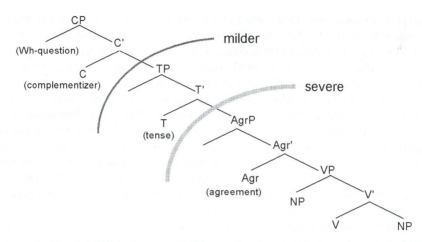

Figure 4.   Degrees of agrammatic severity by pruning sites: CP pruning = milder impairment, TP pruning = more severe agrammatic impairment.

TP and CP. When TP is impaired, CP is also impaired, when TP is intact, AgrP is also intact.[2]

   This pattern suggests a way to describe degrees of agrammatic severity on the syntactic tree, and a way to capture individual differences by the height of the deficit on the tree. The individuals with severe agrammatism are TP-pruned; namely, they are impaired in TP and above, and therefore impaired both in TP and in CP and intact in AgrP. The more mildly impaired agrammatic individuals are CP-pruned; namely, they are only impaired higher up, in CP. Therefore their CP is impaired, and their TP and AgrP are unimpaired (Figure 4). Importantly, a deficit at a specific level on the tree entails a deficit in all levels above it. The higher a patient can access (the higher the pruning site is), the milder the impairment, because more functional nodes can be accessed. The lower the impaired node is on the syntactic tree, the more severe the clinical manifestation of agrammatism, because fewer functional nodes are available.

   Notice that in every other respect, except for this difference with respect to the functional categories, these patients share all the standard clinical signs of agrammatism. The speech of all of them is non-fluent, and impaired in aspects of their grammar—they have short phrase length, they produce ungrammatical sentences, and in particular, they cannot embed or ask questions. So it seems that the impairment of all these participants does indeed belong to the same general clinical generalisation, but in different degrees of severity. The crucial point here is that there is a single principle that distinguishes them from one another—the level in the syntactic tree at which the pruning occurs. This is how the Tree Pruning Hypothesis provides a flexible formulation of a neuropsychological deficit that may have more than a single manifestation. Yet this generalisation is highly constrained, as it has strong predictions with respect to what is *not expected* as a pattern of agrammatic production. Specifically, given that inaccessibility to a certain node pre-

---

[2] In this article we have discussed mainly the syntactic tree as a Guttman scale at the individual patient level. However, there are indications that this can also be considered at the sentence level—when an individual with agrammatism succeeds in producing a sentence with the highest syntactic node, the nodes below it are produced correctly as well (for example, when Hebrew-speaking participants correctly produce the verb in C, the verb is always correctly inflected for tense, see Friedmann, in press).

vents access to higher nodes, we do not expect to find individuals with impaired functions that relate to TP (subject case, tense inflection, subject pronouns), but with intact CP functions such as Wh-question production, and production of CP-embedded sentences. Similarly, if agreement-related structures are impaired, we expect both TP and CP to be impaired.

These results and their interpretation raise two interesting questions. First, if indeed there are (at least) two degrees of severity that can be described by the site of pruning on the syntactic tree, does the trajectory of recovery in agrammatism follow the same generalisation? Namely, do individuals with agrammatism whose syntactic abilities improve spontaneously in the several months after a brain injury or stroke, move from being TP-pruned to being CP-pruned?

The second question relates to whether it is possible to identify individuals who are even more impaired than the individuals with agrammatism who are impaired in TP. Are there individuals who are impaired lower on the tree, at AgrP?

These two questions were assessed in Experiment 2, which tested the trajectory of spontaneous recovery of a young woman with agrammatism.

EXPERIMENT 2: RECOVERY ON THE SYNTACTIC TREE

We tested the production of functional elements and syntactic structures of SB, a young woman with agrammatic aphasia, during the first 18 months following her traumatic brain injury. SB was 20 years old, a native speaker of Hebrew who had 12 years of education. She suffered a TBI and had left craniotomy, which resulted in a vast hypodense area in the left hemisphere including temporal, parietal, and frontal lobes, an enlarged lateral ventricle (according to a CT done 4 months post-injury), and right hemiplegia. She received physical therapy, psychological treatment, and general language treatment that did not include specific treatment of syntax. SB's syntax had been systematically and repeatedly tested since she started speaking, 4.5 months post her injury, and then regularly until 18 months post-injury. Her abilities related to AgrP, TP, and CP were assessed. She was tested in agreement inflection, tense inflection, and relative clause and question production, using the same tests described in Experiment 1.

Results and discussion

The results, as can be seen in Figure 5, showed three distinct stages of recovery. During the first stage, at $4\frac{1}{2}$ months post-injury, all the tested functions were impaired: SB produced agreement and tense inflection substitutions in the completion tasks, and was completely unable to construct either a Wh-question or an embedded relative clause (neither subject nor object relative clauses).

Two months later, at 6.6 months post-injury, she was already able to correctly inflect verbs for agreement, but still had many errors of tense inflections, and could not construct embedding and Wh-questions. In the first three testing sessions after this time point, she made only one or two agreement errors out of 20 items, and in the following 12 testing sessions she made no errors in agreement. This condition continued with between 40% and 59% errors of tense in the next five sessions of testing, until she was 15 months post-injury.

At the third stage, 15 months post-injury, tense inflection had recovered, at which point relative clauses were still not produced (0% production of relative clauses and Wh-questions). At 18 months post-injury, relative clauses started to emerge in elicitation tasks, indicating the occasional access to the highest node of the tree, CP. At this time SB

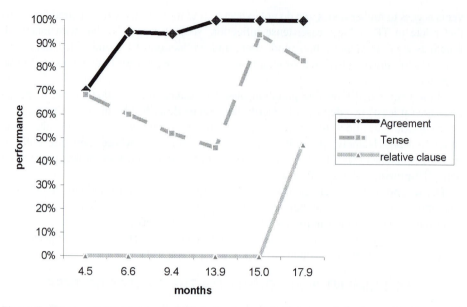

Figure 5. The spontaneous recovery of SB in agreement inflection, tense inflection, and relative clause production.

could also produce some Wh-questions, relative clauses, and sentential complements of verbs (50–75% Wh-questions, 35–60% correct relative clauses, 60% repetition of sentential embedding). This final stage of recovery of CP functions might not have been the result of spontaneous recovery—it rather could be ascribed to the fact that 17 months post-injury SB started receiving treatment that focused on the production of complex sentences.

Thus, it seems that SB's recovery can be described as a gradual climbing up the syntactic tree, obtaining access to higher nodes of the tree at each stage (see Figure 6). During the very first stage, AgrP, TP, and CP were all not accessible. Then, around 6 months after injury, AgrP became available, and TP and CP were still not accessible. Then, 15 months after the injury, TP became available, but CP was still out of reach. The final stage was characterised by access to AgrP and TP, and partial access to CP.

These results answer the two research questions we posed before this experiment. First, they indicate that syntactic recovery might be described by the hierarchy on the syntactic tree. The results also answer our second question: They present an agrammatic patient with a deficit in AgrP (as well as in TP and CP). This suggests that the fact that only individuals with a tree pruned at TP or pruned at CP were reported in the initial study of 18 participants may have resulted from the inclusion criteria for the study: We included in the initial study only individuals at a stable stage who had sentences of at least two words. It might be that the individuals whose agreement is also impaired are either not yet in a stable condition or produce very short sentences. The results also show three different degrees of severity, characterised by three different pruning sites, AgrP, TP, and CP, in one and the same patient during recovery from very severe to mild agrammatism.

These initial findings raise questions for further research regarding treatment and the interaction between treatment and recovery: Should treatment fit the trajectory of recovery? Given preliminary results showing that treatment of higher nodes improves the

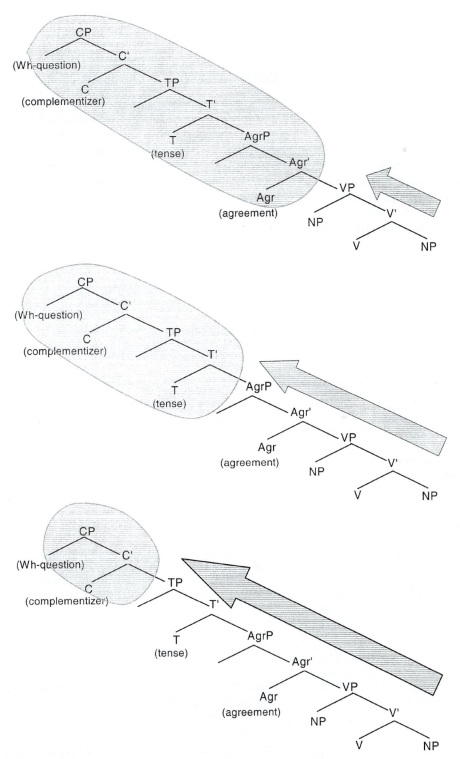

Figure 6. The gradual recovery of SB on the syntactic tree. Top: 4.5 months post brain injury. Middle: 6.5 months post-injury. Bottom: 15 months post-injury.

accessibility of lower nodes (Friedman, Wenkert-Olenik & Gil, 2000), can treatment of higher nodes accelerate spontaneous recovery? At which phase of recovery is treatment most efficient?

CONCLUSION

This study shows that the syntactic tree and the relative positions of various syntactic structures on it are useful descriptive tools not only to account for the dissociations found between different structures and between the same structures in different languages, but also to describe differences in performance between individuals, as well as different stages of recovery within the same individual. The key is which parts of the syntactic tree are required by each syntactic structure: Individuals with agrammatism find it hard to access the highest nodes of the syntactic tree, milder impairment manifests in ability to access higher nodes, and recovery, at least for the one person we followed, means the ability to reach higher and higher on the syntactic tree.

REFERENCES

Bates, E. A., Friederici, A. D., Wulfeck, B. B., & Juarez, L. A. (1988). On the preservation of word order in aphasia: Cross-linguistic evidence. *Brain and Language, 33*, 323–364.

Benedet, M. J., Christiansen, J. A., & Goodglass, H. (1998). A cross-linguistic study of grammatical morphology in Spanish- and English-speaking agrammatic patients. *Cortex, 34*, 309–336.

Berndt, R. S., & Caramazza, A. (1980). A redefinition of Broca's aphasia: Implications for a neuropsychological model of language. *Applied Psycholinguistics, 1*, 225–278.

Caplan, D. (1985). Syntactic and semantic structures in agrammatism. In M-L. Kean (Ed.), *Agrammatism*. New York: Academic Press.

Chomsky, N. (1995). *The minimalist program*. Cambridge, MA: MIT Press.

Crawford, J. R., & Howell, D. C. (1998). Comparing an individual's test score against norms derived from small samples. *The Clinical Neuropsychologist, 12*, 482–486.

De Bleser, R., & Luzzatti, C. (1994). Morphological processing in Italian agrammatic speakers syntactic implementation of inflectional morphology. *Brain and Language, 46*, 21–40.

Ferreiro, S. M. (2003). *Verbal inflectional morphology in Broca's aphasia*. Unpublished master's thesis, Universitat Autonoma de Barcelona, Spain.

Friedmann, N. (1994). *Morphology in agrammatism: A dissociation between tense and agreement*. Unpublished master's thesis, Tel Aviv University, Israel, Dept. Cognitive Psychology.

Friedmann, N. (1998a). *Functional categories in agrammatic production: A cross-linguistic study*. Unpublished doctoral dissertation, Tel Aviv University, Israel.

Friedmann, N. (1998b). *BAFLA – Friedmann's battery for agrammatism*. Tel Aviv University, Israel.

Friedmann, N. (2000). Moving verbs in agrammatic production. In R. Bastiaanse & Y. Grodzinsky (Eds.), *Grammatical disorders in aphasia: A neurolinguistic perspective* (pp. 152–170). London: Whurr.

Friedmann, N. (2001). Agrammatism and the psychological reality of the syntactic tree. *Journal of Psycholinguistic Research, 30*, 71–90.

Friedmann, N. (2002). Question production in agrammatism: The Tree Pruning Hypothesis. *Brain and Language, 80*, 160–187.

Friedmann, N. (2005). Speech production in Broca's agrammatic aphasia: Syntactic tree pruning. In K. Amunts & Y. Grodzinsky (Eds.), *Broca's region*. Oxford: Oxford University Press.

Friedmann, N. (in press). Agrammatic aphasia and the psychological reality of the syntactic tree. In G. Hatav (Ed.), *Theoretical Hebrew linguistics*. Jerusalem: The Hebrew University Magnes Press [in Hebrew].

Friedmann, N., & Gil, M. (2001). *Verb movement in agrammatic comprehension and production*. Paper presented at the 2nd "Science of Aphasia" Conference, Giens, France.

Friedmann, N., & Grodzinsky, Y. (1997). Tense and agreement in agrammatic production: Pruning the syntactic tree. *Brain and Language, 56*, 397–425.

Friedmann, N., & Shapiro, L. P. (2003). Agrammatic comprehension of simple active sentences with moved constituents: Hebrew OSV and OVS structures. *Journal of Speech Language and Hearing Research, 46*, 288–297.

Friedmann, N., Wenkert-Olenik, D., & Gil, M. (2000). From theory to practice: Treatment of agrammatic production in Hebrew based on the tree pruning hypothesis. *Journal of Neurolinguistics, 13*, 250–254.

Goodglass, H. (1976). Agrammatism. In H. Whitaker & H. A. Whitaker (Eds.), *Studies in neurolinguistics, 1* (pp. 237–260). New York: Academic Press.

Goodglass, H., & Berko, J. (1960). Agrammatism and inflectional morphology in English. *Journal of Speech and Hearing Research, 3*, 257–267.

Grodzinsky, Y. (1990). *Theoretical perspectives on language deficits.* Cambridge, MA: MIT Press.

Guttman, L. (1944). A basis of scaling quantitative data. *American Sociological Review, 9*, 139–150.

Hagiwara, H. (1995). The breakdown of functional categories and the economy of derivation. *Brain and Language, 50*, 92–116.

Kolk, H. (2000). Canonicity and inflection in agrammatic sentence production. *Brain and Language, 74*, 558–560.

Menn, L., & Obler, L. (Eds.). (1990). *Agrammatic aphasia: A cross-language narrative sourcebook.* Philadelphia: John Benjamins.

Pollock, J. Y. (1989). Verb movement, Universal Grammar and the structure of IP. *Linguistic Inquiry, 20*, 365–424.

Ruigendijk, E., Kouwenberg, M., & Friedmann, N. (2004). Question production in Dutch agrammatism. *Brain and Language, 91*, 116–117.

Thompson, C. K., & Shapiro, L. P. (1994). A linguistic specific approach to treatment of sentence production deficits in aphasia. *Clinical Aphasiology, 22*, 307–323.

Thompson, C. K., & Shapiro, L. P. (1995). Training sentence production in agrammatism: Implications for normal and disordered language. *Brain and Language, 50*, 201–224.

Thompson. C. K., Shapiro, L. P., Ballard, K. J., Jacobs, B. J., Schneider, S. S., & Tait, M. E. (1997). Training and generalised production of Wh- and NP-movement structures in agrammatic aphasia. *Journal of Speech, Language, and Hearing Research, 40*, 228–244.

Thompson, C. K., Shapiro, L. P., Tait, M. E., Jacobs, B. J., & Schneider, S. L. (1996). Training *Wh*-question production in agrammatic aphasia: Analysis of argument and adjunct movement. *Brain and Language, 52*, 175–228.

Wenzlaff, M., & Clahsen, H. (2004). Tense and agreement in German agrammatism. *Brain and Language, 89*, 57–68.

APHASIOLOGY, 2005, 19 (10/11), 1052–1065

Using a computer to communicate: Effect of executive function impairments in people with severe aphasia

Marjorie Nicholas

MGH Institute of Health Professions, and Boston University School of Medicine, USA

Michele P. Sinotte and Nancy Helm-Estabrooks

Boston University School of Medicine, USA

Background: Some individuals with severe non-fluent aphasia do not respond in a functional way to any form of communication therapy. Others show improved ability to communicate with treatment focused on alternative communication modalities such as drawing, gesturing, or using a computer. An important difference between these two patient groups may lie in their nonverbal executive function abilities. Executive functions refer to a range of cognitive abilities including goal formulation, planning, carrying out goal-directed plans, and monitoring the effects of actions.

Aims: We aimed to determine whether individuals with severely restricted verbal output due to aphasia could significantly improve their functional communication skills by using an alternative communication computer program called *C-Speak Aphasia*. We examined several factors to determine how they related to individual patients' ability to communicate expressively using *C-Speak Aphasia*, including linguistic factors related to semantic processing and extent of executive system dysfunction.

Methods and Procedures: Results from five patients who received at least 6 months of treatment to learn *C-Speak Aphasia* are presented. Communication skills on five untrained tasks were repeatedly probed throughout training to assess carryover of treatment effects. Response to treatment was then examined with respect to baseline measures of language and non-linguistic executive functioning.

Outcomes and Results: Using *C-Speak Aphasia* three of the five participants communicated significantly more information on selected probe tasks than they did without the computer. Executive function skills were more relevant to treatment response than severity of aphasia or semantic knowledge. Subjects with more intact executive function skills responded better to treatment with this alternative communication method than subjects with relatively greater impairment in these skills.

Conclusions: These results suggest that executive function impairments may underlie poor response to treatment of alternative modes of communication, and that non-linguistic measures of executive functioning should be part of every aphasia assessment when attempting to determine candidacy for certain types of treatment programmes.

When aphasia is severe, the ability to communicate even basic social information such as expressing a birthday greeting on the telephone is no longer possible for many individuals. Furthermore, for many people with aphasia, restoration of functional verbal expression is not an achievable goal. Treatment of communication for many of these

---

Address correspondence to: Marjorie Nicholas, Graduate Program in Communication Sciences and Disorders, MGH Institute of Health Professions, Charlestown Navy Yard, 36 1st Avenue, Boston, MA 02129-4557, USA. Email: mlnicholas@mghihp.edu

people focuses on the development of alternative modalities for expression such as drawing, gesturing, or using communication aids such as a computer. A computer-based alternative communication system that is appropriate for people with aphasia must be picture based rather than text based, because of the difficulties with reading and writing that are almost always part of the language disorder of aphasia. One such computer program, known as *C-Speak Aphasia* (Nicholas & Elliott, 1998) is a picture-based software program that was developed specifically for people with aphasia. The purposes of the current study were to investigate whether people with severe aphasia could significantly improve communication by using *C-Speak Aphasia* and to investigate factors that may be relevant to response to training with this alternative communication program.

Rapid advances in technology have resulted in the development of many picture-based communication devices. However, attempts to train people with aphasia to use these communication systems have met with only mixed success (Johannsen-Horbach, Ceglas, Mager, Schempp & Wallesch, 1985; Koul & Harding, 1998; Naeser et al., 1998; Shelton, Weinrich, McCall, & Cox, 1996; Steele, Weinrich, Wertz, Kleczewska, & Carlson, 1989; Steele, Kleczewska, Carlson, & Weinrich, 1992; Weinrich, Steele, Carlson, Kleczewska, Wertz, & Baker, 1989a; Weinrich, Steele, Kleczewska, Carlson, Baker, & Wertz, 1989b). In almost every one of these studies, some people learned to communicate well with the alternative system, while others did not.

Few controlled studies of treatment efficacy or functional outcomes have been published. The program known as C-ViC (Computer-assisted Visual Communication) has by far received the most attention by research groups (Naeser et al., 1998; Shelton et al., 1996; Steele et al., 1989, 1992; Weinrich et al., 1989a, 1989b), but there are no published studies specifically addressing use of C-ViC for functional communication purposes. Nor are there any published reports of well-controlled studies of functional outcomes for any other alternative communication program used by people with aphasia.

In our thinking about patients with severe aphasias we have traditionally assumed that the language disorder alone is responsible for the poor communication abilities of these individuals. In recent years, however, emerging evidence suggests that it is the language disorder in conjunction with non-linguistic cognitive deficits that may be responsible for unsuccessful communication. Clinical experience tells us that most patients with aphasia do not have *only* aphasia. Rather, patients with left hemisphere damage resulting in aphasia often show other non-linguistic deficits on neuropsychological testing. However, the relation between aphasia severity and associated non-linguistic deficits is far from uniform across patients.

We speculate that the presence of additional cognitive deficits, and in particular executive system dysfunction commonly associated with frontal lobe impairment, may help to explain some of the differences between patients with severe aphasia who learn to be good communicators and those who do not (Van Mourik, Verschaeve, Boon, Paquier, & Van Harskamp, 1992). To illustrate this point, consider the example of a person who suddenly finds herself in a foreign country and is unable to comprehend or speak the language of the environment. She would be able to think of and initiate alternative ways to express herself, perhaps by drawing pictures, or pantomiming, or pointing to objects in the area. She would be able to monitor whether her message was received correctly, and would adjust her output accordingly. In effect, she would be using her intact executive function skills, including problem solving, monitoring, and flexibility, to find a solution to a communication dilemma. Persons with aphasia often find themselves in a similar situation: unable to comprehend and unable to express themselves via language. Yet some individuals do *not* figure out alternative ways to communicate on their own; they are unable to find a solution to their communication problem. Even after months of training focused specifically on using alternative modalities, many patients remain unable to use these means of communication to convey even the most rudimentary ideas.

The relation between executive function skills and response to treatment of communication deficits has been the focus of only a few studies. Research by Purdy (1992, 2002) indicated that patients with executive function impairments did not spontaneously shift to using alternate modes of communication such as gesturing or pointing to items on a communication board despite having been successfully trained to do so in treatment tasks. Furthermore, in a lesion study of patients trained on the C-ViC program, Naeser and colleagues found that extent of lesion in selected language areas of the left hemisphere in combination with lesion in the supplementary motor area (SMA) was related to response to training on C-ViC (Naeser et al., 1998). Patients with more extensive lesion in SMA were less able to initiate use of C-ViC to communicate their own messages than patients without lesion to this area. It is likely that this "initiation" skill may reflect an important set of executive functions.

In the current study we investigated whether individuals with severely restricted verbal output due to aphasia could significantly improve their functional communication skills by using the *C-Speak Aphasia* program as an alternative means of expression. We also examined several factors to determine how they related to individual patients' ability to communicate expressively using *C-Speak Aphasia* including linguistic factors related to semantic processing and extent of executive system dysfunction. We tested the hypotheses that: (1) functional communication would be improved significantly using the *C-Speak Aphasia* system, and (2) measures of executive functioning would be related to response to *C-Speak Aphasia* training, and that participants with impairments in EF would be less able to use *C-Speak Aphasia* to improve functional communication than participants with relatively intact EF skills. An important aspect of the design was that generalisation of treatment effects to real-life functional communication contexts was repeatedly assessed throughout treatment using a set of functional communication probe tasks.

The *C-Speak Aphasia* program used in this study is conceptually based on the C-ViC program (Steele et al., 1989). Using *C-Speak Aphasia*, patients learn to select icons from semantic category groups and put them together to create novel messages in the form of statements, commands, and questions. Each message can be spoken aloud by the computer's speech synthesiser by clicking on the message display area. *C-Speak Aphasia* also contains specialised sets of screens to assist the patient in social communication activities such as conversing on the telephone, writing, sending email messages, and expressing autobiographical information. *C-Speak Aphasia* is operated using the *Speaking Dynamically Pro* application available from the Mayer-Johnson Company (King Software Development, 1997). Figure 1 shows a sample *C-Speak Aphasia* screen with a message in the message display area.

METHODS AND PROCEDURES

This study used a multiple baseline design where participants served as their own controls. The amount of information that each participant expressed on five different functional communication tasks was compared across two conditions (using *C-Speak Aphasia*, referred to as "On-Computer", and not using it, referred to as "Off-Computer"). Extensive data from five participants are presented here.

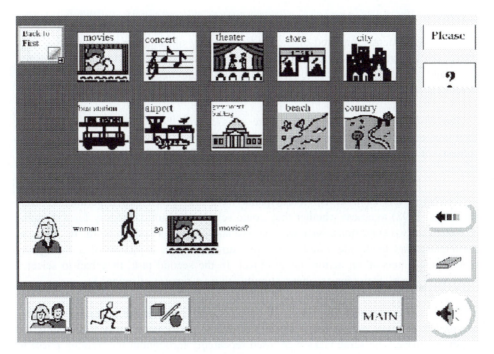

Figure 1.   Sample *C-Speak Aphasia* screen.

Participants

All participants were at least 1 year post-onset of a large left-hemisphere stroke resulting in severe non-fluent aphasia. All had phrase lengths of less than one word in spontaneous speech; four participants produced primarily verbal stereotypies when speaking. Participants displayed a range of auditory comprehension abilities, but all had either moderate or severe impairments of auditory comprehension on formal testing. Further details are presented in Table 1.

TABLE 1
Participant characteristics

Participant No.	Gender	Age	Handedness	Years post-onset	Educ (yrs.)	Lesion region	Aetiology
1	M	27	Right	7.5	12	L MCA	L ICA dissection
2	F	67	Right	1.6	18	L MCA	Embolic CVA
3	F	53	Right	2.3	20	LMCA + small R parietal	L ICA dissection
4	M	60	Left	1.5	17	L MCA	Embolic CVA
5	M	51	Left	4.2	17	L MCA	Embolic CVA

Baseline assessments

Baseline assessments consisted of standardised testing of language and nonverbal cognitive skills related to executive functioning, two semantic knowledge experimental tasks, and repeated assessments of five functional communication probe tasks to insure baseline stability.

Standardised testing. Participants were assessed with the Boston Diagnostic Aphasia Examination, (BDAE-3), (Goodglass, Kaplan, & Barresi, 2000), and five non-linguistic subtests of the Cognitive Linguistic Quick Test (CLQT), (Helm-Estabrooks, 2000): symbol cancellation, symbol trails, design memory, mazes, and design generation.

Semantic experiment tasks. Participants were also given two experimental tasks (Nicholas, 1998) to assess whether they could select a semantic category for a stimulus presented in two conditions, once as a picture and once as a spoken word. In one task, participants had to decide whether a given stimulus (e.g., a picture of a firefighter) represented a person, an action, or an object. In the second task, they had to select a subcategory (e.g., fruit) for an object stimulus (e.g., a picture of grapes.)

Functional communication tasks. Five functional communication tasks were also assessed three times at baseline to ensure stability of performance prior to initiating the treatment phase. The same tasks were used repeatedly throughout the training phase to probe for generalisation of treatment effects to functional communication abilities. These tasks are described in more detail in the "Measuring Response to Treatment" section.

C-Speak Aphasia treatment programme

Each participant received the treatment programme for a period of at least 6 months, usually at the rate of two hour-long sessions per week. There were three training modules: (1) generative language, in which the participant learns how to produce statements, ask questions, and give commands using *C-Speak Aphasia* and learns to use the personalised "autobiography" screen; (2) communicating on the telephone using *C-Speak Aphasia*; and (3) communicating via writing and/or email. A training manual was developed previously and describes the structured treatment approach that begins with literal dictation of multi-icon messages for which the patient receives maximum guidance and extensive feedback. The training progresses gradually to open-ended conversational exchanges for which the patient receives no guidance and only normal conversational feedback.

Each participant receives the generative language module first. More time was spent in this module because it is here that the participant learns the organisation of most of the vocabulary items in *C-Speak Aphasia*. All individual vocabulary items are represented as pictures with the English word written above the picture. The training emphasises the production of actor-action-object messages beginning in the initial training session. *C-Speak Aphasia* does not contain vocabulary for verb tensing, prepositions, or pronouns. Only basic syntactic constructions are specifically trained such as subject-verb-object. As a result, many of the messages created by users are agrammatic.

The early training procedure also emphasises the use of *C-Speak Aphasia* to communicate novel information that is unknown to the clinician. For example, as early as the first session, the participant is asked to communicate something about a meal they have eaten that day prior to the session. In this way, participants are exposed from the beginning of training to the primary function of *C-Speak Aphasia*, i.e., to communicate novel information using picture selections. Participants are trained on each step until performance is at least 80% correct without guidance.

In the telephone module, the participant learns to use a combination of pre-programmed phrases such as ''I'm using the computer to help me speak. Please be patient'', that are combined with novel messages using other vocabulary icons. Similarly, in the assisted writing module, participants combine stock phrases (e.g., ''Thanks for your letter'') with novel vocabulary selections. Messages are then either printed to a printer or can be sent as text email messages. Training progresses from literal dictation to self-initiated utterances with a performance criterion of 80% correct without guidance.

Measuring response to treatment

Response to treatment can be measured in a variety of ways, including accuracy levels within treatment sessions, how quickly a transition is seen from clinician-directed to patient-initiated utterances, and generalisation of performance to probe tasks. For the purposes of this report we present data only for this last measure. The probe tasks were designed to reflect a range of real-life functional communication activities. Generalisation of skills learned in the training sessions was measured by repeatedly probing performance on the following five tasks: (1) responding to a set of seven autobiographical questions, (2) describing a set of five pictures, (3) describing a 1-minute non-verbal video showing a mother and two children in a kitchen, (4) making two telephone calls, and (5) writing a birthday card and a grocery list. At baseline, and during each probe session, performance using *C-Speak Aphasia* (on-computer) was compared to performance without the computer (off-computer) on each of the five tasks. All modalities of expression were permissible in both conditions, except for *C-Speak Aphasia* in the off-computer condition. That is, an individual who tended to draw or gesture or otherwise supplement communication was able to use any of these expressive modalities in both conditions. Probe sessions were conducted after every 100 ''utterances'' of the training procedure, which was approximately once a month. Each participant was videotaped while performing probe tasks 1–3 and audiotaped for task 4. Only graphic productions on paper were scored for task 5. The order of the two probe conditions (on-computer and off-computer) was counterbalanced across individuals and probe sessions.

On the probe tasks, performance was evaluated in terms of how many discrete information units the participant was able to express. Performance was noted in terms of modality of expression and credit was given for clear expression of information in any modality. For example, on the picture description task to describe the picture of a man drinking coffee, the participant could produce a gesture representing drinking, could say ''man'', and click on the picture of coffee on the computer. In this example, the participant would be given three points for expression of three different and relevant bits of information.

OUTCOMES AND RESULTS

Baseline assessments

Performance on baseline language measures and the semantic experiment tasks were similar across participants. All participants had at least moderate impairments of auditory comprehension according to the BDAE-3 scores. Furthermore, four participants performed fairly well on the picture condition of the semantic knowledge experimental tasks, indicating relative preservation of semantic conceptual knowledge. Except for Patient 3, all participants were over 75% accurate at making these semantic decisions when the stimulus was a picture in both experiments.

However, performance on the CLQT non-linguistic tasks was more variable (see Table 2). For example, Patient 1 performed at or above normal cut-off on all five subtests, while both Patients 3 and 4 performed at normal cut-off on only one of the five CLQT tasks (design memory). Normal cut-off scores are based on performance of a sample of non-brain-damaged adults grouped by age as reported in the CLQT manual.

Generalisation of skills to the functional communication probe tasks

After examination of the training session data and performance on the probe tasks, one subject was deemed to be an excellent responder to the C-Speak training (Subject 1), two demonstrated improvements on some tasks but clearly not to the extent of the good responder (Subjects 2 and 5), and two were deemed to be poor responders (Subjects 3 and 4). Notable performance variability across participants was seen on the five functional communication tasks assessed in the repeated probe sessions.

Figure 2 shows performance on the autobiographical task by all participants. For this task, participants responded to seven questions pertaining to personal biographical information (e.g., name, address, birthday). Subjects 1, 2, and 3 were able to communicate more information in the on-computer condition, although performance was quite variable for subjects 2 and 3. Subject 5 was quite good at communicating personal information both off and on the computer; thus the availability of C-Speak Aphasia did not augment communication for him.

Figure 3 shows performance on the picture description task. For this task, participants looked at pictures and were asked to describe them to someone else who couldn't see the picture. Each picture showed a person doing some activity (e.g., a man drinking coffee; a child writing a letter). The target information for each picture was therefore approximately three information units (a person, an action, and an object.) Subjects 1, 2, and 5 improved in their ability to perform this task using C-Speak Aphasia quite early in treatment. Subject 3 began to show minimal change from baseline starting at probe session 4. This patient was able to communicate whether a man or woman was in the picture but remained unable to communicate information about what the person was

TABLE 2
Scores on the CLQT with reference to normal cut-off scores

Subtest	Subject 1		Subject 2		Subject 3		Subject 4		Subject 5		Normal cut-off score
Symbol Cancellation	12	+	11	=	5	–	8	–	11	=	11
Symbol Trails	10	+	3	–	7	–	3	–	7	–	9
Mazes	8	+	4	–	5	–	4	–	7	=	7
Design Generation	6	=	6	=	3	–	3	–	3	–	6
Design Memory	6	+	4	–	6	+	5	=	5	=	5
Total number of sub-tests at or above cut-off score	5		2		1		1		3		

Above the cut-off (+), equivalent to the cut-off (=), below the cutoff (–).

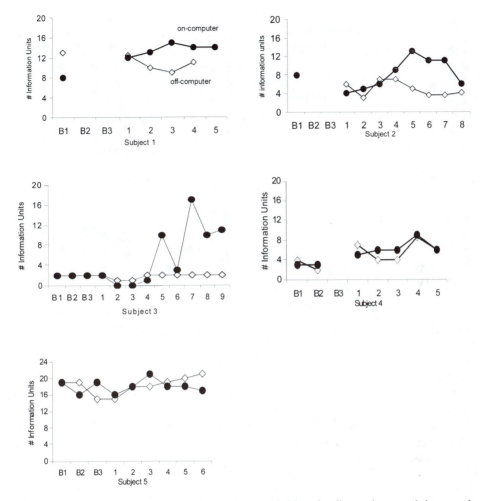

Figure 2.   Performance on the autobiographical task. (B1, B2, B3 are baseline sessions, remainder are probe sessions.) On-computer = black circles; Off-computer = white diamonds.

doing. At probe session 9 she also began to communicate more information off-computer by drawing some recognisable pictures.

Figure 4 shows the performance on the video description task. For this task, participants watched a brief video of a kitchen scene in which a mother and two children carried out various activities without any dialogue. After viewing the video, the participant was asked to describe what took place. Some participants are missing baseline data for this task because it was not ready at the start of the project. However, as can be seen in Figure 4, Subject 1 was able to communicate much more information using *C-Speak Aphasia* on the computer (21 relevant information units) than he could in the off-computer condition (6 relevant information units). Subjects 2 and 5 also communicated more information in the on-computer condition. Subject 3 was also aided slightly by using the computer starting at probe session 5. Subject 4 showed no advantage of using the computer.

Figure 5 shows performance by the five participants on the telephone calls probe task. For this task, participants were required to make two separate telephone calls, and were given specific information to communicate to the clinician on the other end of the phone

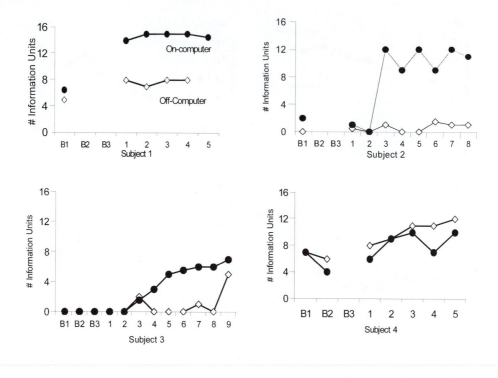

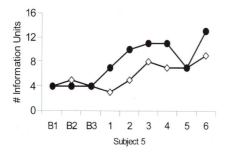

Figure 3. Performance on the picture description task. (B1, B2, B3 are baseline sessions, remainder are probe sessions.) On-computer = black circles: Off-computer = white diamonds.

line (e.g., their name and address, and to ask questions of another person.) They also had written material in front of them to remind them of what they were supposed to communicate on the phone. Only information heard on the other end of the call was scored (verbal and/or using *C-Speak Aphasia*) to reflect the way telephone communication occurs in real-life contexts. Again, Subjects 1, 2, and 5 showed improvement in their scores using CSA as compared to the off-computer condition. In contrast, Subjects 3 and 4 were not able to use the computer to augment communication on the telephone at all, even though each had received many months of treatment and more than five probe sessions.

The computer has not assisted any of the participants in communicating more information on the writing tasks of making a birthday card and writing a grocery list. Although some participants have used the computer to assist their performance, for example by

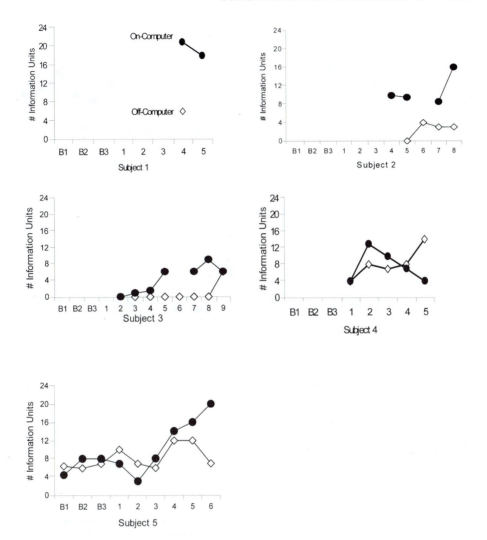

Figure 4.   Performance on the video description task. (B1, B2, B3 are baseline sessions, remainder are probe sessions.) Baselines were not available for Subjects 1–4. On-computer = black circles; Off-computer = white diamonds.

finding items on the computer and then copying words or printing out words on a printer, this has not resulted in higher scores in the on-computer condition, except perhaps to some extent for one subject.

Table 3 summarises some of these data for the five participants. Difference scores were calculated by subtracting the mean baseline score from the mean score achieved during all the probe sessions. Therefore, scores close to zero indicate little change from baseline during the treatment phase and higher scores represent greater increases. Composite change scores represent the totals of change scores summed across the five tasks. Note that Subject 1 shows no change in the off-computer condition in his composite score and a large increase in the amount of information communicated in the on-computer condition. A similar pattern is seen in Subject 2. All subjects except for

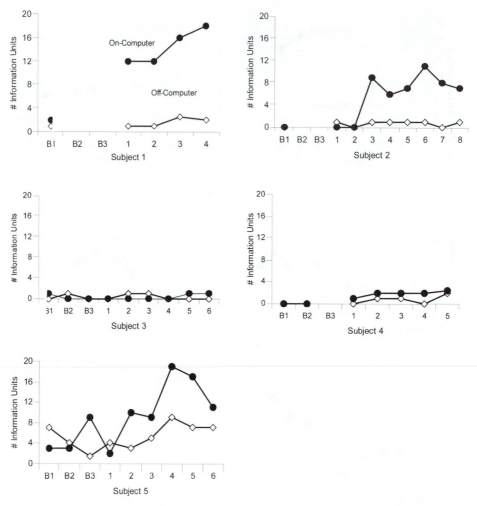

Figure 5. Performance on the telephone calls task. (B1, B2, B3 are baseline sessions, remainder are probe sessions.) On-computer = black circles; Off-computer = white diamonds.

Subject 4 showed greater changes in the on-computer condition than in the off-computer condition.

Relation between response to treatment and baseline measures of language and cognition

Examination of performance across the probe sessions on all probe tasks indicates that participants with better preservation of non-linguistic cognitive skills responded better to *C-Speak Aphasia* training. For example, Subject 1 scored at or above the normal cut-off score on each of the five non-linguistic measures of the CLQT and showed clear improvements on probe tasks using the *C-Speak Aphasia* program. In contrast, Patients 3 and 4 who made the least progress in training and showed only minimal benefit of the computer in the probe sessions performed above normal cut-off on only one CLQT subtest.

TABLE 3
Difference scores

	Autobiog. questions		Picture descriptions		Video description*		Telephone calls		Writing tasks		Summary score (across all 5 tasks)	
	Off	On	Off	On	Off	On	Off	On	Off	On	Off	On
S 1 Off-comp.	−2.4		2.8		0.0		0.6		−1.3		−0.03	
S 1 On-comp.		5.6		8.2		13.5		12.5		−0.1		39.7
S 2 Off-comp.	−3.1		0.6		2.5		0.8		2.1		2.8	
S 2 On-comp.		0.1		6.3		11.0		6.0		4.3		27.7
S 3 Off-comp.	−0.2		0.9		0.9		0.0		1.6		3.2	
S 3 On-comp.		4.0		3.8		4.2		0.1		0.9		13.1
S 4 Off-comp.	2.9		3.7		4.2		0.8		2.2		13.8	
S 4 On-comp.		3.4		2.9		3.6		1.9		1.6		13.4
S 5 Off-comp.	0.8		2.1		2.5		1.7		0.0		7.2	
S 5 On-comp.		0.2		5.9		4.5		6.3		0.0		16.8

Mean probe score minus mean baseline score for the off-computer and on-computer probes.
*Because baselines were not available for this task for Subjects 1–4, the first score earned in the off-computer condition was used as the mean baseline score for these calculations.

In contrast, performance on the language measures from the BDAE and the semantic experimental tasks bore little relationship to performance on the probe tasks. Patient 4, for example, performed quite well on making semantic decisions on the experimental tasks, and responded moderately well to training within the context of the treatment session, yet he showed no ability to use *C-Speak Aphasia* to improve communication skills on the probe tasks. For example, he was able to locate the pictures of his family members on the computer and use these icons to create messages during training, yet when asked to answer a question about who was in his family on the probe task, he did not spontaneously attempt to use the computer to augment his answer.

These impressions concerning the relative importance of language versus cognitive skills to the carryover of treatment effects were confirmed when we correlated mean baseline language and nonverbal CLQT scores to the composite change scores observed on the probe tasks that are presented in the last column of Table 3. There were no significant correlations between either the BDAE auditory comprehension mean score or the semantic experiment scores measured at baseline and the composite change scores of the probe tasks. In contrast, the summed CLQT score (sum of the five CLQT nonverbal subtests) was correlated with the composite change score, but only in the on-computer condition ($r = .85$, $p < .05$). To explore this relationship further, we subsequently correlated the individual CLQT subtest scores with the composite change scores. In this analysis, only the CLQT Design Generation score was significantly correlated with the composite score of the on-computer condition ($r = .92$, $p < .05$), although the Symbol Cancellation subtest approached significance ($r = .74$, $p = .076$). These results should be viewed with caution, however, since this analysis was performed on data from only five participants.

We speculate that performance on the Design Generation task of the CLQT may be particularly relevant because it requires executive function skills that may be especially important to the use of *C-Speak Aphasia* for communication. This task requires the patient to connect four dots with four lines and to make a series of different designs within a given time period. Several skills are required for optimal performance, including creativity in making new designs, remembering the "rules", and monitoring performance to avoid perseveration, all within a short time frame. Both Subjects 1 and 2 who showed good response to the C-Speak training, performed at the normal cut-off on this measure; Subjects 3, 4, and 5 performed below normal cut-off on this task. Of these three people, Subjects 3 and 4 were generally poor responders to CSA treatment based on the probe task data.

CONCLUSIONS

The results of this study indicated that some participants with severe non-fluent aphasia significantly improved communicative performance by using the *C-Speak Aphasia* program. Using the computer as an alternative and augmentative communication device, three of the five participants were able to communicate significantly more information on selected probe tasks. The advantage in communication ability afforded by using the *C-Speak Aphasia* program was most pronounced on the telephone calls probe task, but was also seen clearly on the picture description and video description probe tasks. The results also support our hypothesis concerning the relatively greater importance of executive functioning over language skills to treatment response. In this group of participants with relatively severe non-fluent aphasia, participants with more intact executive function skills responded better to treatment with this alternative communication method than participants with relatively greater impairment in these skills. Executive function skill as measured by the CLQT design generation task appeared to be more relevant to treatment response than semantic abilities or degree of auditory comprehension impairment in the correlational analysis.

These results suggest that patients with severe aphasia and relatively intact executive function skills are more likely to become independent users of systems like *C-Speak Aphasia* for augmenting spontaneous communication. Patients with severe non-fluent aphasia and impaired executive function skills may still be able to benefit from an alternative communication system like *C-Speak Aphasia*, but they will require more support and are unlikely to master independent use.

These results are consistent with Purdy's results (1992, 2002), and extend her finding of poor use of augmentative communication strategies (gesturing and using a notebook) to poor use of an alternative communication system on a computer in patients with documented executive function impairments. An additional clinical implication of these findings is that non-linguistic measures of executive functioning should be part of every aphasia assessment when attempting to determine candidacy for certain types of treatment programmes.

REFERENCES

Goodglass, H., Kaplan, E., & Barresi, B. (2000). *The Boston Diagnostic Aphasia Examination, 3rd Edition.* Philadelphia: Lea & Febiger.

Helm-Estabrooks, N. (2000). *Cognitive Linguistic Quick Test.* San Antonio, TX: The Psychological Corporation.

Johannsen-Horbach, H., Ceglas, B., Mager, U., Schempp B., & Wallesch, C. (1985). Treatment of chronic global aphasia with a nonverbal communication system. *Brain and Language, 24,* 74–82.

King Software Development. (1997). *Speaking Dynamically Pro.* Solana Beach, CA: Mayer-Johnson Co.

Koul, R. K., & Harding, R. (1998). Identification and production of graphic symbols by individuals with aphasia: Efficacy of a software application. *AAC Augmentative and Alternative Communication, 14,* 11–23.

Naeser, M. A., Baker, E. H., Palumbo, C. L., Nicholas, M., Alexander, M. P., Samaraweera, R. et al. (1998). Lesion site patterns in severe, nonverbal aphasia to predict outcome with a computer-assisted treatment program. *Archives of Neurology, 55*, 1438–1448.

Nicholas, M. (1998). *Category selection in patients with nonfluent aphasia: Implications for use of a picture-based alternative communication system.* Unpublished doctoral dissertation, Emerson College.

Nicholas, M., & Elliott, S. (1998). *C-Speak Aphasia. A communication system for adults with aphasia.* Solana Beach, CA: Mayer-Johnson Co.

Purdy, M. (1992). The relationship between executive functioning ability and communicative success in aphasic adults [Doctoral Dissertation, University of Connecticut, 1990]. *Dissertation Abstracts International, 53*, 5164.

Purdy, M. (2002). Executive function ability in persons with aphasia. *Aphasiology, 16*(4/5/6), 549–557.

Shelton, J. R., Weinrich, M., McCall, D., & Cox, D. M. (1996). Differentiating globally aphasic patients: Data from in-depth language assessments and production training using C-ViC. *Aphasiology, 10*(4), 319–342.

Steele, R. D., Kleczewska, M. K., Carlson, G. S., & Weinrich, M. (1992). Computers in the rehabilitation of chronic, severe aphasia: C-ViC 2.0 cross-modal studies. *Aphasiology, 6*(2), 185–194.

Steele, R. D., Weinrich, M., Wertz, R. T., Kleczewska, M. K., & Carlson, G. S. (1989). Computer-based visual communication in aphasia. *Neuropsychologia, 27*, 409–426.

Van Mourik, M., Verschaeve, M., Boon, P., Paquier, P., & Van Harskamp, F. (1992). Cognition in global aphasia: Indicators for therapy. *Aphasiology, 6*(5), 491–499.

Weinrich, M., Steele, R. D., Carlson, G. S., Kleczewska, M., Wertz, R. T., & Baker, E. (1989). Processing of visual syntax in a globally aphasic patient. *Brain and Language, 36*, 391–405.

Weinrich, M., Steele, R. D., Kleczewska, M. K., Carlson, G. S., Baker, E., & Wertz, R. T. (1989). Representation of ''verbs'' in a computerised visual communication system. *Aphasiology, 3*, 501–512.

APHASIOLOGY, 2005, 19 (10/11), 1066–1073

Achieving conversational success in aphasia by focusing on non-linguistic cognitive skills: A potentially promising new approach

Gail Ramsberger

University of Colorado – Boulder, CO, USA

Background: Recent reports from a variety of labs have demonstrated that some patients with aphasia have concomitant non-linguistic cognitive compromises, especially in the area of attention/executive functions. Recent findings also suggest that attention/executive functions may play an important role in the conversational success of persons with aphasia.

Aims: This paper provides a review of recent work being carried out in a number of centres having to do with treatment of attention/executive function problems in persons with aphasia.

Main Contribution: Although results of the studies reviewed herein must be interpreted with caution, there is growing support for the notion that attention/executive function skills in persons with aphasia are remediable, and that there is an important relationship between attention/executive function and functional communication in people with aphasia. The results suggest that treatment of attention/executive function in aphasia—even in people many years post-onset—may result in measurable changes in attention/executive function skills and in the transactional success of conversational communication.

Conclusions: Of course further research must be completed in order to provide clinicians with adequate evidence for clinical decision making. However, this line of research represents a promising new direction in aphasia rehabilitation.

There are a variety of therapeutic options available in aphasia rehabilitation. These include the more traditional approaches that seek to "fix" the broken linguistic processor, as well as those approaches that attempt to teach strategies to compensate for impaired language skills (Chapey, 2001). Regardless of the specific approach used in therapy, the ultimate goal of all aphasia rehabilitation is to improve communication abilities in real-life situations.

In 1994, Ramsberger described two cases illustrating that language impairment in persons with aphasia cannot fully account for functional communicative performance. K and P were both healthy, active adults when they acquired aphasia in their 20s and 30s, respectively. At 6 months post-onset, their linguistic profiles were remarkably similar, with global aphasia (output limited to an occasional single word and poor comprehension). Despite the similarity of language impairment, the functional communication of these two individuals was strikingly different. While P remained dependent on family members for nearly all aspects of his life, K was resuming many of her premorbid activities and responsibilities, as well as developing new interests. She socialised with

---

Address correspondence to: Gail Ramsberger Sc.D., BC-ANCDS, Associate Professor, Department of Speech, Language & Hearing Sciences, UCB 409 University of Colorado, Boulder, CO 80309-0409, USA. Email: Gail.Ramsberger@colorado.edu

---

http://www.tandf.co.uk/journals/pp/02687038.html   DOI:10.1080/02687030544000254

friends, paid bills, shopped, ran the household, and had begun doing volunteer work in the community; and all of this was achieved with very little, if any, assistance. Although most experienced clinicians have undoubtedly observed cases similar to these, as a discipline we have to a great extent until recently failed to acknowledge the degree to which language skills and functional communication abilities may be independent of each other. Assessment of both language processing and functional communication is now standard practice in aphasia rehabilitation and functional outcomes are a widely accepted expectation in aphasia rehabilitation.

Currently, there are several options available for assessing functional communication abilities in persons with aphasia (e.g., ANELT, ASHA-FACS, CADL-2). These tools provide valuable information about the patient's ability to carry out common communicative tasks of daily living (e.g., following written instructions on a bottle of medication, using the telephone, handling money, finding a desired object in a store, etc.) (Blomert, Kean, Koster, & Schokker, 1994; Frattali, Thompson, Holland, Wohl, & Ferketic, 1995; Holland, Frattali, & Fromm, 1999). Curiously, however, none of the functional communication measures currently available takes into consideration the important role that communicative partners play in real-life communication. Furthermore, none of these functional communication assessments includes a measure of conversational interaction.

Kagan (1995) argues that conversational interaction is a vital form of functional communication through which we establish and maintain interpersonal connections and demonstrate our knowledge and capabilities. One of the most common complaints reported by people with aphasia and their families is the difficulty encountered when ''just sitting around and talking about things''. While several authors have described techniques aimed at improving conversational success (e.g., Holland, 1988; Simmons, Kearns & Potechin,1987), it was not until 2002 that a reliable and valid measure of conversational success in aphasia was developed (Ramsberger & Rende, 2002a).

The availability of a means for quantifying transactional success in conversation provided the opportunity to empirically study functional communication in the conversation of people with aphasia. Not surprising to experienced clinicians, Ramsberger and Rende (2002b) found that the language deficit in persons with aphasia was only moderately related to conversational success.

What else could be contributing to success in conversation? While there are probably multiple variables that might impact on how successful a person with aphasia will be in conversational interaction (i.e., skill of the communicative partner, topic of the conversation, motor impairments, etc.), one particularly relevant factor is that of executive functioning. Executive functions regulate and control higher cognitive processing and include such sub-functions as selectively attending to appropriate stimuli and inhibiting distracting ones, switching between cognitive sets, coordinating the performance of multiple tasks, and updating and monitoring incoming information (Baddeley, 1996; Miyake, Friedman, Emerson, Witzki, Howerter, & Wagner, 2000). They are usually involved in complex and novel activities where organising, planning, sequencing, and monitoring behaviour in a flexible manner are required (Purdy, 2002). While the casual conversation of two people with normal communication abilities may not typically qualify as a ''complex'' or ''novel'' activity, the conversational interaction of a person with aphasia may very well fit this description, as will be illustrated below.

In an initial step to explore the possible role that executive function skills may play in the conversational success of persons with aphasia, Ramsberger and Rende (unpublished) observed 16 semi-structured conversations and described behaviours that appeared to impact transactional success. While some of the identified behaviours may have been related to specific language impairments associated with aphasia, Ramsberger and Rende identified possible attention/executive functions that might also contribute to these behaviours.

A common behaviour observed in many of the conversations was the non-aphasic partners requesting confirmation of their understanding. This often resulted in successful transfer of information; however, in many instances the person with aphasia confirmed incorrect information. Partners with aphasia also did not always take into account information expressed by their non-aphasic partners indicating confusion. For example, aphasic partners frequently did not respond to direct questions posed by non-aphasic partners. Or the non-aphasic partner might produce an obvious look of confusion, but the aphasic partner would not stop to offer clarification. Similarly, aphasic partners frequently did not correct errors that they themselves produced. Interestingly, these types of behaviours appeared inconsistent with the aphasic partner's level of auditory comprehension as measured on traditional aphasia tests. Could a difficulty with monitoring and/or self-regulation skills be contributing to this apparent breakdown in linguistic and non-linguistic comprehension in conversation?

Another behaviour that was observed in some of the more successful conversations was that the aphasic partner would take time at the beginning of the interaction to confirm shared knowledge with the non-aphasic partner, establish a communication strategy (e.g., a single letter written on a piece of paper would serve to identify a character whose name could not be verbalised), or establish the parameters of the dialogue (e.g., you ask me questions that I can answer with yes or no). These kinds of behaviours appeared to be related to the ability to develop a plan or strategy.

It was evident that conversational interaction placed numerous demands on attention skills and the ability to coordinate multiple tasks. Aphasic partners had to simultaneously keep track of what they had said, what the non-aphasic partner had said, and what still needed to be communicated while attempting to converse using a disordered linguistic processor. Conversations were frequently forced to go temporarily off track as the aphasic partner attempted to find the correct word, or think of an alternative way of expressing an idea. More successful aphasic partners appeared to be rapidly moving between multiple types of communication in order to construct a more complete concept. For example, one aphasic partner was unable to find the appropriate words to convey the idea that someone had wanted to join a women's club. She thought for a minute and then said, ''P..TA'' with a questioning inflection while tilting her head to one side and making an exaggerated facial expression, suggesting that she wasn't satisfied with her production. The non-aphasic partner immediately asked, ''Do you mean PTA?'' To which the aphasic partner responded with hand gesture and facial expressions that clearly indicated ''not quite''. The two then worked together, with the non-aphasic partner asking questions to which the aphasic partner could respond with ''yes'' or ''no'', and in a matter of seconds the non-aphasic partner understood that the aphasic partner was talking about a club for women. The partners continued to work together in this fashion until the non-aphasic partner understood the complete idea and then the aphasic partner resumed the conversation at the point she had left off.

Similarly, some aphasic partners seemed to be more capable of diverging from a strict linear expression of ideas. This appeared quite beneficial in situations where the non-aphasic partner was having obvious difficulty understanding a particular concept and/or the aphasic partner was having trouble expressing a particular idea. Less successful individuals with aphasia frequently couldn't move beyond such roadblocks and the partners often agreed to discontinue their interaction after several minutes of frustration. More successful persons with aphasia, on the other hand, would discontinue focusing on the challenging idea and broach a new idea, thus keeping the interaction moving forward. Such displays of cognitive flexibility appeared essential to sustaining dialogue; an important feature of aphasic conversation since the longer two partners interact, the more likely they are to experience transactional success.

Having identified these six attention/executive functions (i.e., monitoring, self-regulation, planning, attention, cognitive switching/flexibility, and regulation of cognitive resources), Ramsberger and Rende (2002b) then sought to identify measures of these constructs. There are many widely used tests of attention/executive function available— however, most of these tools were not developed with the intention of assessing people with aphasia (Miyake, Emerson, & Friedman, 2000). Consequently, many of these tests place demands on linguistic processing, and the results are thus confounded when used in the assessment of aphasic individuals. For example, the *Wisconsin Card Sorting Test* (Heaton, 1981) has been shown to be highly related to the phonological working memory (Grön, 1998), and the *Stroop Test* (Stroop, 1935; Regard, 1981) requires the patient to read aloud. For this reason, Ramsberger and Rende (2002b) chose to develop and/or modify existing tools to make them more appropriate for testing language-impaired subjects. These tasks required minimal verbal instruction in order to establish task set, verbal responses were not required, and although verbal mediation of performance may have been beneficial, it was not necessary.

With data provided by 20 individuals with varying forms and severity of aphasia, performance on eight of the nine measures of executive functioning was found to be significantly related to transactional success in conversation (measured using the method described by Ramsberger & Rende, 2002a), and only two measures were significantly related to aphasia severity. Of these eight measures, five were more highly related to transactional success in conversation than to aphasia severity.

While executive function does not appear to be well predicted by performance on typical measures of aphasia, it does appear highly related to transactional success in conversation. The obvious next question is whether it might be possible to effect improved transactional success in the conversation of persons with aphasia by placing therapeutic emphasis on attention/executive function.

The bulk of the reports regarding attention/executive function treatment have investigated the efficacy of therapy provided to individuals with traumatic brain injury. Park and Ingles (2001) carried out a meta-analysis of 30 such studies published between 1966 and 1997 (total of 359 patients). Although Park and Ingles' review concluded that direct retraining of attention produced only small, statistically non-significant improvements in traumatically brain-injured patients, they finished by saying that "it is very possible that there are circumstances in which direct training can restore cognitive function" (p. 205). Robertson and Murre (1999) have suggested that individuals with mild to moderate brain injury may be more appropriate for direct training methods that aim to re-establish neural circuits, while compensation approaches might be more successful with more severely impaired patients. In fact, many of the patients in the studies reviewed by Park and Ingles had severe brain injuries, and group analysis of specific training outcomes may have obscured positive treatment effects for milder patients. This clearly illustrates the importance of studying the efficacy of treatment approaches in well-defined clinical populations and single case studies.

The Cochrane review of cognitive rehabilitation for attention deficits following stroke (Lincoln, Majid, & Weyman, 2003) found only two controlled trials (total 42 patients) that met their criteria for inclusion after an exhaustive search of the literature from 1966 to 1998. The conclusion of this review was that "cognitive training can improve alertness and sustained attention but there is no evidence that it helps people to do daily activities without help after stroke" (p. 5). The authors go on to recommend that further research is needed in this area, with separate data for different diagnostic groups, and appropriate outcome measures of both attention deficit and the effect of the deficit on functional abilities.

There are only four reports in the literature describing treatment of attention/executive function in patients with aphasia. The first set of studies carried out by Sturm and colleagues addressed the important issue of generalisation of attention training. Sturm and Willmes (1991) used a computer-based complex reaction training programme with patients who had focal vascular lesions and found improved performance on the treatment tasks and dependent measures of the attention constructs targeted in treatment, but very little generalisation to untreated constructs or verbal and non-verbal intelligence tests.

In a subsequent study Sturm, Wilmes, Orgass, and Hartje (1997) gathered evidence from 38 patients with focal vascular lesions, with the results suggesting that specific attention disorders in patients with localised vascular lesions need specific training. Sturm and his colleagues suggest that although brain-damaged patients exhibit deficits to very specific aspects of attention that demand very specific intervention approaches, it is "nearly impossible to look for specific deficits [such as these] in activities of daily living" (p. 100). This observation does not, however, rule out the importance of asking whether specific attention treatment results in functionally significant improvements.

The only other reports of cognitive (non-linguistic) treatment in patients with aphasia are case studies provided by Helm-Estabrooks and Albert (1991) and Helm-Estabrooks, Connors, and Albert (2000). In their 1991 study, Helm-Estabrooks and Albert provided cognitive therapy to a gentleman with severe aphasia at 3½ years post-onset. The treatment consisted of a variety of tasks demanding attention and concentration. After only 10 sessions (supplemented by home assignments) this patient demonstrated significant improvement on dependent measures of auditory comprehension and non-verbal cognition. Encouraged by this gentleman's treatment outcome, Helm-Estabrooks and colleagues (2000) designed two additional case studies to look at the impact of attention treatment on auditory comprehension. The patients in this investigation were also very long post-onset (18 and 16 months) and they had incurred their aphasia as a result of unilateral left hemisphere stroke. These patients received 32–34 sessions of a hierarchically organised attention-training programme using non-linguistic materials that began with tasks of sustained attention and progressed to tasks of selective and alternating attention. Results showed improved pre–post treatment performance on the dependent measures of auditory comprehension and visual analytic reasoning. While results from both of these case reports must obviously be interpreted cautiously, they do suggest that there was generalisation not only across cognitive domains, but also from non-linguistic training activities to language processing.

Recently, in the aphasia research laboratory at the University of Colorado in Boulder, a series of four single-case studies were conducted to explore the feasibility of using a computer-based attention/executive function treatment with persons with chronic aphasia (Ramsberger, unpublished data; Hardin & Ramsberger, 2004). Individuals selected for this preliminary study represented a broad range of aphasia types and severities.

The first three individuals received 40 hours of individual, clinician-directed treatment delivered over the course of 4 weeks, using initial modules from the PSSCogRehab program (Bracy, 1994). Pre-treatment testing of these three participants with the *Connors Continuous Performance Test* (Connors, 1990),[1] a review of previous assessments, and informal language assessments revealed that they each presented with different cognitive and linguistic profiles. However, despite the range of abilities in this group, it was possible to easily establish task set for the different treatment tasks from the PSSCog ReHab program (Bracy, 1994). Furthermore, all three were able to perform all of the treatment tasks administered and they showed some benefit from participation in the twenty treatment sessions.

Before treatment, Participant A performed within or near normal range on most measures of impulsivity, inattention, and vigilance. However, her mean reaction time was atypically slow and inconsistent. On post-treatment testing, Participant A's mean reaction time performance was within the normal range with improvements of about one standard deviation from pre-treatment testing. In addition, response consistency scores improved by almost two standard deviations on the two post-treatment administrations of the *Connors Continuous Performance Test*. Pre-treatment testing revealed that Participant B's performance was characterised by impulsivity, inattention, and a somewhat cautious response style. After treatment Participant B performed from one-half to more than two standard deviations better on some measures of impulsivity, inattention, and response style. Finally, Participant C's pre-treatment performance reflected problems in attention, impulsivity, and vigilance. Although her attention and impulsivity scores did not improve after 20 sessions of the treatment, her vigilance scores did improve to be within the normal range.

Encouraged by these findings, Hardin and Ramsberger (2004) carried out an additional case study to look more carefully at the generalisation of attention/executive function training. Using the same treatment tasks, but a less intense treatment schedule (51, 1-hour sessions delivered over the course of 12 weeks), additional measures of attention/ executive function, linguistic processing, and conversational success were added to the protocol. The participant in this study was female with borderline fluent aphasia. M had received linguistically focused treatment since the onset of her aphasia approximately 8 years before. She was receiving no other treatment while engaged in the attention/ executive function treatment.

M's results confirmed the earlier findings, in that she had no difficulty in establishing task set for the training tasks and, like the other three cases, she showed improvement on all of the training tasks over the course of treatment. These improvements appeared to generalise to untrained measures of attention/executive function as well, with perfor- mance on the *Comprehensive Trail Making Test* (Reynolds, 2002) improving by 15 percentile points; and the full-scale response score on the *Integrated Visual and Auditory Continuous Performance Test* (Sandford & Turner, 1995) improving by 24 percentile points. While there was a change of only 2.5 percentile points on *the Porch Index of Communicative Ability* (Porch, 1967), transactional success in conversation improved dramatically. Prior to treatment M was able to convey only 42% of the main ideas in semi-structured conversation, but after treatment she successfully transferred 75% of the main ideas in conversational interactions.

---

[1] The *Connors Continuous Performance Test* is a computerised, 14-minute visual performance task that requires the subject to press the space bar or mouse button for any letter except the letter "X". The test consists of six blocks with three sub-blocks of 20 trials each. Frequency of "X" presentation and inter-stimulus intervals are systematically varied across blocks and sub-blocks.

Although results of the studies reviewed herein must be interpreted with caution, there is growing support for the notion that attention/executive function skills in persons with aphasia are remediable, and that there is an important relationship between attention/executive function and functional communication in people with aphasia. The results suggest that treatment of attention/executive function in aphasia—even in people many years post-onset—may result in measurable changes in attention/executive function skills and in the transactional success of conversational communication. Of course further research must be completed in order to provide clinicians with adequate evidence for clinical decision making. However, this line of research represents a promising new direction in aphasia rehabilitation.

REFERENCES

Baddeley, A. D. (1996). Exploring the central executive. *Quarterly Journal of Experimental Psychology, 49A*, 5–28.

Blomert, L., Kean, M. L., Koster, C., & Schokker, J. (1994). Amsterdam-Nijmegen everyday language test: Construction, reliability and validity. *Aphasiology, 8*, 381–407.

Bracy, O. L. (1994). *PSSCogRehab* [computer software]. Indianapolis, IN: Psychological Software Services Inc.

Chapey, R. (2001). *Language intervention strategies in aphasia and related neurogenic communication disorders*. New York: Lippincott Williams & Wilkins.

Conners, C. K. (1990). *Conners Continuous Performance Test*. North Tonawanda, NY: Multi-Health Systems.

Frattali, C. M., Thompson, C. K., Holland, A. L., Wohl, C. B., & Ferketic, M. M. (1995). *The American speech-language-hearing association functional assessment of communication skills for adults (ASHA-FACS)*. Rockville, MD: ASHA.

Grön, G. (1998). Auditory and visual working memory performance in patients with frontal lobe damage and in schizophrenic patients with low scores on the Wisconsin Card Sorting test. *Psychiatry Research, 80*(1), 83–96.

Hardin, K. H., & Ramsberger, G. (2004). *Treatment of attention in aphasia: A case study*. Poster presented at Clinical Aphasiology Conference, Park City, UT.

Heaton, R. (1981). *A manual for the Wisconsin Card Sorting Test*. Odessa, FL: Psychological Assessment Resources.

Helm-Estabrooks, N., & Albert, M. L. (1991). *Manual of aphasia therapy*. Austin, TX: Pro-Ed.

Helm-Estabrooks, N., Connor, L.T., & Albert, M. L. (2000). Treating attention to improve auditory comprehension in aphasia. *Brain and Language, 74*, 469–472.

Holland, A. L. (1988). *Conversational coaching in aphasia*. Paper presented at the Deep South Conference on Communicative Disorders, Baton Rouge, LA.

Holland, A. L., Frattali, C. M., & Fromm, D. (1999). *Communication activities of daily living* (2nd ed.). Austin, TX: Pro-Ed.

Kagan, A. (1995). Revealing the competence of aphasic adults through conversation: A challenge to health professionals. *Topics in Stroke Rehabilitation, 2*, 15–28.

Lincoln, N. B., Majid, M. J., & Weyman, N. (2003). Cognitive rehabilitation for attention deficits following stroke (Cochrane Review). In *The Cochrane Library, Issue 4*. Chichester, UK: John Wiley & Sons, Ltd.

Miyake, A., Emerson, M. J., & Friedman, M. A. (2000). Assessment of executive functions in clinical settings: Problems and recommendations. *Seminars in Speech and Language, 21*, 169–183.

Miyake, A., Friedman, N. P., Emerson, M. J., Witzki, A. H., Howerter, A., & Wagner, T. D. (2000). The unity and diversity of executive functions and their contributions to complex ''frontal lobe'' tasks: A latent variable analysis. *Cognitive Psychology, 41*, 49–100.

Park, N. W., & Ingles, J. L. (2001). Effectiveness of attention rehabilitation after and acquired brain injury: A meta-analysis. *Neuropsychology, 15*, 199–210.

Porch, B. (1967). *Porch Index of Communicative Ability*. Palo Alto, CA: Consulting Psychologists Press.

Purdy, M. (2002). Executive function ability in persons with aphasia. *Aphasiology, 16*, 549–557.

Ramsberger, G. (1994). A functional perspective for assessment and rehabilitation of persons with severe aphasia. *Seminars in Speech and Language, 15*(1), 1–17.

Ramsberger, G., & Rende, B. (2002a). Measuring transactional success in the conversation of people with aphasia. *Aphasiology, 16*, 337–353.

Ramsberger, G., & Rende, B. (2002b). *Executive functions: A key component of conversational success in aphasia.* Poster presentation at the American Speech, Language, & Hearing Convention, Atlanta, Georgia.

Regard, M. (1981). *Cognitive rigidity and flexibility: A neuropsychological study.* Unpublished PhD dissertation, University of Victoria.

Reynolds, C. R. (2002). *Comprehensive Trail-Making Test.* Austin, TX: Pro-Ed.

Robertson, I. H., & Murre, J. M. (1999). Rehabilitation of brain damage: Brain plasticity and principles of guided recovery. *Psychological Bulletin, 125*, 544–575.

Sandford, J. A., & Turner, A. (1995). *Manual for the Integrated Visual and Auditory Continuous Performance Test.* Richmond, VA: Braintrain.

Simmons, N., Kearns, K., & Potechin, G. (1987). Treatment of aphasia through family member training. In R. Brookshire (Ed.), *Clinical aphasiology conference proceedings, 17* (pp. 106–116). Minneapolis, MN: BRK.

Stroop, J. R. (1935). Studies of interference in serial verbal reactions. *Journal of Experimental Psychology, 18*, 643–662.

Sturm, W., & Willmes, K. (1991). Efficacy of a reaction training on various attentional and cognitive functions in stroke patients. *Neuropsychological Rehabilitation, 1*, 259–280.

Sturm, W., Wilmes, K., Orgass, B., & Hartje, W. (1997). Do specific attention deficits need specific training? *Neuropsychological Rehabilitation, 7*, 81–103.

APHASIOLOGY, 2005, 19 (10/11), 1074–1089

Analysing the language therapy process: The implicit role of learning and memory

Jacqueline Ann Stark

Austrian Academy of Sciences, Vienna, Austria

Background: Analysis of language recovery has focused primarily on the linguistic aspects of language therapy provided to people with aphasia. The preservation and influence of cognitive skills has been taken for granted, although factors such as memory, attention, and learning are fundamental to an understanding of the language rehabilitation process.

Aims: The goals of this paper are to elucidate the ELA-syntax treatment protocol, which aims at ameliorating oral sentence production, and to demonstrate how significant gains in performance might be attributed to aspects of its structure and content, in particular, its use of verbal recall in the therapy procedure.

Methods & Procedures: A qualitative analysis of the structure of a single ELA therapy session and data from a single-case study, TH, will be presented in support of the issues being addressed. Transcriptions of single therapy sessions from the beginning, middle, and end of the three protocols are analysed with particular emphasis on sentence recall.

Outcomes & Results: From early on in language therapy, TH demonstrated a relatively good ability to recall, i.e., convey the content of the sentences worked on in therapy sessions. This performance contrasted with his poor initial spontaneous production of each sentence. TH's severe verb retrieval difficulties improved and the length of the sentences produced in therapy increased from an average of 5.25 to 10.0 words. A carryover to discourse and pragmatic-level tasks and to written sentence production is also observed.

Conclusions: The use of "delay" and a form of personalised cueing appear to play a crucial role in facilitating the retrieval of information from memory for oral sentence production. Incorporating the task of recalling the content of a therapy session at the beginning of the next session and at the end of each session provides an immediate and repeated measure of a participant's learning abilities and his/her response to the ongoing therapy programme. It is postulated that this distinct feature of the treatment programme facilitates the use of language in everyday life.

Numerous principles underlying language therapy are derived from learning and memory research, although they are rarely explicitly stated as such. In the same vein, the rationale for providing language therapy to aphasic individuals according to a specific treatment protocol is often assumed. Being explicit about the components of a language therapy protocol requires simultaneous consideration of numerous factors. These include an understanding of the type and severity of the processing deficits, hypotheses regarding

---

Address correspondence to: Jacqueline Ann Stark PhD, Department of Linguistics and Communication Research, Austrian Academy of Sciences, Kegelgasse 27/1, 1030 Vienna, Austria.
Email: jacqueline-ann.stark@univie.ac.at

I am deeply grateful to Nadine Martin and Ruth Fink for organising the workshop with me and for collaborating on this special issue, and in particular for their comments and constructive criticism of this paper. Particular thanks go to Lotti Viola for transcribing and processing the data. I would also like to thank Susan Etlinger and Caroline Brew for their review of and helpful comments on this manuscript.

    DOI:10.1080/02687030544000263

the focus of therapy, description of therapy tasks and steps, the therapy materials used, the duration of the therapy, and the type of feedback and cues provided in the therapy setting. These aspects and others discussed by Byng (1993, 1995), Byng and Black (1995), and Ferguson (1999) provide a good starting point for being explicit about the relevant questions of "why" and "how" a specific therapy protocol is provided, "what" is done in terms of the structure of the therapy including the tasks, and moreover "how" and "why" an aphasic person responds (or does not respond) to the therapy. Basso (2005, this issue, p. 982) insightfully asserts that "... the content of therapy has not aroused as much interest as whether or not therapy is efficacious, but it goes without saying that efficacy mainly depends on what is done, and not for how long or with what frequency it is done" and, moreover, that "... we should concentrate our efforts on understanding what treatment is beneficial to such and such functional damage and why" (cf. also Rapp, 2005, this issue).

The complexity of the language therapy process becomes apparent in a qualitative analysis of the structure of single therapy sessions. This paper discusses the structure of a language therapy programme in which immediate and delayed recall of sentences plays a crucial role. The role of learning and memory in the therapy process is implicated by the good performance of the participants at the end of a session in recalling the verbal materials practised in that therapy session, and the reproduction, i.e., verbatim recall, of the sentences worked on in the previous therapy session at the beginning of a new therapy session. The rationale for the structure of the ELA-syntax programme is examined with reference to the following issues:

(1) What factors determined the content and sequence of therapy steps especially those involving verbal recall?
(2) What role does verbal recall of the content of a therapy session play in the restitution of language functions?
(3) How or why are significant changes in language performance achieved by the therapy programme under discussion? What are these changes?

LEARNING AND MEMORY

Learning and memory are fundamental to all aspects of therapeutic intervention. Anderson (2000, p. 4) defines learning as "the process by which long-lasting changes occur in behavioral potential as a result of experience". This definition views *memory* as "... the record of the experience that underlies learning" (p. 5). Whereas learning refers to some underlying change, *performance* refers to "... a behavioral manifestation of that change". This tripartite division of the terms learning, memory, and performance captures the key elements of the language therapy process. Complex interactions between learning and memory can be revealed in a detailed analysis of language therapy sessions. Performance can be evaluated by comparing pre- with post-therapy language assessments and by analysing changes in performance over time within and across therapy sessions. The distinction between learning and performance is particularly important to make because an aphasic individual's performance in test and therapy contexts is often not equivalent, and often is worse in the testing situation.

Andrewes (2001) characterises "memory" as "... the hub of a wheel that is surrounded by the spokes representing all the other cognitive functions" (p. 207). Some aspects of this "hub" that are relevant to the role of memory in the language therapy process include:

(a) Memory system type (working, short-term or long-term memory, declarative versus episodic).
(b) Memory stages (acquisition, retention phase, and the testing or retrieval phase).
(c) Encoding and retrieval interactions (e.g., "levels of processing" framework, elaboration of encoding, transfer-appropriate processing).
(d) Practice effects (e.g., massed versus distributed practice, the role of effort, errorful learning versus errorless learning, reduction of verbalisation, etc.).
(e) Transfer of information to untrained items or generalisation across settings, i.e., modalities.

There is an increasing awareness of the importance of learning and memory to the rehabilitation process (cf. Baddeley, 1993).[1] Relevant issues include learning potential, rate of learning, learning versus facilitation of a process, learning according to different methods and the maintenance and retention of learned material.[2] Lesser (1988, p. 388) stresses that "for the planning of intervention and management one of the most important aspects ... is the ability to learn". Horner and LaPointe (1979) outline a procedure for assessing learning potential in severely impaired aphasic persons which encompasses the following variables: rate of learning, stimulability, response pattern, carryover from the clinic to everyday life, and generalisation from trained to untrained items. Others question the very nature of generalisation, whether it is *learning* or a *facilitation* process (cf. Sullivan & Brookshire, 1989).

The roles of learning and memory in the therapy process tie into another broad issue: "How" does any particular therapy approach effect change? In a clinical forum article on learning in aphasia therapy, Ferguson (1999) and several authors (M. Boyle, J. Gordon, D. Howard, C. Linebaugh) respond to Ferguson's article entitled *"It's not so much what you do, but how you do it"* (*Aphasiology*, *13* (2), 1999, pp. 125–150). Ferguson notes that the focus of therapy is on "what" will be targeted in therapy, and that the "how"—i.e., the extent to which a particular therapy process is crucial to therapy outcome—is largely missing from aphasia therapy reports (1999, p. 126). Howard and Hatfield (1987) note this problem as well, maintaining that even when the clinician knows *what* is wrong, this does not in any simple way determine *what* to do about it.

ELA-SYNTAX PROGRAMME

The ELA-Syntax Programme targets the essential components of oral sentence production using picture stimuli from the *Everyday Life Activities* ("ELA") *Photo Series* (Stark, 1992, 1995, 1997, 1998), which depict everyday life activities and objects. The programme is meant to serve as a "framework" with seven steps for providing therapy to improve word retrieval and the ability to construct sentences. Word-finding abilities are worked on intensively within the natural context of a sentence production task. A unique

---

[1] Studies that directly address issues of learning and memory of aphasic individuals have compared their performance with that of healthy controls and other populations on tasks such as paired associate learning, digit span, word span, pointing span, and list learning. See Ettlinger and Moffett, 1970; Carson, Carson, and Tifkovsky, 1968; Risse, Rubens, and Jordan, 1984. Burgio and Basso (1997) provide a survey of the literature on memory and aphasia.

[2] See Lesser, 1988; Horner and LaPointe, 1979; Friedman, Lacey, and Nitzberg Lott, 2003; Freed and Marshall, 1995, 1998; Freed, Celery, and Marshall, 2004; Marshall, Freed, and Philips, 1994; Marshall, Karow, Freed, and Babcock, 2002; Fillingham, Hodgson, Sage, and Lambon Ralph, 2003; Lacey, Glezer, Nitzberg Lott, Miller, and Friedman, 2004; Prescott, Selinger, and Loverso, 1982.

aspect of this programme is that it includes in each session three steps that provide an opportunity to recall materials—words and sentences—worked on in therapy: (1) within a single session, (2) across two therapy sessions, and (3) following a session, i.e., the homework. Each session has the same overall structure and consists of the following sequence of steps:

- Step 1. Memory – Last session: At the beginning of a new session the participant is asked to recall the sentences worked on in the previous session.
- Step 2. Old cards: Oral sentence production is practised with the four to six photo cards used in the previous session. The participant is asked to say what is happening on each photo card at least twice (four to six cards).
- Step 3. New cards – Constructing/building up a sentence: Four to six new picture stimuli varying in verb argument structure and semantic reversibility from one- to three-place predicates are worked on in each session. The participant is asked to describe what is happening on a picture card. The therapist waits for a response and gets involved in the process only after the participant has provided a response to work on: an agrammatic sentence, a phrase, a noun, a verb, a gesture in combination with a verbal response. Each card is worked on intensively, with the participant repeating and producing the sentence several times alone as well as together with the therapist.
- Step 4. Taking apart the sentence in the form of answering questions (posed in random order) regarding the verb and the thematic roles: "Who is doing something?", "What activity is the person doing", etc. The number of questions varies according to the content of the sentence. After the questions have been asked, the participant is asked to say the entire sentence once again. The content of Step 4 is comparable to an "oral mapping programme" in that the therapist poses questions concerning all the participants of the sentence and the activity depicted.

Steps 3 and 4 are carried out for each stimulus consecutively for each of the new cards. These two steps constitute the main part of each session in terms of the intensity of interactions between the participant and therapist: cueing, feedback, repeating, etc. and also in terms of time allotment: Each sentence is built up incrementally, practised, and then taken apart and finally produced as a sentence again.

- Step 5. Auditory comprehension check: After Steps 3 and 4 have been completed for all of the stimuli selected for that session, the photo cards are placed on the working space in front of the participant and he/she is asked to point to the card that matches the sentence spoken to him/her.
- Step 6. New cards – Second time: Each of the (new) photo cards is shown again individually and the participant is asked to say once again, what is happening in a sentence. Each sentence is produced at least twice. Help is provided when the participant demonstrates difficulty with a particular aspect of the sentence.
- Step 7. Memory – New cards: At the end of the session the participant is asked to recall the (new) sentences worked on in that session. The participant is allowed as much time as he/she needs to access and produce the sentences worked on in that session. Non-specific cues are provided after the participant has indicated that he/she has terminated his search.

Homework is an important aspect of the treatment programme. Following each therapy session the participant is given the homework assignment of writing down the sentences worked on in the actual therapy session from memory as well as he/she can, or of "dictating", i.e., reporting the content of the sentences to a relative or caregiver by any means possible (cf. PACE, Davis & Wilcox, 1985). This person records the sentences for the participant. The homework is given to the therapist at the beginning of the next session.

Each therapy session in the programme is structured to elicit sentences to describe picture stimuli at least six times, i.e., several repetitions in six different steps within a single session. Within this framework, changes in language processing within a single session and across sessions can be observed and documented longitudinally. For Steps 2, 3, 4, and 6, the picture stimuli provide the context and content to be verbalised. The sequencing of steps is designed to allow a comparison of a participant's production of the same sentences for the different steps. The selection and sequence of the steps used in each therapy session was based on pilot studies of various orderings with other individuals. The aim was to vary tasks and, to a lesser extent, modality (oral and auditory) used to access new and old information from memory in the context of oral sentence production. The resulting sequence of steps used in the present study allowed the participant to repeatedly retrieve new as well as old information from memory. An attempt to characterise the assumed processes (e.g., memory stages, memory system types, etc.) and components required by each therapy step is provided in Table 1.

In particular, the recall steps (1 and 7) and the homework help the therapist to determine what the participant has learned in the actual therapy session and what can be recalled from the most recent therapy session. Sentence production in the untreated written modality (the homework), provides the therapist with information about carryover from a treated to an untreated modality. In the following section the treatment programme and its effects will be illustrated through the case study of TH.

ILLUSTRATIVE CASE STUDY: TH

TH is a 42-year-old, right-handed male who, prior to onset of his aphasia, worked as a radio announcer and freelancer, whose speaking voice and language were his commodity. TH developed endocarditis following an abscess in the jawbone, which went to his heart. He suffered a left intracerebral haemorrhage frontolateral after a mycotic aneurysm (2/11/2001). Following a clipping of the aneurysm (2/11/2001), TH suffered a massive left CVA (infarction of the left middle cerebral artery). Initially he presented with global aphasia, which developed into Broca's aphasia. At 14.5 months post-onset he was referred to our unit.

Assessment

Extensive pre-therapy language testing was carried out. This included a semi-standardised interview, several picture descriptions (Cookie Theft from *BDAE*, Goodglass & Kaplan, 1983), and other pictures, *ELA* Sentence Production Task (SPT, $n = 80$ stimuli), a sentence–picture matching task (*ELA* Sentence Comprehension Task, SCOT, $n = 40$ stimuli, Stark, 1992), *Amsterdam Nijmegen Everyday Language Test (ANELT)* (Blomert, Kean, Koster, & Schokker, 1994), *Boston Naming Test* (Kaplan, Goodglass, & Weintraub, 1983), *Action Naming Test* (Obler & Albert, 1979), and selected tasks from other test batteries. Results of this testing revealed severe agrammatic sentence production, asyntactic comprehension, and apraxia of speech. TH's spontaneous speech consisted of single words and utterances consisting of one and two words, mainly nouns. Verb retrieval was severely impaired. Auditory comprehension as judged by TH's responses in

TABLE 1
Processes and components of therapy

	Step 1	Step 2	Step 3	Step 4	Step 5	Step 6	Step 7	Homework (written)
(Re-) Acquisition of new informat. (or facilitation)			✓✓✓	✓✓		✓		
Retention[#] of information	✓✓✓	✓✓	⟲	✓✓✓	✓	✓✓✓	✓✓✓	✓✓✓
Production of new information[$]			✓✓✓	✓✓		✓	✓	✓*
Production of old information[$]	✓✓✓	✓✓✓	✓	✓		✓✓	✓✓	✓✓✓*
Auditory processing[§]				✓✓✓	✓✓✓			
Retrieval of new information			✓✓✓	✓✓		✓	✓	
Retrieval of old Information	✓✓✓	✓✓✓	✓	✓	✓	✓✓	✓✓	✓✓✓
Verbal recall of newly acquired information			✓✓✓	✓✓✓		✓✓✓	✓✓✓	✓*/**
Verbal recall of old information	✓✓✓	✓✓✓	✓	✓		✓	✓	✓✓✓*/**
Working memory	✓	✓	✓✓✓	✓	✓✓✓	✓✓✓	✓✓	✓
Short-term memory		✓	✓	✓✓✓	✓	✓	✓✓✓	
Long-term memory	✓✓✓	✓✓✓	✓			✓	✓✓	✓✓✓
Picture stimuli		✓✓✓	✓✓✓	✓✓✓	✓✓✓	✓✓✓		

Processes and components assumed to be involved in the therapy steps according to degree of involvement in the task from great involvement (✓✓✓) to involved to a lesser extent (✓).

[#] The maintenance of memories after their *initial* encoding (Anderson, 2000).

[§] Understanding the instructions and feedback/interactions is required in all steps/tasks.

[$] A categorical distinction between 'new' and 'old' information is difficult to draw; after several repetitions of single words and the whole sentence, the newly (re-)acquired information is no longer 'new'. The term 'new' is used in the sense that picture stimuli depicting *new* activities and *new* objects are used for a limited time—a single therapy session. The persons depicted remain the same; therefore, they represent old information.

* It depends on when the homework is written (or dictated): right after therapy or a day later.

** When the participant dictates the sentences to a caregiver it is primary involvement.

conversation was relatively intact; however, on formal testing TH's responses to semantically reversible sentences (two- and three-place predicates) resulted mainly in reversed role errors.

Treatment

Three ELA-Syntax protocols were administered to TH. Each one consisted of 60 one-hour therapy sessions provided three to four times a week. All language testing and therapy sessions were audio- and videotaped. Preceding and following the 60 sessions, language testing was carried out using the same tests and tasks. The *third* therapy protocol differed from the first two protocols in that for each new stimulus after each sentence was composed (Step 3) and the questions pertaining to the constituents of that sentence (Step 4) had been answered, the orally produced sentence was written down and read aloud by TH before proceeding to the next stimulus.

Data analysis

Due to the large amount of data collected for a qualitative analysis of the process of language recovery, two transcribed therapy sessions from the initial, middle, and final stages of each programme were randomly selected for this discussion. Selected language samples from pre-therapy (before the first protocol was administered) and post-therapy testing (following the third protocol) are given in the Appendix. An extensive discussion of pre- and post-therapy test results in relation to the administered therapy is presented elsewhere (Stark, 2005).

Results

Table 2 documents the evolution of TH's recall performance over time from protocol 1 (early to mid to late) to protocol 3 (early to mid to late). The numbers in columns one to five and seven refer to a measure of recalled content as a ratio of the number of sentences for which the content of the sentence was correctly conveyed out of the number of photo cards, i.e., sentences presented in each session for each step of the protocol. The numbers in column six are the average word length of TH's sentences produced in response to the *new* cards for that session, i.e., Steps 3, 4, and 6. Steps 1 and 7 are considered for oral sentence recall (from memory without pictures) and Steps 3, 4, and 6 for oral sentence production (with picture stimuli). (Due to time constraints for each therapy session, this number varied from four to six old cards and four to six new photo stimuli.)

There are several points worth noting:

(1) The totals across conditions indicate that TH shows a strong ability to recall sentences learned the previous session (old sentences) from memory (recall, Step 1 = 90%).

(2) TH's production of the old sentences to picture stimuli (prod., Step 2) immediately following their recall from memory (90%) reveals a better performance (93%) than both recall steps (1 and 7). This result is evidence of a learning effect for the treated sentences.

(3) TH also shows good recall from memory of newly learned sentences at the end of the session (recall, Step 7 = 87.5%) and good production of sentences to picture stimuli (prod., Step 6 = 84%) for a second trial.

(4) The difference between TH's spontaneous production of the content of the new sentences (prod., Step 3 = 60%) and the content of the previously learned sentences (prod., Step 2 = 93%) is significant (Wilcoxon Signed Ranks Test, Asymp. Sig. = .000).

(5) Significant differences are found across the therapy sessions assessed in Table 2 for sentence production performance for practised stimuli within and across sessions: Step 3 (60%) → Step 6 (84 %) → Step 2 (93%) (Friedman Test, df 2, Asymp. Sig. = .000).

(6) Recall performance (Step 1)—with up to 2.5 days intervening—is actually higher than at the end of an hour of therapy (Step 7): 92% versus 87.5%.

(7) The average length of TH's sentences produced in Steps 3 and 6, i.e., for the new stimuli, increased from 5.25 (for the two early sessions from protocol 1) to 10 words per sentence (for the two late sessions from protocol 3).

TABLE 2
Verbal recall vs oral sentence production

Therapy prot.	Stage/time	Recall Step 1	Recall Step 7	Product. Step 2	Product. Step 3	Product. Step 6	Average sentence length	Total
Prot 1	Early	2/4	2/4	2/4	1/4	2/4	6	9/20
	Early	2/4	1/4	3/4	0/4	2/4	4.5	8/20
	Mid	3/4	4/5	4/4	2/5	4/5	6	17/23
	Mid	5/5	2/5	5/5	2/5	1/5	6	15/25
	Late	5/5	5/5	4/5	1/5	4/5	6.2	19/25
	Late	5/5	3/4	5/5	2/4	4/4	7.2	19/23
Prot 2	Early	3/5	5/5	4/5	3/5	4/5	7.2	19/25
	Early	5/5	4/4	5/5	3 /4	4/4	6.5	22/22
	Mid	4/5	5/5	4/5	4/5	5/5	6.6	22/25
	Mid	5/5	4/5	5/5	4/5	3/5	8	21/25
	Late	5/5	6/6	5/5	3/6	6/6	8.8	25/28
	Late	6/6	6/6	6/6	4/6	6/6	7.5	28/30
Prot 3	Early	4/4	5/5	4/4	4/5	5/5	8.3	22/23
	Early	4/5	5/5	5/5	4/5	5/5	9.3	23/25
	Mid	5/5	5/5	5/5	4/5	5/5	9.2	24/25
	Mid	5/5	5/5	5/5	3/5	5/5	8.6	23/25
	Late	5/5	5/5	5/5	5/5	5/5	9.2	25/25
	Late	5/5	5/5	5/5	4/5	5/5	10.8	24/25
Total		78/87	77/88	81/87	53/88	75/88		
		(90%)	(87.5%)	(93%)	(60%)	(84%)		

Evolution of verbal recall of the content of sentences *versus* oral sentence production for three therapy protocols according to early, middle and late stage of therapy.

(8) Comparison of therapy protocol 1 (all steps) and protocol 3 (all steps) reveals significant differences in performance (Friedman Test, *df* 2, Asymp. Sig = .002). Separate comparison of the early, middle, and late sessions across the three protocols reveals significant differences for each stage.

Qualitative differences in communicative proficiency are reported by TH's wife and son, and by friends and colleagues. These are described as an increased ability for TH to express himself adequately, increased participation in conversations at home, on visits, and at work, initiation of more spontaneous interactions (e.g., asking questions), and an increase in his active vocabulary. His spontaneous speech is more informative and fluent, and his word retrieval has improved for nouns, verbs, adjectives, and prepositions; it has become less telegraphic. As initial language testing and the first therapy programme were carried out after the phase of spontaneous recovery (15 months) was complete, it can be assumed that gains in TH's language performance can be attributed to the therapy provided. Qualitative analysis of the individual therapy sessions gives credence to this assumption.

DISCUSSION

In this section I will address questions (2) and (3) posed in the introduction:
(2) What role did the recall of information play in the therapy process? (3) How and why did the therapy protocol administered to TH lead to a quantitative and

qualitative improvement in language performance and verbal communicative competence?

Beginning with the third question—TH initially presented with severe agrammatic sentence production in which verbs were strikingly absent. The ELA syntax programme provided TH with the opportunity for intensive practice in accessing verbs, prepositions, and nouns in the context of a sentence production task. Because of its central role in sentence production, impaired verb retrieval constrains sentence formulation and production. Bock and colleagues (Bock, 1987; Bock & Warren, 1985) demonstrate the crucial role of accessibility of lexical items, in this case of verbs for producing sentences. Any programme directed at improving oral sentence production necessarily addresses several aspects of sentence processing simultaneously, which can be selectively impaired and which are interrelated in actual language production. In TH's case, the ability to access the appropriate verb to describe a depicted activity was compromised, particularly in the context of a sentence production task. It was assumed that the sentence production component of this therapy protocol would provide intensive and systematic practice in accessing the main verb and, in so doing, would stimulate production of other obligatory and optional constituents. If TH could access the lexical items and select a syntactic construction (predominantly a simple active declarative sentence for this task), the correct sequencing of the words should follow. This was predicted because the ordering of the nouns produced by TH in sentence production tasks was correct.

It is hypothesised that an inability to access a verb in the process of producing a sentence, coupled with a rapid decay rate for a target verb rehearsed immediately before attempting to produce a sentence, is the cause of TH's difficulty. Pre-therapy (protocol 1) test data for oral sentence production (ELA-SPT) reveals 61/80 verb omissions (and the rest of the errors consisted of substitutions and perseverations). Evidence for verb retrieval problems is also provided by qualitative analysis of his performance in therapy sessions. Longitudinally an improvement in performance is observed. Grammatically correct sentences of varying length and complexity were already produced at the end of the first therapy protocol. By the end of the third protocol, TH could correctly produce sentences using reversible three-place predicates with additional information, i.e., adjuncts (locative and other prepositional phrases) consisting of up to 12 to 14 words, for example: "The man is giving the woman flowers for her birthday". However, errors are still made in the selection of prepositions, personal pronouns, etc. Attempts to produce complex sentences, e.g., subject relatives, are noted.

In the initial phase of therapy, TH's written version of the practised sentences (homework) was as telegraphic as his oral production of the sentences. His written performance improved significantly, although writing was not worked on in therapy. By the end of the second protocol, TH started using written language, for instance to facilitate the oral production of a target verb or noun.

To understand the role of memory in this treatment programme, I will review and discuss the three steps that involved the recall of sentences: Step 1 – verbal recall of the sentences worked on in the previous session; Step 7 – verbal recall of new information, i.e. sentences produced to new picture stimuli; and Homework – written (re-)production of the information treated in the most recent therapy session (see Table 1). Each of these steps provides an opportunity to regenerate recently activated information from long-term and/or short-term memory. Functionally, Steps 1 and 7 mirror actual communication between two persons sharing information (oral and written): Reporting to another person what one has seen or experienced in the absence of the other person is a basic activity in interpersonal communication. Theoretically, it is of interest to know exactly what the participant is doing in each step. In Step 7, the participant must reproduce sentences on the basis of what is still activated from the repetitions within the session, especially from Step 6. This step, then, taps into short-term memory for recently practised sentences. After going through all the new cards for that session, the participant is asked to tell the therapist which sentences were worked on. Two observations are consistent with the involvement of memory. First, a recency effect is often observed; the last sentence worked on in Step 6 (second trial, new stimuli) is almost always reproduced first. Second, the order of presentation of the new photo cards is often maintained in recall, indicating that this information was somehow encoded in short-term memory.

Studies by Potter and Lombardi (1990) and Lombardi and Potter (1992) are relevant to the recall of information in Step 7 and the homework. They examined highly accurate immediate recall of sentences by non-aphasic, healthy subjects. Their experiments confirmed their hypothesis that the surface syntax of the to-be-recalled sentence is not directly represented in memory, but is regenerated using normal mechanisms of sentence production. Moreover, the selection of the verb determines the syntactic structure when a sentence is regenerated from its conceptual representation (Lombardi & Potter, 1992). They stress that accurate short-term memory for a sentence depends on two things: (1) a conceptual representation of the sentence (cf. Marshall & Cairns, 2005 this issue), and (2) recent activation of a set of lexical units. In recall the speaker expresses the conceptual representation in a manner similar to normal speech production, whereby lexical units still active from previous productions are retrieved and produced (cf. Bock, 1987; Bock & Warren, 1985). As judged by the good recall performance in Step 7 (and to a greater extent in Step 1), the implications for learning are that the intensive practice, combined with adhering to the wording of the sentences worked on in each session, strengthened conceptual representations of the sentences and the activation of lexical units. In Step 3 we also worked intensively on ''thinking for speaking'' by providing semantic and a type of personalised cueing, which result in an exhaustive search (cf. Marshall & Cairns, 2005 this issue). Information or traces that are *available* in memory storage are made more *accessible* for sentence production (cf. Tulving & Pearlstone, 1966).

In contrast to the recall task of Step 7, the recall task of Step 1—to recall the sentences from the last therapy session—taps long-term memory. Good recall performance is obtained even when as many as 3 days intervene before the sentences have to be reproduced. Several factors are relevant in this context, e.g., the effort expended in the encoding phase and the fact the actual situation of the initial encoding phase, i.e., the learning context, is reinstated for Step 1. Thus, the retrieval situation reinstates the learning context both in terms of the task instructions and the same physical location.

It is postulated that the sequence of steps in the ELA-syntax programme, in combination with the structured practice, spontaneously form the basis of good recall. For the steps requiring oral recall, TH regularly reproduced between four and six sentences varying in sentence length and structure for the four to six practised stimuli. The actual time to reproduce the sentences varied for TH. The first three or four sentences are now easily reproduced, and if difficulties arise, they are due to the retrieval of a single lexical item which results in longer response times for the last one or two sentences. Thus, based on the results in Table 2, it is clear that verbal recall plays an important role in the therapy programme and in the restitution of language functions in general. A greater carryover to other language tasks and to verbal communication in everyday life should follow, because the tasks used in the therapy reflect what a speaker is doing when actually communicating with other persons: searching, selecting, accessing, and retrieving information (verbs, etc.) from long-term memory to convey information on a variety on topics.

To understand how and/or why the changes in performance were achieved, the role of recall in the recovery process must be emphasised. The following features of the ELA-syntax programme are assumed to play a crucial role in improving oral sentence production:

(1) Delay: In this context, delay refers to the therapist allowing the participant ample time to carry out an exhaustive search of his mental lexicon. This motivates him/her to keep trying to retrieve a word and to rely less on facilitating cues supplied by the therapist. We have observed that over time the speed and accuracy of accessing the target word increase, and the participant is at times surprised by his own success and proud of his performance (cf. Stark, 2005). We have also observed that the ability to generate one's own cues improves when given more time to respond. The more opportunities an aphasic individual has to put the self-generated or autocues to use, the more automatic they will become in initiating language production and producing language (Robertson & Murre, 1999).

In an analysis of instances of word retrieval difficulties, Marshall (1976, p. 447) noted that delay was the most effective facilitator of retrieval behaviour (i.e., 90.6% success), although it was used sparingly and mainly by less-impaired aphasic persons. Initially the use of delay, i.e., waiting for a response from the participant before providing feedback, requires the therapist to hold back. This may be a crucial aspect for the participant in the therapy setting. In contrast, in everyday communication an aphasic individual is often not given ample time to respond.

(2) Own production: The participant's response (verbal and/or nonverbal) is practised, unless it is an incorrect description of the activity depicted on a photo card. The process of retrieving some information pertaining to the depicted activity is initiated by the participant. The therapist waits for a response, before he/she provides feedback. The self-reliance is not only important for improving verbal communication skills but also for motivating a participant to rely on his/her own cues, i.e., autocues or self-generated cues. These cues have been demonstrated to facilitate language production (Berman & Peelle, 1967; Freed & Marshall, 1995, 1998; Golper & Rau, 1983).

Thus, with the ELA-syntax programme the therapist starts with the response provided by the participant. With emphasis on the participant's own production, the process is an effortful one and errors are made in the process of producing sentences. Although errorless learning has been applied successfully with people with anomia for remediation of word retrieval deficits—albeit on the single word level (Fillingham et al., 2003; Lacey et al., 2004)—it is difficult to conceptualise a therapy protocol based on errorless learning aimed at remediating oral sentence production. Also, there is some disagreement about whether learning should be errorless or errorful, since the latter is believed to lead to "deeper" learning. Bjork (1994, p. 185) asserts for example that: "Manipulations that speed the rate of acquisition during training can fail to support long-term posttraining performance, while other manipulations that appear to introduce difficulties for the learner during training can enhance posttraining performance." In the case of errorless learning, a participant's *own production* would have to be substituted, e.g., by repetition of correct target sentences. However, even when only repeating sentences, errors would also be made. Moreover, the task of repeating auditorily presented sentences is a completely different one from spontaneously producing a sentence. Thus, the ELA-syntax programme involves errorful and effortful learning. Both delay and own production are in accordance with what is suggested by cueing hierarchies being used with participants, in that the "... recovery process is best served by eliciting the desired response with a minimal cue ..." i.e., "... to retrieve the desired word with no more external facilitation than is essential" (Linebaugh & Lehner, 1977, p. 19).

(3) "Personalised" cues: Several studies (Berman & Peelle, 1967; Freed et al., 2004; Freed & Marshall, 1995) have shown that the use of self-generated, personalised cues results in a better immediate performance and also maintenance of the target word(s) over a longer time interval. In a study by Mäntylä and Nilsson (1983), healthy subjects showed almost perfect recall performance after a single trial when the word-learning task involved the subjects making up their own cues by which they should remember the target items. While looking at a photo card, TH would comment and then retrieve the target word, e.g.: "In Melbourne ... I also ...". Also, in adaptation of the self-generated personalised cues, cues were provided that were based on personal information known to the therapist. Such personalised cues proved to be very successful. These cues could be unspecific in terms of semantic content. The personal reference point is the important factor in triggering the access of the target word, for example: "you like it very much", "your son did the same thing yesterday", or "we spoke about it last week" (cf. episodic memory). These personalised, less specific cues and associative or semantic build-ups aided the participant in producing the target word on his own. These cues are related to *delay* and also *own production* in terms of the self-initiation of language. The idea behind the first three points is that, despite variability in performance, what the participant produces on his own will be maintained better and be more accessible in future attempts to produce words.[3]

(4) Levels of processing framework: The first three variables are related to this point because they refer to the manner in which a response is elicited (see also point 5 below) and the types of cues provided, factors that are crucial for the ELA-syntax programme. The elicitation of the first response to every photo card from the aphasic individual (Step 3) aims to facilitate a deeper level of processing. The levels of processing framework (Craik & Lockhart, 1972) maintains that "... memory-encoding operations should be conceptualised as the *processes* underlying perception and comprehension, and that retrieval is the corollary of encoding" (Craik, 2002, p. 306). Craik and Lockhart suggested that "... remembering reflected the qualitative types of analysis that had been performed during initial encoding processes of perception and comprehension, and that deeper processing was associated with higher levels of subsequent remembering" (1972, p. 678). The qualitative type of processing required in the sentence production task is enhanced by the use of picture stimuli, which are remembered better than verbal material and, thus, add to the level of processing: deeper codes are more meaningful, more durable, and also more discriminable. Intensive, albeit distributed, practice is used in the steps requiring oral sentence production (Steps 2, 3, 4, and 6).

The effectiveness of a retrieval cue for encoding and retrieval depends on the compatibility with the item's initial encoding or with "... the extent to which the retrieval situation reinstates the learning context" (Craik & Lockhart, 1972, p. 678; Lockhart, 2002). Both in terms of the actual therapy setting and the content of the sessions, the ELA-syntax programme provides the same context for encoding and retrieving treated sentences. In three steps (2, 3, and 6) the learning context is reinstated in a very systematic manner. This is assumed to be vital for the subsequent retrieval of information. Further developments of the levels of processing framework such as *elaboration of*

---

[3] Evidence for this comes from observations of the participant using a semantically less adequate verb to describe an activity. In those cases the therapist suggests a more adequate verb. However, the participant reverts back to his initially produced verb on successive turns to produce the sentence, for example, for other steps of the programme.

encoding apply in accounting for the good recall performance. For example, the semantic and other cues used to elicit a verb or noun can be considered elaborations, which create additional records to help retrieve the original record (Anderson, 2000, p. 201).

(5) The use of picture stimuli: The therapy materials, i.e., the ELA photo cards, on which this therapy programme is based depict relevant everyday activities. The use of picture stimuli is assumed to facilitate verbal expression and to add to the depth of processing by providing an additional activation modality for the participant when retrieving the sentences worked on in a therapy session: "People have particularly good memory for their interpretation of pictorial material" (Anderson, 2000, p. 214). Stimuli of simple action pictures provide contextual information to which the participant can relate, and they also activate old memories that clients have not thought about for some time. This is observed in their remarks and sentences produced to specific photo cards which in turn facilitate retrieval, for example: "Three years ago …", "Twenty years ago my father rode his motorcycle from X to Y", "My son … also …". The facilitatory effect of the photo cards on sentence production is particularly apparent in Step 6, when the new cards are worked on a second time: The sentences are produced more quickly and with less effort with a picture support than without one. These two possibilities have been carried out and compared in trial therapy sessions. Also, in recalling the sentences in Step 7 the participant's pointing to the original placement of the removed cards on the workspace in front of him/her also helps to recall a specific sentence. This is related to visually reinstating the learning context.

These five interrelated points reiterate several of the factors I have hypothesised to play a role in achieving good recall of learned or facilitated sentences observed with TH and other clients who have participated in the ELA-therapy protocols. With regard to the mechanisms and principles involved in the language therapy process, Robertson and Murre (1999) state that experience-dependent plasticity forms the basis for changes, e.g., learning. They maintain that the brain is capable of a large degree of self-repair through synaptic turnover. Furthermore, they maintain that synaptic turnover is to some extent experience dependent and, thus, a key mechanism underlying both learning and recovery of function: Recovery processes following brain damage share common mechanisms with normal learning and experience-dependent plasticity processes: "… not only do brain damaged individuals learn to do things in different ways, they may also learn to do what they did before in more or less similar ways as before" (Robertson & Murre, 1999, p. 545).

Although Robertson and Murre's (1999) principles of guided language rehabilitation are less well articulated with regard to memory and language, at least two of the five principles apply with respect to the ELA-syntax programme: bottom-up targeted stimulation and top-down targeted stimulation. With regard to bottom-up specific stimulation, for example, adhering to the sequence of steps (intra and inter Steps 1–7) requires structured repetitive training and this "… would result in a more rapid and complete pattern completion because such repetitive training would consistently activate the same sets of neurons in a damaged network, allowing faster completion through Hebbian learning mechanisms" (Robertson & Murre, 1999, p. 553). An example of top-down targeted stimulation, which was intensively practised, is the attending to and responding to specific questions required by Step 4.

CONCLUSION

Therapy studies are often presented in a manner that makes it difficult for the reader to imagine what actually happened in each session. Single results are presented as if they were independent of the other variables in the study. However they seldom are: Numerous factors play a role in the complex therapy process and it is often difficult to tease them apart. What I have attempted to do in this paper is to discuss a therapy protocol that we have been providing with good results in several aphasic individuals, in which the good recall performance was so striking in contrast to their spontaneous productions and in which there is also a generalisation from oral sentence production to written sentence production. The participants' performance triggered numerous questions as to *how* and *why* their language and communication improved and *why* at the end of an intensive therapy session the recall of the sentences practised in that session was often their best performance. Highlighting the role of learning and memory in the therapy process is only the starting point for understanding what we are doing when we provide language therapy to aphasic individuals.

REFERENCES

Anderson, J. R. (2000). *Learning and memory: An integrated approach, Second Edition.* New York: John Wiley & Sons.

Andrewes, D. (2001). *Neuropsychology: From theory to practice.* Hove, UK: Psychology Press.

Baddeley, A. (1993). A theory of rehabilitation without a model of learning is a vehicle without an engine: A comment on Caramazza and Hillis. *Neuropsychological Rehabilitation, 3,* 235–244.

Berman, M., & Peelle, L. M. (1967). Self-generated cues: A method for aiding aphasic and apractic patients. *Journal of Speech and Hearing Disorders, 32*(4), 372–376.

Bjork, R. A. (1994). Memory and metamemory: Considerations in the training of human beings. In J. Metcalfe & A. P. Shimamura (Eds.), *Metacognition: Knowing about knowing.* Cambridge, MA: MIT Press.

Blomert, L., Kean, M-L., Koster, C., & Schokker, J. (1994). Amsterdam-Nijmegen Everyday Language Test: Construction, reliability and validity. *Aphasiology, 8,* 381–407.

Bock, K. (1987). An effect of the accessibility of word forms on sentence structures. *Journal of Memory and Language, 26,* 119–137.

Bock, J. K., & Warren, R. K. (1985). Conceptual accessibility and syntactic structure in sentence formulation. *Cognition, 21,* 47–67.

Burgio, F., & Basso, A. (1997). Memory and aphasia. *Neuropsychologia, 35*(6), 759–766.

Byng, S. (1993). Hypothesis testing and aphasia therapy. In A. L. Holland & M. Forbes (Eds.), *Aphasia treatment: World perspectives* (pp. 115–130). London: Chapman & Hall.

Byng, S. (1995). What is aphasia therapy? In C. Code & D. Muller (Eds.), *The treatment of aphasia* (pp. 1–17). London: Whurr.

Byng, S., & Black, M. (1995). What makes a therapy? Some parameters of therapeutic intervention in aphasia. *European Journal of Disorders of Communication, 30,* 303–316.

Carson, D. H., Carson, F. E., & Tifkovsky, R. S. (1968). On learning characteristics of the adult aphasic. *Cortex, 4,* 92–112.

Craik, F. I. M. (2002). Levels of processing: Past, present … and future? *Memory, 10*(5/6), 305–318.

Craik, F. I. M., & Lockhart, R. S. (1972). Levels of processing: A framework for memory research. *Journal of Verbal Learning and Verbal Behavior, 11,* 671–684.

Davis, G. A., & Wilcox, M. J. (1985). *Adult aphasia rehabilitation: Applied pragmatics.* Windsor, UK: NFER-Nelson.

Ettlinger, G., & Moffett, A. M. (1970). Learning in dysphasia. *Neuropsychologia, 8,* 465–474.

Ferguson, A. (1999). Learning in aphasia therapy: It's not so much what you do, but how you do it! *Aphasiology, 13,* 125–150.

Fillingham, J. K., Hodgson, C., Sage, K., & Lambon Ralph, M. A. (2003) The application of errorless learning to aphasic disorders: A review of theory and practice. *Neuropsychological Rehabilitation, 13*(3), 337–363.

Freed, D., Celery, K., & Marshall, R. C. (2004). Effectiveness of personalised and phonological cueing on long-term naming performance by aphasic subjects: A clinical investigation. *Aphasiology, 18*(8), 743–757.

Freed, D., & Marshall, R. C. (1995). The effect of cue origin on the facilitation of aphasic subjects' verbal labelling. *Clinical Aphasiology, 23,* 227–236.

Freed, D., & Marshall, R. C. (1998). The effect of personalized cueing on long-term naming of realistic visual stimuli. *American Journal of Speech-Language Pathology, 4*(4), 105–108.

Friedman, R., Lacey, E., & Nitzberg Lott, S. (2003). Learning and maintenance in aphasia rehabilitation. *Brain & Language, 87,* 181–182.

Golper, L. A., & Rau, M. T. (1983). Systematic analysis of cuing strategies in aphasia: Taking your ''cue'' from the patient. In R. Brookshire (Ed.), *Clinical aphasiology* (pp. 52–61). Minneapolis: Brookshire Publishers.

Goodglass, H., & Kaplan, E. (1983). *The assessment of aphasia and related disorders* (2nd ed.). Philadelphia: Lea & Febiger.

Horner, J., & LaPointe, L. (1979). Evaluation of learning potential of a severe aphasic adult through analysis of five performance variables using novel pictorial stimuli. In R. Brookshire (Ed.), *Clinical aphasiology* (pp. 101–115). Minneapolis: Brookshire Publishers.

Howard, D., & Hatfield, M. (1987). *Aphasia therapy.* Hove, UK: Lawrence Erlbaum Associates Ltd.

Kaplan, E., Goodglass, H., & Weintraub, S. (1983). *Boston Naming Test.* Philadelphia: Lea & Febiger.

Lacey, E. H., Glezer, L. S., Nitzberg Lott, S., Miller, E. A., & Friedman, R. B. (2004).The role of effort in errorless and errorful learning. *Brain and Language, 91*(1), 189–190.

Lesser, R. (1988). The assessment of verbal comprehension. In F. C. Rose, R. Whurr, & M. A. Wyke (Eds.), *Aphasia* (pp. 346–401). London: Whurr Publishers.

Linebaugh, C. W., & Lehner, L. H. (1977). Cueing hierarchies and word retrieval. In R. Brookshire (Ed.), *Clinical aphasiology* (pp. 19–31). Minneapolis: Brookshire Publishers.

Lockhart, R. S. (2002). Levels of processing, transfer-appropriate processing, and the concept of robust encoding. *Memory, 10*(5/6), 397–403.

Lombardi, L., & Potter, M. (1992). The regeneration of syntax in short-term memory. *Journal of Memory and Language, 31,* 713–733.

Mäntylä, T., & Nilsson, L-G. (1983). Are my cues better than your cues? Uniqueness and reconstruction as prerequisites for optimal recall of verbal materials. *Scandinavian Journal of Psychology, 24,* 303–312.

Marshall, R. C. (1976). Word retrieval of aphasic adults. *Journal of Speech and Hearing Disorders, 41,* 444–451.

Marshall, R. C., Freed, D. B., & Philips, D. (1994). Labelling of novel stimuli by aphasic subjects: Effects of phonologic and self-cueing procedures. *Clinical Aphasiology, 22,* 335–343.

Marshall, R. C, Karow, C., Freed, D., & Babcock, P. (2002). Effects of personalised cue form on the learning of subordinate category names by aphasic and non-brain-damaged subjects. *Aphasiology, 16*(7), 763–771.

Obler, L. K., & Albert, M. L. (1979). *Action Naming Test, Experimental Edition.* Unpublished manuscript.

Potter, M., & Lombardi, L. (1990). Regeneration in the short-term recall of sentences. *Journal of Memory and Language, 29,* 633–654.

Prescott, T. E., Selinger, M., & Loverso, F. L. (1982). An analysis of learning, generalisation and maintenance of verbs by an aphasic patient. In R. Brookshire (Ed.), *Clinical aphasiology* (pp. 178–182). Minneapolis: Brookshire Publishers.

Risse, G. L., Rubens, A. B., & Jordan, L. S. (1984). Disturbances of long-term memory in aphasic subjects. A comparison of anterior and posterior lesions. *Brain, 107,* 605–617.

Robertson, I. H., & Murre, J. M. J. (1999). Rehabilitation of brain damage: Brain plasticity and principles of guided recovery. *Psychological Bulletin, 125*(5), 544–575.

Stark, J. (1992, 1995, 1997, 1998). *Everyday Life Activities Photo Series, Set 1, 2, 3.* Vienna: Jentzsch.

Stark, J. (2005). *Recovery of language in a Broca's aphasic: A longitudinal case study.* Manuscript in preparation.

Sullivan, M. P., & Brookshire, R. H. (1989). Can generalisation differentiate whether learning or facilitation of a process occurred? In T. Prescott (Ed.), *Clinical aphasiology, Vol. 18* (pp. 247–256). Boston: College Hill.

Tulving, E., & Pearlstone, Z. (1966). Availability versus accessibility of information in memory for words. *Journal of Verbal Learning and Verbal Behavior, 5,* 381–391.

APPENDIX: TH'S PRE- AND POST-THERAPY LANGUAGE SAMPLES

Cookie Theft

Pre-therapy Protocol 1: Washing [laughs about scene] uh sink [laughs] . boy and girl . . .um foot . um .um . uh . uh cookies.. um .. fall. Uh. Mum and um . um . boy.. uh ..um . uh .. uuh. ~ chair.

Post-therapy Protocol 3: Um ... hm ... the . woman is... drying and disses and ... no! Uh... tap uh .. long, long uh way... uh ... floor, yes? And uh .. rinsing in the .. tap .. and ... floor... no! And um... woman... and .. tap uh.. no! Uh ... uh .. water in the ... fl- uh foor... floor, yes? Yes? And uh .... boy and girl are ... eating uh cookies, yes? And uh. . boy... uh... falling in the... sairs uh.. table, yes? And uh .. no! Uh ... uh... uh.. um ..... falling ... up.. in the.. um... floor, yes? And uh... girl cookies! Uh ... boy .. and uh .. cookies ... uh ... eating and ... boy, no! Falling ... on the .. table, yes?

Therapist: Uh-hum.

TH: Yes, fine!

ANELT

Stimulus to be responded to: ''You are at the florist/in a flower shop. You want to have a bouquet of flowers delivered to a friend. I am the salesperson. What do you say?''

Pre-therapy Protocol 1: Um ... [laughs] My .. uh .... flowers . uh ... uh love. Jane.

Post-therapy Protocol 3: Hum .. Hello! Um... um...I...want um ... uh... uh... uh.. big big flowers, alright? And uh... um...uh.. she is.. um.. uh.. hossipul, yes? Uh.. please uh.. um.. me.. pay, yes? Alright? How much? Oh, Jesus, alright. Uh .... um.. money hm.. OK. Uh... please wait. Jesus. Um .. money.. alright. Please, alright, Thanks.

Oral Sentence Production

Target: The girl is riding a bike
Pre-therapy Protocol 1: Uh ..sun and...bike .and...wo- uh girl...and....sunny...and...um... .sunny.
Post-therapy Protocol 3: Um ... the girl is riding the bike .. in the park.

Target: The girl is giving the man a newspaper
Pre-therapy Protocol 1: ......um .. paper .. and ... girl .. uh... hm ... paper ... um ....
Post-therapy Protocol 3: The girl is .. giving the man . a newspaper.

Subject index